NATURAL RESOURCES AND HUMAN RIGHTS

Natural Resources and Human Rights

An Appraisal

JÉRÉMIE GILBERT

OXFORD

UNIVERSITY PRESS

OXFORD
UNIVERSITY PRESS

Great Clarendon Street, Oxford, OX2 6DP,
United Kingdom

Oxford University Press is a department of the University of Oxford.
It furthers the University's objective of excellence in research, scholarship,
and education by publishing worldwide. Oxford is a registered trade mark of
Oxford University Press in the UK and in certain other countries

Published in the United States of America by Oxford University Press
198 Madison Avenue, New York, NY 10016, United States of America

British Library Cataloguing in Publication Data
Data available

Library of Congress Control Number: 2018949657

ISBN 978–0–19–879566–7

Printed and bound by
CPI Group (UK) Ltd, Croydon, CR0 4YY

Links to third party websites are provided by Oxford in good faith and
for information only. Oxford disclaims any responsibility for the materials
contained in any third party website referenced in this work.

Acknowledgements

Writing a monograph is often a very lonely experience. However, I was privileged to receive valuable comments and feedback on each chapter from many colleagues working on topics (as academic researchers as well as advocates and activists) that are at the heart of this book. I thank them deeply for helping me shape both the book and my own ideas on the relationship between human rights law and the management of natural resources.

Priscilla Claeys looked at the draft of Chapter 1, and her work on food sovereignty and the transnational peasants' movement has been instrumental in shaping some of my arguments in this chapter. I also thank her for the invitation to join the prolonged negotiations regarding the eventual adoption of the UN Draft Declaration on the Rights of Peasants and Other People Working in Rural Areas; this advocacy and lobbying work has greatly enhanced my understanding of the issues facing small-scale farmers and peasants.

Lorenzo Cotula gave me some excellent reviews and advice on Chapter 2 about the complex relationship between property rights and natural resources. I highly recommend his writing and advocacy work on the relationship between investment law, human rights, and natural resources governance.

Elisa Morgera provided some extremely valuable comments that helped to navigate the complex relationship between biodiversity law and human rights, issues at the heart of Chapter 3 on the governance of natural resources. Her ground-breaking work on benefit-sharing provided me with a sound foundation from which to approach the complex relationship between biodiversity law and human rights law.

Shane Darcy provided excellent feedback to help me understand some of the key issues that developed in Chapter 4 on the relationship between international humanitarian law, international criminal law, and human rights law. His work and writing on some of the issues at stake, including crimes of pillage of natural resources, are extremely valuable.

Stefan Disko provided helpful, first-rate comments addressing the complex relationship between international cultural heritage law and human rights law discussed in Chapter 5. His research and work are must-reads for anyone interested in the dynamics between cultural heritage and human rights law.

Marie-Catherine Petersman gave me some extremely insightful comments that greatly improved Chapter 6, which looks at the relationship between environmental law and human rights. Her work on this relationship was vital in its support of my arguments here.

Daniel Aguirre supported me through the final stages of the book and whipping the introduction and conclusion into shape. His comments, along with several discussions we had, hands-on training, and work with concerned communities in Myanmar greatly helped me to shape this book.

I also thank Edel Hugues, Joshua Curtis, Christine Bell, David Keane, and Shane Darcy for their early comments on the book proposal and their support throughout this project.

Writing a monograph also takes a significant amount of time and energy, as well as copious doubts and mood swings. I thank my family—Audrey, Léo, and Millie—for their constant support throughout the highs and the lows. I also thank Léo for his constant encouragement, interest, and support while I was writing this book.

Finally, I thank my current institution, the University of Roehampton, for being very supportive of my academic research and appreciating its value; the British Library, an institution that provided me with access to valuable resources during the writing of this book; and the *Netherlands Quarterly of Human Rights* to allow the reproduction of my 2013 article 'The Right to Freely Dispose of Natural Resources: Utopia or Forgotten Right?', 31/3: 295–322, as part of the first chapter.

Table of Contents

List of Abbreviations

ACHPR	African Charter on Human and Peoples' Rights
ACHR	American Convention on Human Rights
ACoHPR	African Commission on Human and Peoples' Rights
ASEAN	Association of Southeast Asian Nations
BIT	Bilateral Investment Treaties
CAO	Compliance Advisor/Ombudsman
CBD	Convention on Biological Diversity
CCD	Convention to Combat Desertification
CDM	Clean Development Mechanism
CEACR	Committee of Experts on the Application of Conventions and Recommendations
CEDAW	Committee on the Elimination of Discrimination against Women
CERD	Committee on the Elimination of Racial Discrimination
CESCR	Committee on Economic, Social and Cultural Rights
CITES	Convention on International Trade in Endangered Species of Wild Fauna and Flora
CMS	Convention on the Conservation of Migratory Species of Wild Animals, or Bonn Convention
CSR	Corporate Social Responsibility
DRC	Democratic Republic of Congo
ECHR	European Convention for the Protection of Human Rights and Fundamental Freedoms
ECtHR	European Court of Human Rights
EMRIP	Expert Mechanism on Indigenous Issues
FAO	Food and Agriculture Organization
FDI	Foreign Direct Investment
FPIC	Free, Prior, and Informed Consent
GR	Genetic Resources
HRC	Human Rights Committee
HRL	Human Rights Law
IACHR	Inter-American Commission on Human Rights
IACtHR	Inter-American Court of Human Rights
ICC	International Criminal Court
ICCA	Indigenous and Community Conserved Area
ICCPR	International Covenant on Civil and Political Rights
ICERD	International Convention on the Elimination of all forms of Racial Discrimination
ICESCR	International Covenant on Economic, Social and Cultural Rights
ICJ	International Court of Justice
ICL	International Criminal Law
ICMM	International Council on Mining and Metals
ICRW	International Convention for the Regulation of Whaling
ICSID	International Convention on the Settlement of Investment Disputes

IFC	International Finance Corporation
IGC	Intergovernmental Committee
IHL	International Humanitarian Law
IHRL	International Human Rights Law
ILCCR	ILO Conference Committee on the Applications of Standards
ILO	International Labour Organization
IPCC	Intergovernmental Panel on Climate Change
IPR	Intellectual Property Rights
ITPGRFA	Treaty on Plant Genetic Resources for Food and Agriculture
ITTA	International Tropical Timber Agreement
IUCN	International Union for Conservation of Nature
NCP	Non-Compliance Procedure
NIEO	New International Economic Order
OAS	Organization of American States
OAU	Organization of African Unity
OECD	Organisation for Economic Co-Operation and Development
OHCHR	Office of the UN High Commissioner for Human Rights
PCA	Permanent Court of Arbitration
PCIJ	Permanent Court of International Justice
PFII	Permanent Forum on Indigenous Issues
REDD+	Reducing Emissions from Deforestation and Forest Degradation
SDGs	Sustainable Development Goals
UDHR	Universal Declaration of Human Rights
UN	United Nations
UNCCD	UN Convention to Combat Desertification
UNCED	UN Conference on the Environment and Development
UNCLOS	UN Convention on the Law of the Sea
UNCTAD	UN Conference on Trade and Development
UNDRIP	UN Declaration on the Rights of Indigenous Peoples
UNECE	UN Economic Commission for Europe
UNEP	UN Environment Programme
UNESCO	UN Educational, Scientific and Cultural Organization
UNFCCC	UN Framework Convention on Climate Change
UNFF	UN Forum on Forests
UNSC	UN Security Council
VGGT	Voluntary Guidelines on the Responsible Governance of Tenure of Land, Fisheries and Forests in the Context of National Food Security
WHC	World Heritage Convention
WIPO	World Intellectual Property Organization
WTO	World Trade Organization

Table of Cases

INTERNATIONAL COURT OF JUSTICE

EUROPEAN COURT OF HUMAN RIGHTS

COURT OF JUSTICE OF THE ECONOMIC
COMMUNITY OF WEST AFRICAN STATES

EUROPEAN COURT OF JUSTICE

INTERNATIONAL CRIMINAL TRIBUNALS

HUMAN RIGHTS COMMITTEE (INDIVIDUAL)

ICISD ARBITRATION

NATIONAL CASES

Australia

Table of Instruments

Introduction

Exploitation of natural resources is certainly not a new phenomenon. However, with the advent of a more global dominant market economy, the demand for raw materials and natural resources has increased considerably. This increase comes from a number of related phenomena, including the globalization of agricultural production, increased investment in energy and biofuel security ventures, and demands for resources from newer hubs of global capital. The rise in prices coupled with new resource discoveries is transforming the demand for natural resources. Changes in commodity markets, agricultural investment strategies, land prices, and a range of other market forces have led to a dramatic increase in the acquisition and exploitation of natural resources such as water, forests, minerals, biogenetic resources, and land itself. Increased pollution and the irremediable change on our climate also cause land degradation, desertification, droughts, freshwater scarcity, and loss of biodiversity, all of which intensify the pressure to control the planet's remaining resources, leading to what was labelled as a 'quest for what is left'.[1]

The role and place of international human rights law (IHRL) in this 'quest' are not usually addressed, as the norms concerning natural resources are dominated by international trade, investment, environmental, and governance issues. The international legal framework focuses on either the commercial or the environmental aspects of natural resources, but little attention is paid to human rights. While the management of natural resources is linked to broad issues of economic development, as well as to political stability, peace, and security, it is also intimately connected to the political, economic, social, and cultural rights of individuals and communities relying on these resources. This book argues that natural resources and their effective management are necessary for securing the realization of human rights, and that IHRL can play an important role to ensure the sustainable management of natural resources.

---

[1] Michael T. Klare, *The Race for What's Left: The Global Scramble for the World's Last Resources* (Picador, 2012).

Natural Resources and Human Rights: An Appraisal. Jérémie Gilbert. © J. Gilbert 2018. Published 2018 by Oxford University Press.

1. Context: Resources Conflicts, the 'Curse', and Resource Grabbing

The regulation of natural resources, and the way these are exploited and generate benefits, directly relates to the structural allocation of wealth and power.[2] Natural resource endowment should be synonymous with wealth and development, yet this wealth is often labelled a 'curse'. The 'resource curse' denotes the paradox under which regions, or countries, rich in raw natural resources tend to display lower levels of economic development than other countries with fewer natural resources.[3] Also labelled 'the paradox of plenty', the resource curse specifically concerns countries with high-value, non-renewable resources like minerals and fuels, and which tend to have less economic growth and worse development outcomes than countries with fewer natural resources.[4] The focus on lucrative extractive industries (such as oil or gas) engenders a decline in the development of other sectors of the economy.[5] There is a strong correlation between authoritarianism and control over natural resources in countries rich in natural resources: authoritarian policies create a heavy dependence on exports of natural resources, creating a collapse in other parts of the economy.[6]

There is also a correlation between abundance of high-value natural resources and conflict.[7] The fight to control natural resources has resulted in conflicts between national authorities and regional factions or more general civil wars.[8] The link between natural resources and conflicts is so deeply entrenched that some of these conflicts

---

[2] See Peter Newell and Joanna Wheeler (eds), *Rights, Resources and the Politics of Accountability* (Zed Books, 2006); Melanie Pichler, Cornelia Staritz, Karin Küblböck, Christina Plank, Werner Raza, and Fernando Ruiz Peyré (eds), *Fairness and Justice in Natural Resource Politics* (Routledge, 2016).

[3] See Jeffrey Sachs and Andrew Warner, 'The Curse of Natural Resources', 45 *European Economic Review*, 2001, 827–38; Richard Auty, *Sustaining Development in Mineral Economics: The Resource Curse Thesis* (Routledge, 1993).

[4] See Terry Lynn Karl, *The Paradox of Plenty: Oil Booms and Petro-States* (University of California Press, 1997); Sevil Acar, *The Curse of Natural Resources: A Developmental Analysis in a Comparative Context* (Palgrave, 2017); Brenda Shaffer and Taleh Ziyadov (eds), *Beyond the Resource Curse* (University of Pennsylvania Press, 2011); Victor Menaldo, *The Institutions Curse: Natural Resources, Politics, and Development* (CUP, 2016).

[5] See Thad Dunning, *Crude Democracy: Natural Resource Wealth and Political Regimes* (CUP, 2008); Macartan Humphreys, Jeffrey D. Sachs, and Joseph E. Stiglitz (eds), *Escaping the Resource Curse* (Columbia University Press, 2007); Michael Ross, *The Oil Curse: How Petroleum Wealth Shapes the Development of Nations* (Princeton University Press, 2012).

[6] For example, a survey of 141 countries over a 40-year period found that a 1 per cent increase in natural resource dependence can increase the likelihood of authoritarian government by nearly 8 per cent. See Leonard Wantchekon, 'Why Do Resource Dependent Countries Have Authoritarian Governments?', 5(2) *Journal of African Finance and Economic Development*, 2002, 57–77. See also Paul Collier and Anthony Venables (eds), *Plundered Nations? Successes and Failures in Natural Resource Extraction* (Palgrave Macmillan, 2011); Markus Kröger, *Contentious Agency and Natural Resource Politics* (Routledge, 2013).

[7] See Ian Bannon and Paul Collier (eds), *Natural Resources and Violent Conflict: Options and Actions* (World Bank Publications, 2003); Paul Le Billon, *Geopolitics of Resource Wars: Resource Dependence, Governance and Violence* (Routledge, 2005).

[8] Examples include Biafra, Cabinda, Katanga, or the Democratic Republic of Congo and Sudan. See Nicholas Shaxson, *Poisoned Wells: The Dirty Politics of African Oil* (Palgrave Macmillan, 2008).

have been labelled 'resource wars'.[9] The fight to gain control over natural resources is either a goal in itself or a way to fuel the conflict in providing resources to support the war effort.[10] Many theories regarding the drivers and consequences of conflicts over natural resources have been put forward, including theories regarding scarcity, competition, greed, grievances, and vulnerability.[11] The causal relationship between natural resource scarcity and violent conflicts makes it also relevant to ensure long-term peace and security. [12]

The exploitation of high-value natural resources, and notably extractive resources such as oil and rich minerals, often leads to denial of civil and political rights, as well as prevailing insecurities, for example, military interventions in extractive areas.[13] More generally, the poor management of natural resources also often leads to ill-planned development, misappropriation of land, corruption, bad governance, mis-aligned budget priorities, lack of strong institutional reforms, and weak policies.[14] Development connected to natural resources often requires the construction of mega-projects (dams, nuclear plants, hydroelectric facilities, wind farms, land reclamation large-scale farming) that are intended to make use of natural resources, particularly for large-scale commercial gain. These often have significant consequences on the rights of the local communities, leading to forced displacement, loss of access to essential sources of livelihood, and destruction of significant cultural assets.

The increased value of natural resources has led to large investment in the field of natural resources from corporations investing into natural resources assets, specialized investments portfolio on natural resources, pension funds, and new financial practices to support these investments. Investments in agribusiness, forest plantation, biotechnologies, or other forms of natural resources investments have become extremely substantial.[15] Due to the important financial returns that the

---

[9] See Michael Klare, *Resource Wars: The New Landscape of Global Conflict* (Henry Holt and Company, 2002); Christa N. Brunnschweiler and Erwin H. Bulte, 'Natural Resources and Violent Conflict: Resource Abundance, Dependence, and the Onset of Civil Wars', 61(4) *Oxford Economic Papers*, 2009, 651, 674.

[10] See Paul Le Billon, *Fuelling War: Natural Resources and Armed Conflicts* (Routledge, 2013).

[11] See Baechler Günther, *Violence Through Environmental Discrimination* (Springer, 1999); Thomas Homer-Dixon, *Environment, Scarcity, and Violence* (Princeton University Press, 1999); Paul Collier, V. L. Elliott, Håvard Hegre, Anke Hoeffler, Marta Reynal-Querol, and Nicholas Sambanis, *Breaking the Conflict Trap: Civil Wars and Development Policy* (World Bank/OUP, 2003); Colin Kahl, *States, Scarcity, and Civil Strife in the Developing World* (Princeton University Press, 2006).

[12] See Päivi Lujala and Siri Aas Rustad (eds), *High-Value Natural Resources and Post-Conflict Peacebuilding* (Routledge, 2012); Helen Young and Lisa Goldman (eds), *Livelihoods, Natural Resources, and Post-Conflict Peacebuilding* (Routledge, 2015); Carl Bruch, Carroll Muffett, and Sandra S. Nichols (eds), *Governance, Natural Resources and Post-Conflict Peacebuilding* (Routledge, 2016).

[13] See Patricia I. Vasquez, *Oil Sparks in the Amazon: Local Conflicts, Indigenous Populations, and Natural Resources* (University of Georgia Press, 2014); Abiodun Alao, *Natural Resources and Conflict in Africa: The Tragedy of Endowment* (University of Rochester Press, 2007).

[14] See Aled Williams and Philippe Le Billon (eds), *Corruption, Natural Resources and Development: From Resource Curse to Political Ecology* (Edward Elgar Publishing, 2017).

[15] See Alex Loftus and Hug March, 'Financialising Nature?', 60 *Geoforum*, 2015, 172–5; Sian Sullivan, 'Banking Nature? The Spectacular Financialisation of Environmental Conservation', 45(1) *Antipode*, 2013, 198–217; Sarah Bracking, 'How Do Investors Value Environmental Harm/Care? Private Equity Funds, Development Finance Institutions and the Partial Financialization of Nature-Based Industries', 43(1) Development and Change, 2012, 271–93.

exploitation of natural resources can create, as well as the parallel depletion and rarefication of these resources, the price and value of natural resources have usually greatly increased, attracting more investments and financialization.[16] As part of these changes in the global economy in the trade of natural resources, the last few decades have witnessed the multiplication of international, regional, and bilateral trade agreements governing the exploitation and management of natural resources.[17] As examined in this book, all these legal frameworks governing the trade and investments over natural resources have a direct impact on the human rights of local communities.

2. Scope of the Book

The book examines how IHRL can provide a relevant legal framework, and a new approach to the issue of natural resources management.[18] It offers a comprehensive analysis of the different norms, procedures, and approaches developed under IHRL that are relevant to the management of natural resources and proposes a coherent human rights-based approach to natural resources management.[19] Although IHRL has not been developed to specifically address the management of natural resources, international and regional human rights institutions are increasingly focusing on the connection between IHRL and natural resources management. For example, in 2012, the Inter-American Commission on Human Rights (IACHR) and the African Commission on Human and Peoples' Rights adopted a joint 'Declaration on a Human Rights-Based Approach to Natural Resources Governance'.[20] In 2015, the UN Special Rapporteur on rights to freedom of peaceful assembly and of association issued a specific report on the issue of natural resources exploitation.[21] These are only illustrations of a larger phenomenon as international human rights institutions have started to address the correlation between natural resources and IHRL in a much more systematic and proactive way. Although analysis regarding

---

[16] See A. Greiner and W. Semmler. *The Global Environment, Natural Resources, and Economic Growth* (OUP, 2008); Edward B. Barbier, *Natural Resources and Economics Development* (CUP, 2005).

[17] See *World Trade Report 2010: Trade in Natural Resources* (World Trade Organization, 2010)

[18] Natural resources management refers to the sustainable utilization of major natural resources, such as land, water, air, minerals, forests, fisheries, and wild flora and fauna.

[19] 'A human rights-based approach is a conceptual framework for the process of human development that is normatively based on international human rights standards and operationally directed to promoting and protecting human rights.' Office of the High Commissioner for Human Rights, *Frequently Asked Questions about Human Rights-Based Approach to Development Cooperation* (United Nations, 2006), p. 15. See also Office of the High Commissioner for Human Rights, 'Applying a Human Rights-Based Approach to Climate Change Negotiations, Policies and Measures', Guidance Note, 2015.

[20] Inter-American Commission on Human Rights and the African Commission on Human and People's Rights, 'Declaration on a Human Rights-Based Approach to Natural Resources Management', Adopted in preparation to the Rio+20 Summit, March 2012; see also Resolution on a Human Rights-Based Approach to Natural Resources Governance, 51st Ordinary Session held from 18 April to 2 May 2012 in Banjul, The Gambia.

[21] See Report of the Special Rapporteur on the Rights to Freedom of Peaceful Assembly and of Association, Maina Kiai, The Rights to Freedom of Peaceful Assembly and of Association in the Context of Natural Resource Exploitation Projects, UN Doc. A/HRC/29/25 (2015)

the emergence of specific human rights, such as the right to water, the right to food, or public participation exists,[22] comprehensive analysis on the potential role that IHRL can play in the management of natural resources is needed. From this perspective, the book offers an in-depth analysis of these developments, and how these could contribute to a more comprehensive human rights-based approach to the management of natural resources.

In analysing the nexus between natural resources and IHRL, the book brings together areas of the law which rarely meet: namely 'international natural resources law' and IHRL. International natural resource law is a generic term used to refer to the overall legal framework governing the management of natural resources.[23] It includes the specialized fields of the law of the sea, mining law, energy law, international law of water resources and fisheries, international environmental law, biodiversity law, and intellectual property rights. Moreover, the management of natural resources is also key element of trade and investment law.[24] In this expanding, fragmented field of international law, the role and place of human rights deserve to be examined and appraised. The book offers an appraisal of the role that IHRL can play when it comes to natural resource governance, and notably how IHRL is placed within the larger field of international norms that dominate the management of natural resources. In summary, the aims of the book are:

(1) to offer a comprehensive review of the human rights norms, procedures, principles, and institutions that are relevant to the management of natural resources;

(2) to set out the substance of a human rights-based approach to the management, use, and protection of natural resources; and

(3) to examine the interaction and potential impact of IHRL on other branches of international law governing the management of natural resources.

3. Which Natural Resources? Terminology and Definitions

The term 'natural resources' refers to 'those materials or substances of a place which can be used to sustain life or for economic exploitation'.[25] In terms of international

---

[22] See, for example, Donald M. Zillman, Alastair Lucas, and George (Rock) Pring (eds), *Human Rights in Natural Resource Development: Public Participation in the Sustainable Development of Mining and Energy Resources* (OUP, 2002); Inga T. Winkler, *The Human Right to Water: Significance, Legal Status and Implications for Water Allocation* (Hart Publishing, 2012); Malcolm Langford and Anna F. S. Russell (eds), *The Human Right to Water* (CUP, 2017); George Kent, *Freedom from Want: The Human Right to Adequate Food* (Georgetown University Press, 2005); Wenche Barth Eide and Uwe Kracht, *Food and Human Rights in Development* (Intersentia, 2005).

[23] See Elena Blanco and Jona Razzaque (eds), *Globalisation and Natural Resources Law: Challenges, Key Issues and Perspectives* (Edward Elgar, 2011); Elisa Morgera and Kati Kulovesi (eds), *Research Handbook on International Law and Natural Resources* (Edward Elgar Publishing, 2016).

[24] See Shawkat Alam, Jahid Hossain Bhuiyan, and Jona Razzaque, *International Natural Resources Law, Investment and Sustainability* (Routledge, 2017); Celine Tan and Julio Faundez, *Natural Resources and Sustainable Development: International Economic Law Perspectives* (Edward Elgar Publishing, 2017).

[25] Oxford English Dictionary Online (OUP, 2017). Available at: http://www.oed.com.

law, no international treaty proposes a definitive and universally legally binding definition on the term 'natural resources'. Instead, several definitions have been put forward. For example, the Organisation for Economic Co-operation and Development (OECD) suggests that 'natural resources are natural assets (raw materials) occurring in nature that can be used for economic production or consumption'. The World Trade Organization (WTO) defines natural resources as 'stocks of materials that exist in the natural environment that are both scarce and economically useful in production or consumption, either in their raw state or after a minimal amount of processing'.[26] Adopting a less consumption-based focus, the IACHR has defined natural resources as follows:

Natural resources are substances that exist naturally in the Earth. Natural resources are valuable in manufacturing products, supplying human necessities or comforts, and providing ecosystem services that maintain the health of the biosphere. Natural resources include air, land, water, natural gas, coal, oil, petroleum, minerals, wood, topsoil, fauna, flora, forests and wildlife. Renewable natural resources are those that reproduce or renew and include animal life, plants, trees, water, and wind. Nonrenewable resources are irreplaceable once extracted from water or soil and include gold, silver, fossil fuels, diamonds, natural gas, copper and ore.[27]

This definition is adopted in this book as the aim is to examine all natural resources, not only the resources that can be exploited and used. Although the literature often makes a distinction between essential resources such as water, forest, air and food, and extractives resources such as gas, oil, and other minerals, this book wishes to take a large approach to all natural resources and examine to what extent IHRL can play a role in the management of all these resources. Distinctions are also made between non-renewable resources (such as oil, strategic minerals, and gems), renewable (such as water, forest, and fisheries), and global common pool resources (the air, the oceans, forests, and fisheries). Again, the book adopts an encompassing approach by examining IHRL when it comes to all natural resources, renewable or not, common and not common resources. Inherently, nuances are adopted when the nature of the resources influences the legal framework, but in general the aim of the book is to include all 'substances that exist naturally in the Earth'.

This encompassing approach on the meaning of natural resources and its focus on IHRL does not mean that the book is based on a restrictive anthropocentric approach to nature, which sees it mainly as a 'resource' for humans. Nor does it mean that the only focus is on the exploitation of natural resources. As aptly captured by Ribot: '[T]he step from nature to commodity requires a moment of vision in which the social uses of nature are apprehended. This is the first step in the commodification of what we call natural resources.... Nature as a commodity, however, is a kind of fiction.'[28] Bearing in mind this warning, the book adopts the language of

---

[26] *World Trade Report 2010: Trade in Natural Resources* (World Trade Organization, 2010), p. 46.

[27] Inter-American Commission on Human Rights, 'Indigenous and Tribal Peoples' Rights over Their Ancestral Lands and Natural Resources: Norms and Jurisprudence of the Inter-American Human Rights System', OEA/Ser.L/V/II. Doc. 56/09, 30 December 2009, para. 41.

[28] Jesse Ribot, 'Foreword'. In: Jin Sato (ed.), *Governance of Natural Resources: Uncovering the Social Purpose of Materials in Nature* (United Nations University Press, 2013), p. xv.

'resources' in order to reflect on the role of IHRL to challenge (or not) this dominant vision which treats nature as a resource. This approach does not ignore the fact that the term 'natural resources' usually also includes animals as 'resources',[29] nor that nature itself can have a legal standing on its own.[30] Also it worth noting that the use of terms of such as 'protected areas', 'conservation', or 'wilderness' entails a division between the human and natural world, and a commodification of nature. While these terms and the generic reference to natural resources are used throughout the book it does not imply any endorsement of these approaches to nature. It is none-theless necessary to use these terminologies to engage in a contemporary analysis of the relationship between humans and nature, and the potential role of IHRL in this relationship.

4. Conceptual Framework and Methodology

To be able to analyse the potential content of a human rights-based approach to natural resources, the book is based on three distinct but interrelated conceptual frameworks of analysis.

First, the book adopts a rights-based approach in relying on the interpretation and the judicial development of the rights proclaimed within international and regional human rights treaties. It also includes a strong focus on procedural rights such as the right to information and participation, or the right to consultation and consent. The book relies on different legal sources including, among others, inter-national and regional instruments, texts adopted by intergovernmental bodies, gen-eral comments adopted by treaty monitoring bodies, and recommendations from United Nations (UN) Special procedures, which might be relevant to explore the connection between human rights norms and natural resources. It also includes the work on non-specialized human rights institutions that have adopted human rights statements, documents, and guidelines relating to governance over natural resources. For example, this includes the work of the Food and Agriculture Organization (FAO) which has adopted several guidelines concerning the rights of peasants, farmers, and other agricultural producers over natural resources.[31] This is not limited to

---

[29] See Yoriko Otomo, *Unconditional Life: The Postwar International Law Settlement* (OUP, 2016); Yokiro Otomo and Edward Mussawir (eds), *Law and the Question of the Animal: A Critical Jurisprudence* (Routledge, 2012).

[30] See Roderick Frazier Nash, *The Rights of Nature: A History of Environmental Ethics* (University of Wisconsin Press, 1989); David R. Boyd, *The Rights of Nature: A Legal Revolution that Could Save the World* (ECW Press, 2017).

[31] See *Voluntary Guidelines to Support the Progressive Realization of the Right to Adequate Food in the Context of National Food Security* (Food and Agriculture Organization of the United Nations, 2004). Available at: http://www.fao.org/docrep/009/y7937e/y7937e00.htm; UN Committee on World Food Security, *Voluntary Guidelines on the Responsible Governance of Tenure of Land, Fisheries and Forests in the Context of National Food Security* (Food and Agriculture Organization of the United Nations, 2012). Available at: http://www.fao.org/docrep/016/i2801e/i2801e.pdf; *Voluntary Guidelines for Securing Sustainable Small-Scale Fisheries in the Context of Food Security and Poverty Eradication* (Food and Agriculture Organization of the United Nations, 2014). Available at: http://www.fao.org/cofi/42011-0d2bdfc444f14130c4c13ecb44218c4d6.pdf.

institutional and governmental organizations as many non-governmental and civil society organizations are contributing to the emergence of a human rights-based approach to natural resources management.[32]

The second conceptual framework concerns the rights-holders of a human rights-based approach to natural resources. While the aim of the book is to examine the rights of every human to natural resources, some of the most significant developments connecting IHRL and natural resources relate to the recognition that structural inequities in access to natural resources often lead to the violation of the fundamental rights of specific populations, notably indigenous peoples, rural women, landless peasants, and more generally, marginalized local rural communities. For example, women's access to natural resources is often restricted by discriminatory practices.[33] Indigenous peoples suffer greatly from restrictions and loss of access to natural resources; consequently, some of the most advanced legal developments have been taking place under the framework of the rights of indigenous peoples.[34] Indigenous peoples' rights over their natural resources represents an important element of the human rights-based approach to natural resources, and as such forms an important focus of the book.[35] Additionally, several other categories of specific rights-holders are emerging, including landless peasants, small-scale farmers, pastoralists, fisherfolk, or forest communities. More generally, human rights institutions are increasingly referring to the rights of 'local communities' over their natural resources. These terms, and especially the reference to 'local communities', have usually escaped specific international legal definition.[36] Hence, one of the conceptual frameworks of analysis is to unravel the process by which these different categories of rights-holders have emerged, and to analyse how IHRL is contributing the development of specific categories of rights-holders when it comes to natural resources.

The third level of analysis is on the duty bearers of these emerging rights to natural resources. While public authorities are still the principal duty bearers, there is an

---

[32] See, for example, Rights and Resources Initiative (https://rightsandresources.org/); International Institute for Environment and Development (https://www.iied.org/); World Resources Institute (http://www.wri.org); Natural Justice (http://naturaljustice.org). See also the Natural Resource Charter (https://resourcegovernance.org/approach/natural-resource-charter).

[33] See Committee on the Elimination of Discrimination against Women (CEDAW), General Recommendation No. 34 on the Rights of Rural Women calling States to take measures to 'achieve substantive equality of rural women in relation to land and natural resources', UN Doc. CEDAW/C/GC/34, paras 58–9.

[34] For example, the 2007 UN Declaration on the Rights of Indigenous Peoples (UNDRIP) makes several direct references to natural resources, see Preamble, Arts 8, 25, 26, 27, 28, 29, 31, and 32.

[35] While there is no officially sanctioned definition of indigenous peoples under international law, the current international understanding of indigenous peoples is defined via a variety of characteristics that include self-identification; historical continuity with pre-colonial societies; a strong link to territories; a distinct social, economic, or political system; a distinct dialect/language, culture, and beliefs; non-participation as a dominant group in national society; and resolve to maintain and reproduce their ancestral environments and systems as distinctive peoples. See Working Group on Indigenous Populations, Working Paper by the Chairperson-Rapporteur on the concept of 'indigenous peoples', UN Doc. E/CN.4/Sub.2/AC.4/1996/2 (1996).

[36] See Adriana Bessa, *Traditional Local Communities in International Law* (PhD Thesis, European University Institute, Florence, 2013); Adriana Bessa 'Traditional Local Communities: What Lessons Can Be Learnt at the International Level from the Experiences of Brazil and Scotland?', 24(3) *Review of European Community & International Environmental Law*, 2015, 330–40.

extension of these obligations to non-State actors, notably corporations.[37] The role and place of corporations, investors, and financial institutions are important to the management, exploitation, and ownership of natural resources. Overall, the book offers an analysis of the issue of natural resources management based on these three different approaches: (1) rights-based approach to natural resources management; (2) rights-holders; and (3) duty bearers.

In terms of methodology, the book is based on a constructivist approach to legal norms and legal decisions, meaning that it does not only focus on their direct material effects but it also adopts a broader perspective under which legal norms and legal decisions are examined to see how they affect society more generally.[38] As such, it adopts a practice-oriented approach to analyse the application and potential implementation of legal norms.[39] However, it does mean that the analysis is circumstantially driven as the aim is to offer an international analysis on the relationship between IHRL and natural resources. Consequently, cases or case-specific situations will be referred to whenever it is relevant to illustrate a situation and support the issues-based analysis, but the book does not rely on any specific case study or any specific situation.

5. Structure of the Book

The structure of the book is guided by the overall international legal framework governing the management of natural resources. It looks at the interaction between IHRL and natural resources based on six main concerns: (1) sovereignty, (2) property, (3) governance, (4) access to sources of livelihood/food production, (5) cultural and natural heritage, and (6) conservation.

The first chapter examines the issue of defining sovereignty over natural resources, which has been a key element in the development of international law, notably leading to the emergence of the principle of States' permanent sovereignty over their natural resources. However, concomitantly, IHRL proclaims the right of peoples to self-determination over their natural resources. This has led to a complex and ambivalent relationship between the principle of States' sovereignty over natural resources and peoples' rights to natural resources. This conflicting relationship is analysed in Chapter 1 which looks at the emergence of the right of peoples to freely dispose of their natural resources and evaluate the potential role of this right in contemporary advocacy. It explores how indigenous peoples have called for the revival

---

[37] See Andrew Clapham, *Human Rights Obligations of Non-State Actors* (OUP, 2006); Nadia Bernaz, *Business and Human Rights: History, Law and Policy—Bridging the Accountability Gap* (Routledge, 2017).

[38] See Jutta Brunnée and Stephen J. Toope, 'International Law and Constructivism: Elements of an Interactional Theory of International Law', 39 *Columbia Journal of Transnational Law*, 2000, 19; Benedict Kingsbury, '"Indigenous Peoples" in International Law: A Constructivist Approach to the Asian Controversy', 92(3) *American Journal of International Law*, 1998, 414–57.

[39] See César Rodríguez-Garavito, 'Beyond the Courtroom: The Impact of Judicial Activism on Socioeconomic Rights in Latin America', 89 *Texas Law Review*, 2010, 1669; Jérémie Gilbert, *Strategic Litigation Impacts—Indigenous Peoples' Land Rights* (Open Society Initiative, 2017).

of their right to sovereignty over natural resources, and how the global peasants' movement has pushed for the recognition of the concept of food sovereignty.

The second chapter focuses on the equally challenging issue of property rights and natural resources. Traditionally, most national jurisdictions are based on a model of 'State property', whereby ownership and control of valuable natural resources are vested in the ultimate authority of the State. Nonetheless, IHRL is gradually incorporating the rights to tenure of local communities, including indigenous peoples, landless peasants, and rural women. Looking at concession agreements for natural resource exploitation, Chapter 2 also examines the clashes between IHRL and investment and trade law, which protect the interests of corporate actors over the rights of the local communities.

The third chapter looks at the role of IHRL in the governance of natural resources. Using the compass of the right to development, it explores how IHRL supports the emergence of a right to participation, to consent, and to benefit from the exploitation of natural resources. It explores how the right to participation has been translated into a right for communities to be consulted in decisions affecting the use of natural resources. Chapter 3 also examines how IHRL is engaging with issues of transparency about the fiscal regimes and taxation of natural resources.

The fourth chapter concerns the worst scenario—when the denial of access to natural resources leads to loss of life. The focus is on the correlation between access to essential natural resources to support livelihood and the right to life. It also focuses on situations of resources conflicts in examining the relationships between international humanitarian law and IHRL in conflict situations. Chapter 4 also looks at the relevance of international criminal law to explore potential avenues to ensure the accountability for crimes connected to the exploitation of natural resources.

The fifth chapter focuses on the relationship between natural resources and cultural rights. For many rural communities, natural resources are integral to their worldview, traditions, folklore, or belief systems. Exploitation and management of natural resources can lead to restrictions of their access to resources that are parts of the cultural life of the local communities. Chapter 5 analyses how cultural rights could extend to the protection of these cultural connections to natural resources, especially looking at the potential relevance of the human rights approach to cultural and religious diversity. It also critically examines the relationship between IHRL and international cultural heritage norms in the context of natural resources heritage.

Finally, Chapter 6 offers a reflection on the connection between the international legal framework dedicated to the protection and conservation of natural resources and IHRL. In the context of an increased convergence between international environmental law and human rights,[40] the chapter proposes to analyse how IHRL supports a new approach to the protection of the natural resources. To do so, it focuses on three main issues that have been at the heart of the interaction between environmental concerns and IHRL: pollution and its impact on human health; protection of biodiversity and endangered species; and climate change. While focusing

[40] See Donald K. Anton and Dinah L. Shelton, *Environmental Protection and Human Rights* (CUP, 2011).

on these specific areas, the chapter also offers a wider reflection on the role of IHRL in supporting the development of a more developed legal framework to protect natural resources.

Overall, in focusing its attention on these six specific areas that govern the relationship between international law and natural resources, the book aims to provide an appraisal of the content of IHRL when it comes to the management of natural resources. Although each chapter is self-contained and could be read on its own, together they constitute a cohesive appraisal of the interaction of IHRL with the overarching legal framework which governs the management of natural resources. To support this appraisal, the conclusion offers a reflection on the potential content and value of a human rights-based approach to natural resources.

1

Sovereignty, Self-Determination, and Natural Resources

Reclaiming Peoples' Rights

All peoples may, for their own ends, freely dispose of their natural wealth and resources . . .

Article 1 (2), International Covenant on Civil and Political Rights & International Covenant on Economic, Social and Cultural Rights

1. Introduction

This chapter focuses on the issue of sovereignty over natural resources and how it relates to the right of peoples to freely dispose of their natural resources. Under public international law, the issue of control over natural resources usually falls under the category of sovereignty rights. Sovereignty entails control over natural resources, and jurisdictional rights over resources within the territory.[1] More precisely, territorial sovereignty conventionally includes the ownership and control over natural resources.[2] Sovereignty over natural resources is traditionally one of the attributes of State sovereignty.[3] Conversely, under international human rights law (IHRL) it belongs to peoples as it forms part of the right to self-determination.[4] Hence, there

---

[1] See Jona Razzaque, 'Resource Sovereignty in the Global Environmental Order'. In: Elena Blanco and Jona Razzaque (eds), *Natural Resources and the Green Economy: Redefining the Challenges for People, States and Corporations* (Brill, 2012), pp. 81–110.

[2] See Antonio Cassese, *International Law in A Divided World* (Clarendon Press, 1986), pp. 376–90.

[3] See George Elian, *The Principle of Sovereignty over Natural Resources* (Sijthoff & Noordhoff International Publishers, 1979); James N. Hyde, 'Permanent Sovereignty over Natural Wealth and Resources', 50(4) *American Journal of International Law*, 1965, 854, 867; Karol Gess, 'Permanent Sovereignty Over Natural Resources: An Analytical Review of the United Nations Declaration and its Genesis', 13 *International & Comparative Law Quarterly*, 1964, 398–449.

[4] See Alice Farmer, 'Towards a Meaningful Rebirth of Economic Self-Determination: Human Rights Realization in Resource-Rich Countries', 39 *NYU Journal of International Law and Politics*, 2007, 417, 424; Lillian Aponte Miranda, 'The Role of International Law in Intrastate Natural Resource Allocation: Sovereignty, Human Rights, and Peoples-Based Development', 45(3) *Vanderbilt Journal of Transnational Law*, 2012, 12–17.

Natural Resources and Human Rights: An Appraisal. Jérémie Gilbert. © J. Gilbert 2018. Published 2018 by Oxford University Press.

is a fundamental ambiguity in the language of international law when it comes to sovereignty over natural resources as it is proclaimed as both a fundamental element of Statehood and as a right of the people. It is one of the very few legal principles that has two rights-holders: States and peoples. According to Schrijver in his anthology on the topic, the principle of permanent sovereignty over natural resources creates both rights and duties for States.[5] One of these duties is to ensure that a people benefits from the exploitation and use of the natural resources. However, as he noted, 'so far international law literature has not addressed the question of exercising permanent sovereignty over natural resources in the interest of national development and the well-being of the people to such an extent that meaningful conclusions can be drawn from it.'[6]

In analysing to what extent a people can exercise their sovereignty over their own natural resources, this chapter hopes to bring some enlightenment on the issue. It explores the correlation between the principle of States' sovereignty over natural resources and the rights of a people to freely dispose of their natural resources and tries to analyse how IHRL provides a counter-narrative to the claim of sovereignty over natural resources by States.

The chapter is divided into three sections. Section 2 examines the emergence of the principle of States' permanent sovereignty over natural resources, and how this relates to the notion of 'stewardship', as a role exercised by the State in the interests of its own population.[7] The second section focuses on the right of peoples to freely dispose of their natural resources as expressed in both the International Covenant on Civil and Political Rights (ICCPR) and the International Covenant on Economic, Social and Cultural Rights (ICESCR). It analyses how a compromise between the right of peoples to self-determination and the principle of State sovereignty over natural resources was reached, and the existing international jurisprudence and doctrine on the issue. Finally, the third section examines how the principle of sovereignty over natural resources has been reclaimed by certain groups of peoples, notably indigenous peoples. It then focuses on the concept of food sovereignty to examine how this concept has been integrated into legal doctrine and jurisprudence as an expression of peoples' right to freely dispose of their natural resources in the context of food production, notably for peasants and small-scale farmers.

2. Sovereignty over Natural Resources: The State Approach

Sovereignty over natural resources has two facets: one external, which ensures control of resources of States against external actors, and one internal, defining the governance of natural resources between the government and its citizens. The

---

[5] Nico Schrijver, *Sovereignty over Natural Resources: Balancing Rights and Duties* (CUP, 2008).
[6] Ibid., 311.
[7] See: Marc Bungenberg and Stephan Hobe (eds), *Permanent Sovereignty over Natural Resources* (Springer, 2015); Emeka Duruigbo, 'Permanent Sovereignty and Peoples' Ownership of Natural Resources in International Law', 38 *George Washington International Law Review*, 2006, 33.

following discussion is concerned with the internal aspect as the goal is to examine how international law has approached the relationship between a State and its citizens when it comes to the exercise of sovereignty over natural resources. To do so, it first goes back to the birth and emergence of the principle of permanent sovereignty over natural resources, and then looks at the specific situation of peoples living under non-self-governing territories.

2.1 Permanent sovereignty over natural resources: decolonization and economic order

The development of international law on the issue of sovereignty over natural resources crystallized around the principle of permanent sovereignty over natural resources. It emerged during the 1950–1960s as an important element of the post-colonial agenda of international law.[8] Exploitation and control of natural resources having been central to colonization; it was only logical that it also became vital to the decolonization movement.[9] This renewed focus on sovereignty over natural resources aimed at ensuring that peoples that had lived under colonial exploitation could now gain their rights to benefit from the exploitation of the resources found within their territories.[10]

One of the first international resolutions on the issue was adopted in 1952 and concerned 'the right to exploit freely natural wealth and resources'.[11] The issue of sovereignty over natural resources then became a focal point with the adoption of a UN General Assembly resolution in 1958, which established the Commission on Permanent Sovereignty over Natural Resources.[12] Its mandate was to conduct a full survey of the status of permanent sovereignty over natural wealth and resources as a basic constituent of the right to self-determination.[13] Probably the clearest expression of the close relationship between decolonization and control over natural resources was expressed in the 1960 'Declaration on the Granting of Independence to Colonial Countries and Peoples'. The declaration marked an important step in the affirmation by the newly independent States of their rights to take full control over their natural resources. Its preamble affirms 'that peoples may, for their own ends, freely dispose of their natural wealth and resources without prejudice to any obligations arising out of international economic co-operation, based upon the principle of mutual benefit, and international law'.[14] It is worth noting that in this resolution,

[8] For an in-depth analysis on the role that sovereignty over natural resources played in these years, see Antony Anghie, *Imperialism, Sovereignty and the Making of International Law* (CUP, 2007), pp. 198–ss.
[9] On this point, see Eric Hobsbawm, *The Age of Empire: 1875–1914* (Abacus, 1989); Mats Ingulstad and Lucas Lixinski, 'Raw Materials, Race, and Legal Regimes: The Development of the Principle of Permanent Sovereignty over Natural Resources in the Americas', 29(1) *World History Bulletin*, 2013, 34.
[10] See Gess (n 3).
[11] General Assembly Resolution 626 (VII), 21 December 1951. See Hyde (n 3).
[12] General Assembly Resolution 1314 (XIII) of 12 December 1958.
[13] The initial proposed resolution was entitled 'Recommendations Concerning International Respect for the Rights of Peoples and Nations to Self-Determination'.
[14] Declaration on the Granting of Independence to Colonial Countries and Peoples, General Assembly Resolution 1514, UN GAOR, 15th Session, Supp. No. 16, UN Doc. A/4684 (1960), Preamble.

it is peoples, not States, that have the right to freely dispose of their natural resources. However, the resolution 'Concerted Action for Economic Development of the Less Developed Countries' adopted on the same day invited States to respect the 'sovereign rights of every State to dispose of its wealth and its natural resources'.[15] Therefore, two resolutions of the UN General Assembly adopted on the very same day put forward the need to respect sovereignty over natural resources, but in one resolution peoples are the subjects while in the other States are. This ambiguity as to who are the rights-holders of the principle of permanent sovereignty over natural resources was to remain a central feature in the development of the principle of sovereignty over natural resources.

Two years later, in 1962, the General Assembly adopted resolution 1803 (XVII) entitled 'Permanent Sovereignty over Natural Resources'.[16] The preamble declares that 'any measure in this respect must be based on the recognition of the inalienable right of all States to freely dispose of their natural wealth and resources in accordance with their national interests, and on respect for the economic independence of States'. The preamble also notes that 'the creation and strengthening of the inalienable sovereignty of States over their natural wealth and resources reinforces their economic independence'. Based on such premises, paragraph 1 states:

The right of peoples and nations to permanent sovereignty over their natural wealth and resources must be exercised in the interest of their national development and of the well-being of the people of the State concerned.[17]

It introduced the idea that the interest of the people might be a limitation to States' sovereignty over natural resources. Probably one of the most important elements of the 1962 resolution was the affirmation that States have to exercise their sovereignty over natural resources 'in the interest of the national development and of the well-being of the people'.

The issue of sovereignty over natural resources also became central to the development of international economic law during the 1970s. The issue of sovereignty over natural resources was seen an essential element in the 1974 Declaration on the Establishment of a New International Economic Order (NIEO). The declaration affirmed that the new economic order should be founded on full respect for the 'full permanent sovereignty of every State over its natural resources and all economic activities'.[18] Likewise, Article 2 of the Charter of Economic Rights and Duties of States reads: 'Every State has and shall freely exercise full permanent sovereignty, including possession, use and disposal, over all its wealth, natural resources and economic activities.'[19] Under the new economic order, the emphasis was on the

[15] General Assembly Resolution 1515 (XV), 15 December 1960, para. 5.
[16] The resolution was adopted on 14 December 1962 by 87 votes against 2 (France and South Africa) with 12 abstentions.
[17] General Assembly Resolution 1803 (XVII), 14 December 1962, 'Permanent Sovereignty over Natural Resources', para. 1.
[18] General Assembly, UN Doc. A/RES/S-6/3201 (1974), para. 4(e).
[19] General Assembly Resolution 3281 (XXIX), 'Charter of Economic Rights and Duties of States', UN Doc. A/RES/29/3281 (1974), Art. 2.

affirmation of States' sovereignty over their natural resources and the need to allow all States to enjoy such sovereignty.[20]

The principle of States' sovereignty over their natural resources is also encapsulated in various international treaties, for example, the 1978 Vienna Convention on Succession of States in Respect of Treaties,[21] the 1982 Convention on the Law of the Sea,[22] the 1983 Vienna Convention on Succession of States in Respect of State Property, Archives and Debt,[23] the 1992 UN Framework Convention on Climate Change, and the 1993 Convention on Biological Diversity.[24] More recently, the principle of States' sovereignty over natural resources was reiterated in the adoption of the Sustainable Development Goals (SDGs).[25] Overall, the principle of States' permanent sovereignty over their natural resources is a well-established principle of public international law, and which is affirmed in more than eighty resolutions and instruments of different bodies of the United Nations.[26] In its 2005 ruling in a case between Uganda and the Democratic Republic of Congo (DRC), the International Court of Justice (ICJ) reiterated that permanent sovereignty over natural resources is a principle of customary international law.[27]

One of the main features of all these different resolutions, declarations, and treaties mentioning or focusing on natural resources is the assertion that States enjoy a quasi-absolute sovereignty over their natural resources.[28] Within this framework, one of the only constraints is that they should exercise their sovereignty to support the well-being of their own citizens. The rationale here is that the State, being the legal expression of the peoples, exercises sovereignty over the natural resources because ultimately it is the State that is entrusted with the exercise of this right. The view is that governments are in charge of ensuring the 'best' utilization of the natural resources that represents the 'common heritage of the nation'.[29] Under this 'functionalist' approach, States have a duty to 'meet the basic rights or needs of their citizens, a duty which in turn requires them to exercise control over the natural resources within their territory'.[30] As Cassese notes, '[g]iven that the people of

---

[20] See Isabel Feichtner, 'International (Investment) Law and Distribution Conflicts over Natural Resources'. In: Rainer Hofmann, Stephan Schill, and Christian Tams (eds), *International Investment Law and Sustainable Development* (Edward Elgar, 2015).

[21] Vienna Convention on Succession of States in Respect of Treaties, 17 *International Legal Materials*, 1488 (22 August 1978); see Art. 13.

[22] Convention on the Law of the Sea, 1833 UNTS 397 (10 December 1982), see Arts 56 and 193.

[23] Vienna Convention on Succession of States in Respect of State Property, Archives and Debt, 25 *International Legal Materials*, 1640 (8 April 1983), see Art. 38(2).

[24] Convention on Biological Diversity, 5 June 1992, 1760 UNTS 143, Art. 15.

[25] 'Transforming Our World: The 2030 Agenda for Sustainable Development', Resolution adopted by the General Assembly on 25 September 2015, UN Doc. A/RES/70/1, para. 18.

[26] For review and analysis, see Schrijver (n 5).

[27] Armed Activities on the Territory of the Congo *(Democratic Republic of the Congo v Uganda)*, Judgment, 2005 ICJ, 19 December 2005, para. 244.

[28] The main limitations concern the respect for foreign investments and the protection of the environment. This is discussed in more detail in Chapter 2 and Chapter 6.

[29] The common heritage terminology has been especially developed through the Law of the Sea; see Convention on the Law of the Sea, UN Doc. A/CONF. 62/122 (1982), reprinted in 21 *International Legal Materials*, 1261, Art. 136.

[30] Chris Armstrong, 'Against "Permanent Sovereignty" over Natural Resources', 14(2) *Politics, Philosophy and Economics*, 2015, 129–51.

every sovereign State have a permanent right to choose by whom they are governed, it is only logical that they should have the right to demand that the chosen central authorities exploit the territory's natural resources so as to benefit the people.'[31] However, as analysed in depth by Schrijver, one of the limitations of the principle of permanent sovereignty over natural resources is the fact that while sovereignty provides important prerogatives to States, it does not impose strong duties regarding their obligations towards their peoples.[32]

In the early years of decolonization, new emerging States have pushed for the recognition of peoples' sovereignty over natural resources. However, after such a first phase, the main actors quickly became the States. All the resolutions on the new economic order push for the recognition of the States' sovereignty over natural resources, not the peoples'. While there was an emphasis on the importance of the 'stewardship' principle under which a State should exercise its sovereignty over natural resources for the benefit of its population, the emphasis became very State-centred, returning to a colonial agenda. Indeed, it was a transfer of sovereignty from the colonial States to the new post-colonial States. In this transfer, which took place under the emergence of the principle of permanent sovereignty over natural resources, the rhetoric of peoples' rights was just that—a rhetorical argument allowing the imposition of the States' absolute sovereignty over natural resources with very little connection to the rights of peoples over these resources.

2.2 Non-self-governing territories and natural resources

The obligation to ensure that sovereignty over natural resources is exercised to ensure the benefit of the people has been mainly examined in the context of non-self-governing territories.[33] While generally there is only a limited amount of jurisprudence regarding the application of the principle of permanent sovereignty over natural resources, the issue of non-self-governing territories has formed a non-negligible element of the jurisprudence of the ICJ.[34] The issue of sovereignty over natural resources was an important element in the 1971 advisory opinion of the ICJ concerning the situation of Namibia under South African rules.[35] In this situation, the ICJ highlighted that the exploitation of uranium and other natural resources in Namibia by South Africa was considered illegal and condemned by the General Assembly.[36] The issue of permanent sovereignty over natural resources was

---

[31] Antonio Cassese, *Self-Determination of Peoples: A Legal Reappraisal* (CUP, 1999), p. 59.

[32] Schrijver (n 5) 306–ss.

[33] Non-self-governing territories are defined in Chapter XI of the United Nations Charter, Art. 73, as 'territories whose peoples have not yet attained a full measure of self-government'.

[34] Regarding the international jurisprudence from the ICJ on natural resources, see Rosalyn Higgins, 'Natural Resources in the Case Law of the International Court', *Themes and Theories* (OUP, 2009).

[35] Legal Consequences for States of the Continued Presence of South Africa in Namibia (South West Africa) notwithstanding Security Council Resolution 276 (1970). For analysis, see Schrijver (n 5) 144–52.

[36] See, for example, UNGA Res. 36/51 of 24 November 1981, and 39/42 of 5 December 1984.

also addressed in the case of *Certain Phosphate Lands in Nauru*.[37] While the parties reached a settlement, in its preliminary observations the Court highlighted the importance to respect the right of the Nauruan people to permanent sovereignty over their natural wealth and resources. Likewise, in a 1995 case concerning East Timor, the ICJ highlighted that the administration of the natural resources by administrative powers must be conducted with the interest of the peoples of the territory.[38] In this particular case, the issue was to determine whether the right of the people of East Timor to permanent sovereignty over its natural wealth and resources had been violated by the negotiation of an agreement between Portugal (then the administrative power) and Indonesia on the exploration and exploitation of the continental shelf in the area of the Timor Gap. While ultimately the Court could not exercise jurisdiction, it nonetheless highlighted that since the territory of East Timor remained a non-self-governing territory, its people had the right to self-determination over their natural resources. All these cases indicate how the ICJ has supported the rights of the people over their natural resources when these territories remain non-self-governing territories.

The situation of the occupied Palestinian territories has also been the focus of several resolutions from the UN General Assembly, highlighting the obligation of Israel to respect the principle of permanent sovereignty in the occupied territories.[39] The UN Human Rights Committee (HRC) also highlighted that the restriction to the access to natural resources, the State party's settlements, the establishment of a partitioning wall, and related-restrictions were all elements infringing on the right to self-determination of Palestinians.[40]

The ongoing dispute regarding the status of the Western Sahara also touches on similar issues as sovereignty over the natural resources is one of the important points of contention. As noted by the UN Under-Secretary for Legal Affairs in 2012, 'if further exploration and exploitation activities were to proceed in disregard of the interests and wishes of the people of Western Sahara, they would be in violation of the international law principles applicable to mineral resource activities in Non-Self-Governing Territories.'[41] In this context, the 2015 decision for the European Court of Justice (ECJ) represents an important milestone.[42] The decision concerned a trade agreement in agricultural and fisheries products that was concluded between Morocco and the European Union (EU). The claim was brought by *Frente Polisario*, the representative organization of the Saharawi, highlighting that the trade agreement was infringing on 'the right to self-determination and the rights which derive from that, in particular, sovereignty over natural resources and the primacy of the

[37] International Court of Justice, Case concerning certain phosphate lands in Nauru (*Nauru v Australia*), Preliminary Objections, Judgment, 26 June 1992.

[38] International Court of Justice, *East Timor (Portugal v Australia)*, Judgment, 30 June 1995

[39] For analysis, see Schrijver (n 5) 152–46.

[40] Human Rights Committee, Concluding Observations: Israel, UN Doc. CCPR/C/ISR/CO/4 (2014), para. 17.

[41] Letter dated 29 January 2002 from the Under-Secretary-General for Legal Affairs, the Legal Counsel, addressed to the President of the Security Council, UN Doc. S/2002/161, para. 25.

[42] European Court of Justice, Judgment of the General Court of 10 December 2015, *Front Polisario v Council* (Case T-512/12).

interests of the inhabitants of Western Sahara'.[43] Although the Court highlighted that there was no absolute prohibition under international law to enter into an agreement regarding natural resources in this context, it also pointed out that such trade agreement could have some serious consequences on the fundamental rights of the population of the concerned territory. The Court rejected the argument put forward by the Council of the EU affirming that 'the issue of whether or not the exploitation of the resources of Western Sahara is carried out to the detriment of the local population only concerns the Moroccan authorities'.[44] Instead, the Court highlighted that were there was a real danger that the trade agreement could result in the exploitation of the resources of Western Sahara to the detriment of its inhabitants, and that the agreement could indirectly encourage this exploitation. Consequently, the court declared that the trade agreement should be annulled as far as it approves the application of that agreement to the Western Sahara. This ruling probably constitutes one of the most advanced legal pronouncements regarding the connection between sovereignty over natural resources and the rights of a people to benefit from it in situations of occupation.

Ultimately, very few peoples, apart from the failed attempts in Katanga,[45] Biafra,[46] and the Western Sahara[47] have claimed their fundamental right to freely dispose of their natural resources against State sovereignty. As Ouguergouz notes, 'apart from the case of a successful secession, it is hard to conceive that an ethnic group could freely dispose of—and therefore exclusively enjoy—natural resources situated in the territory in which it is attached.'[48] This is confirmed by the jurisprudence on the application of the principle of permanent sovereignty over natural resources and its relationship with peoples' rights which predominately focused on the right of peoples still living under occupation or in non-self-governing territories. As Schrijver concludes, 'as regards peoples as right holders, there can be little doubt that originally only peoples still living under colonial rule or foreign occupation were identified as the beneficiaries of the peoples' right to permanent sovereignty over

---

[43] Ibid., para. 189.   [44] Ibid., para. 246.

[45] See René Lemarchand, 'The Limits of Self-Determination: The Case of the Katanga Secession', 56 *The American Political Science Review*, 1962, 2; Thomas Franck and Paul Hoffman, 'The Right to Self-Determination in Very Small Places, 8 *NYU Journal of International Law and Politics*, 1975–76, 404–16.

[46] See David A. Ijalye, 'Was "Biafra" at Any Time a State in International Law?', 65 *American Journal of International Law*, 1971, 551; M. G. Kaladharan Nayar, 'Self-Determination beyond the Colonial Context: Biafra in Retrospect', 10 *Texas International Law Journal*, 1975, 321; Onyeonoro S. Kamanu, 'Secession and the Right of Self-Determination: an O.A.U. Dilemma', 12 *The Journal Of Modern African Studies*, 1974, 355–76.

[47] Hans Morten Haugen, 'The Right to Self-Determination and Natural Resources: The Case of Western Sahara', 3(1) *Lead Law, Environment And Development Journal*, 2007, 70–81; Joshua Castellino, 'A Territorial Interpretation of Identity in International Law: The Case of the Western Sahara,' 29(3) *Millennium Journal Of International Studies*, 1999, 523–59; Laurence S. Hanauer, 'The Irrelevance of Self-Determination Law to Ethno-National Conflict: A New Look at the Western Sahara Case', 9 *Emory International Law Review*, 1995, 133.

[48] Fatasah Ouguergouz, *The African Charter on Human and Peoples' Rights: A Comprehensive Agenda for Human Dignity and Sustainable Development in Africa* (Martinus Nijhoff, 2003), p. 288.

natural resources.'[49] While the ICJ jurisdiction concerns States only, the Court has nonetheless examined whether sovereignty over natural resources is a right to be exercised only by States, or is a right vested in a people. However, this remains limited to situations where States had previously been occupied (or are still occupied) by another State. There is no consequential jurisprudence concerning the application a people against its own State for lack of respect of their right to permanent sovereignty over natural resources.

3. Self-Determination over Natural Resources: Peoples' Rights

In parallel to the development of the principle of States' sovereignty over natural resources, as part of the right to self-determination IHRL proclaims the right of peoples to freely determine the use of their natural resources. As examined in this section, the right to freely use natural resources emerged as part of a compromise between a State-centric and a peoples'-rights approach to sovereignty over natural resources. As such, the right to self-determination over natural resources developed as an ambiguous right, but also as an important contribution to a human rights-based approach to sovereignty over natural resources.

3.1 The emergence of the right to self-determination over natural resources

The issue of control over natural resources was given a prominent place of in IHRL by being inscribed in Article 1 of the two international Covenants as part of the right to self-determination. Common Article 1(2) of the two Covenants states:

All peoples may, for their own ends, freely dispose of their natural wealth and resources without prejudice to any obligations arising out of international economic co-operation, based upon the principle of mutual benefit, and international law. In no case may a people be deprived of its own means of subsistence.[50]

This paragraph is part of the larger right to self-determination. Article 1 on self-determination is often understood as being divided, with paragraph 1 focusing on the so-called 'political' aspect of self-determination, and paragraph 2 focusing on the 'economic' aspect of self-determination. However, this dichotomy is not only erroneous as paragraph 1 includes political, economic, and social development, but it also fails to capture the central importance given to the issue of control over natural resources. Paragraph 2 is very specific to control over natural resources, which clearly is one aspect of economic development, but only partially, since 'economic

---

[49] Nico Schrijver, 'Unravelling State Sovereignty? The Controversy on the Right of Indigenous Peoples to Permanent Sovereignty over their Natural Wealth and Resources'. In: Ineke Boerefijn and Jenny E. Goldschmidt, *Changing Perceptions of Sovereignty and Human Rights* (Intersentia, 2008), p. 88.
[50] International Covenant on Civil and Political Rights, Art. 1, 999 UNTS 171; International Covenant on Economic, Social and Cultural Rights, Art. 1, 993 UNTS 3.

self-determination' is much broader and should include all other aspects of economic development covered in the first paragraph. The inaccurate partition that sees paragraph 1 as the political aspect of self-determination and paragraph 2 as its economic wing has more to do with the historical division between civil and political rights and economic, social, and cultural rights—a divide that was not reproduced in Article 1, which is common to both Covenants. In many ways, the correct label given to paragraph 2 should be 'natural resources self-determination'.

Beyond the purely semantic issue, what matters is that under Article 1 the distinction is not between political and economic self-determination, but rather the emphasis is on the specificity of control over natural resources, which is set aside as a specific right of the people. This specificity of control over natural resources, or the resources aspect of self-determination, proves how this issue is significant and specific. Potentially, it also shows how the two Covenants are ground breaking regarding the comprehension of self-determination, which encompasses the right of a people to freely dispose of their natural resources. Under the current global economic system, which is focused on the exploitation of natural resources, this fundamental aspect of self-determination is undeniably extremely significant. To understand the extent to which the article is far reaching, it is necessary to go back to its drafting history.[51] Originally, the reference to natural resources was integrated into paragraph 3 of draft Article 1 to the two Covenants. It reads that the

right of peoples to self-determination shall also include permanent sovereignty over their natural wealth and resources. In no case may a people be deprived of its own means of subsistence on the grounds of any rights that may be claimed by other States.[52]

The proposed draft faced strong opposition from most of the Western industrialized States. As Nowak notes in his commentary on the ICCPR, the wording of this draft article introduced by Chile 'was heavily amended to the point that its legal meaning has become extremely unclear'.[53] Two principal issues became the centre of deliberation during the drafting process.

The first issue concerned the insertion of the notion of 'permanent sovereignty' in an article concerning peoples' rights, not States'. The first objection to the drafting of this paragraph was a pragmatic one, as it highlighted that including 'permanent sovereignty' was itself a contradiction, since international law was already asserting that States, not peoples, exercised permanent sovereignty over natural resources. As highlighted earlier, States' right to permanent sovereignty over their natural resources was becoming a strong principle of international law and was given prominence in several UN Declarations and Resolutions throughout the 1960s. However, it was argued that the right to self-determination and the concept of permanent sovereignty

---

[51] See E/CN.4/SR.256-257; E/CN.4/L.24; and Official Records of the General Assembly, Ninth Session, Third Committee, 567th, 568th, 573rd, and 576th meetings.

[52] See 'Annotations on the Text of the Draft International Covenants on Human Rights', UN Doc. A/2929 (1955), p. 15, at para. 19.

[53] Manfred Nowak, *UN Covenant on Civil and Political Rights. CCPR Commentary* (N. P. Engel, 1993), p. 24; see also: Manfred Nowak, *UN Covenant on Civil and Political Rights. CCPR Commentary*, 2nd edition (N. P. Engel, 2005).

over natural resources should reflect 'the simple and elementary principle that a nation or people should be master of its own natural wealth or resources'.[54] Ultimately, the reference to 'permanent sovereignty' was removed. In the trade-off, the reference to the fact that a people 'shall' have a right to self-determination over their natural resources was changed to the more positive affirmation that peoples 'have' such a right, making the right much more undeviating.

The second issue relates to the scope of the right to self-determination. Several States saw the inclusion of peoples' right to permanent sovereignty as 'dangerous', since 'it would sanction unwarranted expropriation or confiscation of foreign property and would subject international agreements and arrangements to unilateral renunciation'.[55] This concern resulted in the insertion of two qualifications to peoples' right over natural resources: (1) such a right should not impair or conflict with international treaties that aim at promoting international economic cooperation; and (2) it may not violate international norms protecting the rights of foreign investors. The issue of protecting foreign investments was seen as particularly important, and emphasized that the right to self-determination 'was not intended to frighten off foreign investment by a threat of expropriation or confiscation; it was intended rather to warn against such foreign exploitation as might result in depriving the local population of its own means of subsistence'.[56] Regarding foreign investments, the drafting history of Article 1(2) shows that the aim of the drafters was dual—to ensure that the expropriation or nationalization of foreign investments would be adequately protected and compensated, and that such a right would not undermine foreign investments.[57]

The introduction of a restriction to self-determination to protect foreign investment engendered a much larger debate on the potential limitations to a peoples' right to control their own natural resources. As noted:

It was feared that States might invoke allegedly acquired rights in order to thwart the implementation of the right of peoples to self-determination and to the control of their natural resources. Concepts such as public order or prevention of disorder, which were open to broad interpretations, might easily nullify the whole concept of self-determination.[58]

In general, the limitations added to the right to self-determination over natural resources were seen as a potential Pandora's box that could open the opportunity for States to seriously undermine peoples' rights. As a result, an additional provision was added to each of the Covenants. Article 47 of the ICCPR and Article 25 of the ICESCR further stipulate that:

[n]othing in the present Covenant shall be interpreted as impairing the inherent right of all peoples to enjoy and utilize fully and freely their natural wealth and resources.

---

[54] Annotations on the Text of the Draft International Covenants on Human Rights, UN Doc. A/2929 (1955), p. 15, para. 21.

[55] Annotations on the Text of the Draft International Covenants on Human Rights, para. 20.

[56] Ibid.

[57] See Cassese (n 31) 56.

[58] Annotations on the Text of the Draft International Covenants on Human Rights, UN Doc. A/2929 (1955), p. 25, para. 52.

Hence, when focusing on the rights of a people to freely dispose of their natural resources it is necessary to look beyond common Article 1, as this right is also re-affirmed in other articles of the two Covenants, making it one of the few human rights to be stipulated twice in the same instrument. As Cassese notes, these provisions were inserted in the Covenants much later than Article 1(2) and were aimed at 'rectifying' it.[59]

As an illustration, during the debate that led to the adoption of Article 25 of the ICESCR, the delegate from Ethiopia highlighted that one of the rationales to include such an article was the effort of 'underdeveloped countries to seek to protect their resources against the imperialist powers which sought to exploit them under the cloak of technical assistance or international economic co-operation'.[60] This statement echoes the position of several other countries supporting the inclusion of Article 25, which viewed the restrictions on the rights of peoples to dispose of their own natural resources as a way of ensuring the continuous economic exploitation of such resources. Fourteen States introduced the new draft article after Article 1 had already been adopted.[61] The drafting of this article raised significant debates in the Third Committee of the General Assembly. Several States opposed the introduction of the article, stressing that it would run against the content of Article 1, with the UK representative highlighting 'that the proposed article created an internal contradiction within the Covenant, which would render the Covenant impossible of interpretation'.[62] In the end, the article was adopted with 75 votes in favour, four against, and 20 abstentions.[63] The equivalent Article 46 of the ICCPR was adopted the following month, in November 1966, with less discussion following the prior adoption of Article 25 of the ICESCR.

Hence, the two Covenants offer an ambiguous approach regarding peoples' rights to dispose of their natural resources: it is a qualified right under Article 1, and an absolute right under Article 25 of the ICESCR and Article 46 of the ICCPR. From the very beginning, at the drafting stages, two issues were raised that will haunt the right of peoples to freely dispose of their natural resources: the definition of who the rights-holders are (peoples or States), and its limitations, especially when it comes to the protection of foreign investments.[64]

---

[59] See Cassese (n 31) 57. Some authors have even suggested that Art. 47 was intended to override Art. 1(2).

[60] See Provisional Summary Record, Document A/C.3/SR.1405, 27 October 1966, at 3. See also David Halperin, 'Human Rights and Natural Resources', 9(3) *William and Mary Law Review*, 1968, 770–87.

[61] Chile, Ghana, Guinea, India, Iran, Iraq, Nepal, Nigeria, Pakistan, Sudan, United Arab Republic, United Republic of Tanzania, Venezuela, and Yugoslavia.

[62] Lady Gaitskell, in Provisional Summary Record, Doc. A/C.3/SR. 1405, 27 October 1966, at 5.

[63] For the list of countries, see Provisional Summary Record, Doc. A/C.3/SR. 1405, at 11–12. For detailed analysis of the process, see Halperin (n 60).

[64] This later aspect concerning investments is examined in details in Chapter 2.

3.2 A compromised and ambiguous right

In the development of IHRL, the next step regarding the affirmation of a peoples' right to control their natural resources came with the adoption of the African Charter on Human and Peoples' Rights.[65] Article 21(1) of the African Charter affirms that:

[a]ll peoples shall freely dispose of their wealth and natural resources. This right shall be exercised in the exclusive interest of the people. In no case shall a people be deprived of it.

Compared to the language used in the international Covenants, the African Charter put a greater emphasis on the 'exclusive interest' of the peoples. This goes further than the rights of peoples to use their natural resources for their own ends as it puts forward the notion that the interest of the people should be the exclusive driving force behind any use of natural resources.[66] However, the language used in this article creates ambivalence on whether peoples or States are the rights-holders of the right to self-determination over natural resources. Adding to such ambiguity, paragraph 4 of the same article stipulates that 'States parties to the present Charter shall individually and collectively exercise the right to free disposal of their wealth and natural resources with a view to strengthening African unity and solidarity'. While the right is clearly a right that belongs to the people, it is the States that will ultimately exercise the enjoyment of the right.[67] Under this phrasing, it seems that States are the right holders of a right over natural resources. Kiwanuka sees this as an expression of a State's duty to act as trustee of its own people.[68]

More generally, the phrasing used in the African Charter is representative of the general ambivalence regarding the right to freely dispose of natural resources under IHRL. Clearly, with the adoption of the two Covenants and the African Charter, IHRL supports the claim that the right to freely dispose of natural resources is a right of the people.[69] But at the same time, the human rights framework has not entirely dealt with the controversial issue of how such a right interacts with the international

---

[65] Neither the European Convention on Human Rights nor the American Convention on Human Rights addresses the rights of peoples to control their natural resources. On the drafting history and the reason for the non-inclusion of self-determination, see Thomas Buergenthal, 'The American Convention on Human Rights: Illusions and Hopes', 21 *Buffalo Law Review*, 1971–72, 121; Patrick Thornberry, 'Self-Determination, Minorities, Human Rights: A Review of International Instruments', 38 *International and Comparative Law Quarterly*, 1989, 867–89; A. W. Brian Simpson, *Human Rights and The End of Empire: Britain and The Genesis of the European Convention* (OUP, 2004).

[66] This right was central in the *Ogoni* case under which Nigeria was found to have been violating Art. 21; see *Social and Economic Rights Action Center (SERAC) and the Center for Economic and Social Rights v Nigeria*, Communication 155/96, paras 55–8.

[67] For further discussion, see Peter Jones, 'Human Rights, Group Rights, and Peoples' Rights', 21(1) *Human Rights Quarterly*, 1999, 80–107; Natan Lerner, *Group Rights and Discrimination in International Law* (Martinus Nijhoff, 2003); Frank Thomas, *The Empowered Self: Law and Society in the Age of Individualism* (OUP, 2000); Philip Alston (ed.), *Peoples' Rights* (OUP, 2001).

[68] Richard Kiwanuka, 'The Meaning of Peoples in the African Charter on Human and Peoples' Rights', 82(1) *American Journal of International Law*, 1988, 80–101.

[69] Note that that the American Convention on Human Rights does not address the issue of control of the natural resources (or self-determination) and that the Additional Protocol to the American Convention on Human Rights in the Area of Economic, Social and Cultural Rights ('Protocol of San Salvador') mentions it only in its preamble.

legal principle of States' sovereignty over their natural resources.[70] While IHRL supports and affirms that peoples are ultimately the holders of the right to freely dispose of their natural resources, in practice such a right clashes head on with the international legal principle of State sovereignty over these resources. This goes to the heart of the fundamental complexity of the international legal system, which has been developed by States and for States, while allowing some room for peoples' and individual rights within the system under the banner of IHRL.

Of all the human rights issues that directly challenge States' absolute sovereignty over their peoples and territories, control over natural resources probably remains one of the most contentious. Under the contemporary drive to exploit natural resources and their value, the human rights claim to peoples' rights to freely dispose of their natural resources might even be perceived as utopian.[71] The somewhat imperfect human rights affirmation that people should freely dispose of their natural resources could be seen as idealistic as ultimately governments are *de facto* and *de jure* exercising control over those natural resources.[72] More positively, the affirmation of a right for the people could be seen as a compromise that needs to be reached in order to articulate the fundamental idea that States should exercise control for the interest of their peoples. This approach is confirmed by that adopted by the African Commission on Human and Peoples' Rights (ACoHPR) in its 2001 decision regarding the situation of the Ogoni people in Nigeria.[73] The Commission highlighted that 'the origin of this provision may be traced to colonialism, during which the human and material resources of Africa were largely exploited for the benefit of outside powers, creating tragedy for Africans themselves, depriving them of their birth right and alienating them from the land'. In this particular instance, the African Commission found that the Nigerian authorities had violated Article 21 of the African Charter by giving 'the green light to private actors, and the oil companies in particular, to devastatingly affect the well-being of the Ogonis'.[74]

From this perspective, the affirmation of a people's right over natural resources creates a restriction to States' sovereignty, namely, that States must ensure that their people freely dispose of their natural resources. This compromise remains extremely ambiguous with the affirmation of two rights-holders. Nonetheless, IHRL proposes an alternative to the overarching principle of States' permanent sovereignty over natural resources and puts forward the perspective of a peoples' fundamental right over their own natural resources. Only the practical implementation of the right of a

---

[70] For an enlightening discussion and analysis on whether the right belongs to the peoples or the States, see Emeka Duruigbo, 'Permanent Sovereignty and Peoples' Ownership of Natural Resources in International Law', 38(1) *George Washington International Law Review*, 2006, 33.

[71] Jérémie Gilbert, 'The Right to Freely Dispose of Natural Resources: Utopia or Forgotten Right', 31 *Netherlands Quarterly of Human Rights*, 2013, 314–41.

[72] Most of the national laws assert that the State owns a country's natural resources. See Elizabeth Bastida, Thomas Walde, and Janeth Warden-Fernandezet (eds), *International and Comparative Mineral Law And Policy: Trends and Prospects* (Kluwer, 2005); Aileen McHarg, Barry Barton, Adrian Bradbrook, and Lee Godden (eds), *Property and the Law in Energy and Natural Resources* (OUP, 2010).

[73] African Commission on Human and Peoples' Rights, 155/96: *Social and Economic Rights Action Center (SERAC) and Center for Economic and Social Rights (CESR) v Nigeria* (2001).

[74] Ibid., para. 58.

people to freely dispose of their natural resources can offer guidance on the impact of such an affirmation; the next part of this chapter delves into the operationalization of such a right.

4. Reclaiming Sovereignty: Indigenous Peoples, Peasants, and Food Sovereignty

Despite being at the centre of these controversies, the right of peoples to freely dispose of their natural resources has remained a very toned-down issue in human rights jurisprudence. There are exceptions to this silence, notably when it comes to the rights of indigenous peoples. Indigenous peoples have managed to revive the importance of the right to self-determination over natural resources, highlighting how the right to freely dispose of their natural resources constitutes an essential element of their human rights. The other more recent area where the right to freely dispose of natural resources has been revived relates to the emerging principle of food sovereignty defended by several farmers and peasants' movements across the globe. The following discussion examines (1) how indigenous peoples have managed to revive the human rights approach to sovereignty over natural resources, and (2) how the concept of food sovereignty offers a powerful platform for peasants, small-scale food producers, and other rural groups to reclaim control over natural resources.

4.1 Indigenous peoples and the revival of self-determination over natural resources

The development of the legal framework on indigenous peoples' human rights, and notably its focus on self-determination, has challenged the dominant State-centric approach to sovereignty over natural resources.[75] A 2004 United Nations study on indigenous peoples' permanent sovereignty over natural resources highlighted that indigenous peoples enjoy the right to self-determination over their natural resources, including the right to freely dispose of these resources.[76] It is within this context that one of the most advanced practical applications of this right has taken place. International human rights treaty monitoring bodies frequently refer to the right of indigenous peoples over their natural resources; the HRC has referred several times to Article 1(2) of the Covenant in relation to indigenous peoples. The Committee has integrated Article 1 within both its individual opinions and concluding observations

---

[75] See Maivân Lâm, *At the Edge of the State: Indigenous Peoples and Self-Determination* (Transnational Publishers, 2000); Tomas Hopkins Primeau, and Jeff Corntassel, 'Indigenous "Sovereignty" and International Law: Revised Strategies for Pursuing "Self-Determination"', 17(2) *Human Rights Quarterly*, 1995, 343–65; Alexandra Xanthaki, *Indigenous Rights and United Nations Standards: Self-Determination, Culture and Land* (CUP, 2007).

[76] *Indigenous Peoples' Permanent Sovereignty Over Natural Resources*, UN Doc. E/CN.4/Sub.2/2004/ 30 and Add. 1.

regarding indigenous peoples.[77] For examples, in its Concluding Observations on Canada, the HRC emphasized that 'the right to self-determination requires, *inter alia*, that all peoples must be able to freely dispose of their natural resources and that they may not be deprived of their own means of subsistence (Art. 1, para. 2)'.[78] Likewise, the Committee has invited Norway to report 'on the Saami peoples' right to self-determination under Article 1 of the Covenant, including paragraph 2 of that article'.[79] References to indigenous peoples' right to self-determination were also made in the Concluding Observations on Mexico, Panama, Australia, Denmark, and Sweden.[80]

The Committee on Economic, Social and Cultural Rights (CESCR) has adopted a similar approach, referring to Article 1 of the Covenant in several of its concluding observations;[81] for example, regarding Paraguay it expressed its concerns 'about the fact that the state party has not yet legally recognized the right of indigenous peoples to dispose freely of their natural wealth and resources or put in place an effective mechanism to enable them to claim their ancestral lands (Art. 1)'.[82] The main approach of the HRC and the CESCR has been to connect self-determination with a stronger role in decision making for indigenous peoples when it comes to the management and use of natural resources located on their ancestral territories.[83] This strong connection between self-determination and natural resources is also inscribed in the UN Declaration on the Rights of Indigenous Peoples (UNDRIP). Article 3 mirrors the content of Article 1 of the international Covenants stating that 'Indigenous peoples have the right to self-determination. By virtue of that right they freely determine their political status and freely pursue their economic, social and cultural development.'

The connection between self-determination and natural resources constitutes a strong element of the legal jurisprudence on indigenous peoples' rights. The Inter-American Court of Human Rights (IACtHR) has been particularly active on this front.[84] In the case of the *Saramaka People*, the IACtHR explained that 'property rights must be interpreted so as not to restrict their right to self-determination, by virtue of which indigenous peoples may "freely pursue their economic, social

---

[77] See *Apirana Mahuika et al. v New Zealand*, Communication No. 547/1993, UN Doc. CCPR/ C/70/D/547/1993 (2000); see also Martin Scheinin, 'The Right to Self-Determination Under the Covenant on Civil and Political Rights'. In: Pekka Aikio and Martin Scheinin (eds), *Operationalizing the Right of Indigenous Peoples to Self-Determination* (Institute for Human Rights, 2000).

[78] *Concluding Observations*, Canada, UN Doc. CCPR/C/79/Add.105 (1999).

[79] *Concluding Observations*, Norway, UN Doc. CCPR/C/79/Add.112 (1999).

[80] See Panama, UN Doc. CCPR/C/PAN/CO/3 (2008).

[81] See: Argentina, UN Doc. E/C.12/ARG/CO/3 (2011); Finland: UN Doc. E/C.12/FIN/CO/6 (2014); Guatemala, UN Doc. E/C.12/GTM/CO/3 (2014); Cambodia, UN Doc. E/C.12/KHM/CO/ 1 (2009).

[82] CESCR, Paraguay, UN Doc. E/C.12/PRY/CO/4 (2015).

[83] This aspect is analysed in detail in Chapter 3.

[84] See Lila Barrera-Hernandez, 'Sovereignty over Natural Resources under Examination: The Inter-American System for Human Rights and Natural Resource Allocation', 12 *Annual Survey of International and Comparative Law*, 2006, 43; Lillian Aponte Miranda, 'The U'WA and Occidental Petroleum: Searching for Corporate Accountability in Violations of Indigenous Land Rights', 31(2) *American Indian Law Review*, 2006, 651–73.

and cultural development" and may "freely dispose of their natural wealth and re-sources".[85] A similar approach was adopted in *Case of the Kaliña and Lokono Peoples v Suriname*.[86] The Court stated that:

the right to property protected by Article 21 of the American Convention, and interpreted in light of the rights recognized in Article 1 common to the two Covenants, and Article 27 of the ICCPR which cannot be restricted when interpreting the American Convention in this case, confer on the members of the Kaliña and Lokono peoples the right to the enjoyment of their property in keeping with their community-based tradition.[87]

The ACoHPR has also highlighted the connection between the right to self-determination, control of natural resources, and land rights. In the *Endorois* decision, the ACoHPR found that the non-respect of the right to land of the indigenous community was a violation of Article 21 of the African Charter which states that 'all peoples shall freely dispose of their wealth and natural resources'. In finding a violation of Article 21, the ACoHPR did acknowledge that the right to freely dispose of natural resources is of crucial importance to indigenous peoples and their way of life.[88] This was later confirmed in the African Court's decision regarding the Ogiek community in Kenya, in which the court ruled that the government of Kenya had violated Article 21 of the Charter by restricting access to territories and natural resources that were essential to guarantee the Ogieks' access to food.[89]

This jurisprudence linking self-determination and control over natural resources certainly represents an important development knowing that for most indigenous communities the notion of territory includes a collective rights-based approach to the access, disposal, and use of the natural resources.[90] As examined in more detail in Chapter 3, this connection between self-determination, natural resources, and land rights has been operationalized and been given a practical implementation through the right to free, prior, and informed consent (FPIC). Under this approach, self-determination over natural resources means that indigenous peoples need to consent to the use of the resources located in their territories. Overall, indigenous peoples have managed to revive the rights of peoples to self-determination over their natural resources, not that their sovereignty has been recognized per se but through the recognition that their right to self-determination encompasses their rights to land ownership and to participate, manage, and benefit from the natural resources located on their territories.[91]

[85] *Case of the Saramaka People v Suriname*, Judgment, Inter-American Court of Human Rights Series C No. 172 (28 November 2007), para. 93.
[86] *Case of the Kaliña and Lokono Peoples v Suriname*, Judgment, 25 November 2015 (Merits, Reparations and Costs).
[87] Ibid., para. 124. Interestingly, the Court has also included an examination of Art. 23 of the American Convention relating to the right to participate in government (para. 126).
[88] On the correlation between cultural rights and access to natural resources, see also *Social and Economic Rights Action Center and the Center for Economic and Social Rights/Nigeria*, Communication No. 155/96.
[89] African Court on Human and Peoples' Rights, Application No. 006/2012; *African Commission on Human and Peoples' Rights v Republic of Kenya* (26 May 2017), para. 201.
[90] See Jérémie Gilbert, *Indigenous Peoples' Land Rights under International Law: From Victims to Actors*, 2nd edition (Brill, 2016).
[91] These aspects are examined in detail in Chapter 2 and Chapter 3.

4.2 Food sovereignty, peasants, and natural resources

The development of the rights to self-determination over natural resources forms a central element of the push for the recognition of the right to food sovereignty. The concept of food sovereignty puts forward the rights of peoples to reclaim control of their food production, based on a composite approach to the right to self-determination, the right to food, and the right to development.[92] An important element of the right to self-determination over natural resources concerns access to essential resources to ensure food security. The formulation of Article 1(2) of the two Covenants indicates: 'in no case may a people be deprived of its own means of subsistence.' In this context, Alston argues that common Article 1(2) of the two Covenants should be understood as inviting States 'to take measures to ensure that its own people are not in any case deprived of its own means of subsistence, including food ... and to investigate any situation where such deprivation is alleged to be occurring.'[93] The landmark decision of the ACoHPR in *Social and Economic Rights Action Centre (SERAC) and Another v Nigeria* focused on Article 21 of the African Charter which also affirms that in no case a people shall be deprived of its means of subsistence. In this case, the ACoHPR found that the destruction and contamination of food sources (e.g. water, soil, and crops) by the Nigerian government and by the Nigerian State oil company violated the right to food of the Ogoni people. In the view of the ACoHPR, the government had violated Article 21 of the African Charter because of its failure to protect the right of the Ogoni people to freely dispose of their wealth and natural resources.[94]

The correlation between the right to freely dispose of natural resources and the right to food has found some echoes in the work of the UN Special Rapporteur on the right to food, notably in the context of the global food crisis. De Schutter, the former UN Special Rapporteur, had put the emphasis on the correlation between large-scale acquisition of land by major food-importing States losing confidence in the global market as a stable and reliable source of food and the consequent loss of control by the local people of their capacity to feed themselves. He highlighted how this large-scale acquisition threatens peoples' right to food as well as their fundamental right to freely control the use of their natural resources.[95] In this context the application of the right of peoples to freely dispose of their natural resources is to ensure the realization of their right to food. The focus is on access to natural

---

[92] See Tina Beuchelt and Detlef Virchow, 'Food Sovereignty or the Human Right to Adequate Food: Which Concept Serves Better as International Development Policy for Global Hunger and Poverty Reduction?', 29(2) *Agriculture and Human Values*, 2012, 259–73; Hans Morten Haugen, 'Food Sovereignty—An Appropriate Approach to Ensure the Right to Food?', 78(3) *Nordic Journal of International Law*, 2009, 263–92.

[93] Philip Alston, 'International Law and the Human Right to Food'. In: Philip Alston and Katarina Tomasevski (eds), *The Right to Food* (Martinus Nijhoff, 1984), pp. 9–40.

[94] 155/96 Social and Economic Rights Action Center (SERAC) and Center for Economic and Social Rights (CESR)/Nigeria (27 October 2001).

[95] Report of the Special Rapporteur on the Right to Food, Olivier de Schutter, 'Large-Scale Land Acquisitions and Leases: A Set of Minimum Principles and Measures to Address the Human Rights Challenge', UN Doc. A/HRC/33/13/Add.2.

resources to ensure food security. A study undertaken on behalf of the UN Food and Agriculture Organization (FAO) indicated that the

> normative content of the right to adequate food has major implications for access to natural resources. In much of Africa, access to natural resources is a main source of food for the majority of the rural population. Land and water are central to food production. Forest resources provide a basis for subsistence harvesting as well as for income-generating activities (e.g. through timber production). There is therefore an important relationship between realizing the right to food and improving access to natural resources.[96]

The interconnection between the right to food and the right of peoples to freely dispose of their natural resources has gained momentum with the emergence of the concept of 'food sovereignty', which emphasizes the right to produce food as a key component of the right to food.[97]

Food sovereignty has been advocated by the transnational agrarian movement *La Via Campesina*, and adopted by several civil society organizations working on food security at the NGO forum to the 1996 World Food Summit.[98] According to Claeys, the global food sovereignty movement is 'a transnational movement of rural social organisations that works towards achieving structural changes in the global food system, which has widely relied on the discourse of rights to advance its claims'.[99] Using the human rights-based argument of a combined right to food and self-determination, local communities and small-scale farmers have claimed their right to 'food sovereignty'.[100] Food sovereignty is based on the idea that food production should be a right of local communities, which means that these populations should control the use of the natural resources necessary for food production. It refers to 'the right of people to healthy and culturally appropriate food produced though socially just and ecologically sensitive methods. It entails peoples' right to participate in decision-making, and to define their own food and agriculture systems.'[101] It implies retaking control, or sovereignty, over agricultural policies and decisions regarding food production. It entails control over productive resources (e.g. land, water, seeds) for peasants/family farmers, pastoralists, artisanal fisher-folk, indigenous peoples, landless peoples, rural workers, and forest communities.[102] Food

---

[96] Lorenzo Cotula, Moussa Djiré, and Ringo W. Tenga, *The Right to Food and Access to Natural Resources: Using Human Rights Arguments and Mechanisms to Improve Resource Access for The Rural Poor* (Food and Agriculture Organization of the United Nations, Rome, 2008), p. 21.

[97] See Marc Edelman, James C. Scott, Amita Baviskar, Saturnino M. Borras Jr., Deniz Kandiyoti, Eric Holt-Gimenez, Tony Weis, and Wendy Wolford, *The Journal of Peasant Studies: Global Agrarian Transformations: Critical Perspectives on Food Sovereignty*, 41(6) *The Journal of Peasant Studies*, 2014.

[98] See Annette Desmarais, 'The Power of Peasants: Reflections on the Meanings of La Via Campesina', 24(2) *Journal of Rural Studies*, 2008, 138–49.

[99] Priscilla Claeys, *Human Rights and the Food Sovereignty Movement: Reclaiming Control* (Routledge, 2015), p. 27 (references omitted).

[100] Christina Schiavoni, 'The Global Struggle for Food Sovereignty: From Nyéléni to New York', 36(3) *Journal of Peasant Studies*, 2009, 682–9; Priscilla Claeys, 'The Creation of New Rights by the Food Sovereignty Movement: The Challenge of Institutionalizing Subversion', 46(5) *Sociology*, 2012, 844–60.

[101] Declaration of Nyéléni, February 2007.

[102] See Annette Aurélie Desmarais, Priscilla Claeys, and Amy Trauger (eds), *Public Policies for Food Sovereignty Social Movements and the State* (Routledge, 2017).

sovereignty was initially triggered as a reaction to the dominant model of food security proclaimed by the dominant international institutions such as the World Bank, the International Monetary Fund, and the World Trade Organization.[103] From this perspective, food sovereignty appears as a contrast to the dominant themes such as competition, efficiency, unfettered growth, and consumption, issues which dominate the food security agenda.[104]

One of the central aspects of the concept of 'food sovereignty' is the peoples' right to freely define food and agricultural policies that are best suited to them. While the concept of 'food sovereignty' is not part of the international legal human rights framework per se, the concept has gained increased recognition notably by being included in the Draft United Nations Declaration on the Rights of Peasants and Other People Working in Rural Areas,[105] and in a number of national constitutions.[106] Food sovereignty has also become an important concept in global discussions on the governance of land and natural resources. As highlighted by a recent study from the Food and Agriculture Organization (FAO): 'Because of its different conceptual underpinnings, the political (rather than legal) concept of food sovereignty places more specific emphasis on access to resources. ... the food sovereignty framework provides more far-reaching ammunition than the right to food for calls to improve resource access'.[107] Together, the use of concepts such as the right to food sovereignty, the right to permanent sovereignty over natural resources, and the right to food have managed to re-open the idea that sovereignty over the use of natural resources, in this case to produce food, belongs to the peoples, not only to the States.

5. Conclusion

Despite the fact that over the last few decades there has been a reduction or a loss of States' absolute sovereignty, the principle of State sovereignty still remains one of the central principles of international law.[108] Although the increased movement

---

[103] See María Elena Martínez-Torres and Peter M. Rosset, 'La Vía Campesina: The Birth and Evolution of a Transnational Social Movement', 37(1) *The Journal of Peasant Studies*, 2010, 149–75.

[104] See Hannah Wittman, Annette Aurélie Desmarais, and Nettie Wiebe (eds), *Food Sovereignty: Reconnecting Food, Nature and Community* (Fernwood Publishing/Food First Books: Halifax, 2010).

[105] See the Open-Ended Intergovernmental Working Group on a United Nations declaration on the rights of peasants and other people working in rural areas, Human Rights Council, Promotion and Protection of the Human Rights of Peasants and Other People Working in Rural Areas, UN Doc. A/HRC/RES/21/19 (2012).

[106] For example, the Constitution of Ecuador, the Constitution of Bolivia, and the Declaration of Cochabamba on Food Security with Sovereignty in the Americas, adopted by the General Assembly of the Organization of American States in June 2012.

[107] Lorenzo Cotula, Moussa Djiré, and Ringo W. Tenga, *The Right to Food and Access to Natural Resources: Using Human Rights Arguments and Mechanisms to Improve Resource Access for the Rural Poor* (Food and Agriculture Organization of the United Nations, 2008), p. 24.

[108] See Martti Koskenniemi, 'What Use for Sovereignty Today?', 1(1) *Asian Journal of International Law*, 2010, 61–70; Eric C. Ip, 'Globalization and the Future of the Law of the Sovereign State', 8(3) *International Journal of Constitutional Law*, 2010, 636–55; Saskia Sassen, *Losing Control? Sovereignty in the Age of Globalization* (Columbia University Press, 1996).

of peoples across borders and the expansion of transnational markets might have blurred some aspects of sovereignty, the control and ownership of natural resources remains a very strong component of States' jurisdictional power. From the perspective of international law, the international legal principle of permanent sovereignty over natural resources is relatively young as it was born mainly as part of the decolonization movement. It was first being proclaimed as being a fundamental element of peoples' rights to decolonization to then becoming a more centralized principle of the inter-State economic order to protect national development. Although it has emerged from the postcolonial ideal that States' sovereignty should be guided by the benefit of the people, it nonetheless remained embedded within the notion of sovereignty of the State rather than a right of the peoples. There is a duty attached to the principle of States' permanent sovereignty over natural resources which is to exercise it in the interest of national development and to ensure that the whole population benefits from the exploitation of the resources. However, as highlighted earlier this notion of stewardship attached to sovereignty has in reality been leading to a transfer to the elites and to commercial ventures involved in the exploitation of natural resources. In practice, States' sovereignty over natural resources is exercised by political, administrative, and economic leaders. This absolute control of the resources has led to what has been labelled as 'resource privilege'. As noted by Pogge, the current international legal system allows the perpetuation of an elite which keeps control of the natural resources to the detriment of the local populations. He talks about 'the resource privilege' that is conferred upon elite groups in power.[109]

This chapter examines one of the main challenges to this State-centric sovereignty over natural resources, which arises in the context of indigenous peoples' rights. In the long battle that took place to get the UNDRIP adopted in 2007, indigenous peoples' activists have made sure that self-determination and its connection to natural resources remained an important element of this new declaration. As analysed, there is now a significant doctrine and jurisprudence linking indigenous peoples' right to self-determination and natural resources. Of course, this does not mean that in practice indigenous peoples have regained sovereignty over their natural resources, but it has nonetheless opened a new perspective in reviving the principle of natural resources self-determination which was undermined under the international legal agenda. In this process, the promises of Article 1 of the two international Covenants have been re-born and put into action in the practice of the international human rights treaty bodies. The push by indigenous peoples to reclaim and revive the fundamental human rights to self-determination over natural resources has also served as a catalyst and support to push for new battlegrounds to reclaim control over natural resources. The more recent movement of peasants, small-scale farmers, and local communities to inscribe the right to sovereignty and control over natural resources within the international human rights agenda is an illustration of this potential revival. At the time of writing, it is too early to predict if the promises of IHRL

---

[109] Thomas Pogge, *World Poverty and Human Rights* (Polity, 2008), p. 119.

to recognize the rights of peoples to freely dispose of their natural resources would ever be achieved. The indigenous peoples' and peasant/rural peoples' movements are at a vanguard of a renewed human rights approach to the issue of sovereignty over natural resources—an approach which is challenging the overall focus on States' absolute sovereignty over their resources.

2

Property Rights and Natural Resources

States, Communities, and Corporations

!El agua es nuestra, carajo!
(The water is ours, dammit!)

Protestors in Cochabamba, 2000[1]

1. Introduction

As examined in Chapter 1, most national jurisdictions are based on a model of States' sovereignty over natural resources where control over the use of resources is in the hands of the State. This is expressed under the principle of permanent sovereignty over natural resources. As part of this, States define the rules regarding property rights of the resources within their territory.[2] The origins of most property rights can be traced back to the western Regalian regime, later integrated into the domanial system, under which the ownership of natural resources is vested in the sovereign.[3] Although there are several models of property rights across the globe, most national legal systems generally vest ownership of natural resources in the surface landowners, with the exception of minerals, and energy resources such as oil, gas, and coal, which are usually subject to State ownership.[4] While the precise content of the property rights exercised by private entities might vary depending on which

[1] See Thomas Kruse, 'La "Guerra del Agua" en Cochabamba, Bolivia: Terrenos Complejos, Convergencias Nuevas'. In: Enrique de la Garza Toledo (ed.), *Sindicatos y Nuevos Movimientos Sociales en América Latina* (CLASCO, 2005); Carlos Crespo Flores, 'La Guerra del Agua en Cochabamba: Movimientos Sociales y Crisis de Dispositivos del Poder', 20 *Ecología Política*, 2000, 59–70.
[2] See Richard Barnes, *Property Rights and Natural Resources* (Hart Publishing, 2009), Ch. 6; Lorenzo Cotula, 'Land, Property and Sovereignty in International Law', 25 *Cardozo Journal of International and Comparative Law*, 2017, 219, 286.
[3] See Anthony Scott, *The Evolution of Resource Property Rights* (OUP, 2008).
[4] One of the rare exceptions being the United States, where a regime of private ownership of mineral resources exists. See Ricardo Pereira, 'The Exploration and Exploitation of Energy Resources in International Law'. In: Karen Makuch and Ricardo Pereira (eds), *Environmental and Energy Law* (John Wiley & Sons, 2012), pp. 199–224.

Natural Resources and Human Rights: An Appraisal. Jérémie Gilbert. © J. Gilbert 2018. Published 2018 by Oxford University Press.

resources are concerned, property rights commonly integrate a variety of rights, not only ownership. Property rights over natural resources are often referred to as a 'bundle of rights', which includes use and access, control, management, and exclusion rights.[5] Hence, property rights are not limited to ownership, but also to use, management, and transfer rights.[6] By focusing on this 'bundle of rights' over natural resources, this chapter analyses the content of a human rights-based approach to property over natural resources looking at the interactions between the rights of the public authorities, local communities, and private corporations.

In analysing the historical debates that surround the development of the right to property, the first section examines to what extent a human right to property includes, or not, references to natural resources. It notably examines how collective rights to property are increasingly recognized under international human rights law (IHRL), notably under the banner of indigenous peoples' rights. Based on this analysis, the second section turns its attention to the issue of community resources. Over the last few years, there has been an increased demand on the part of local communities to have recognized their collective rights to property as regards their natural resources.[7] To analyse the role of IHRL in supporting these community-based claims, it focuses on the issues of collective tenure rights over forests and fisheries, two issues that have been at the forefront of the development of a collective property rights approach to natural resources. The third section examines situations where natural resources have been privatized or granted under concession to private corporations. In this context, an important legal issue arises in terms of the rights of the citizens who might lose their fundamental right to access the natural resources that have been transferred to the private sector, especially when these resources concern essential resources such as water.

2. The Human Right to Property: From Eminent Domain to Land Rights

This section analyses the emergence of a human right to property and highlights its complex and controversial nature. It examines the evolution of the correlation between issues of property rights and natural resources, and notably how it has increasingly become connected with property rights to land and natural resources for indigenous peoples.

---

[5] See Edella Schlager and Elinor Ostrom, 'Property-Rights Regimes and Natural Resources: A Conceptual Analysis', 68(3) *Land Economics*, 1992, 249–62.

[6] Safia Aggarwal and Kent Elbow, *The Role of Property Rights in Natural Resource Management, Good Governance, and Empowerment of the Rural Poor* (United States Agency for International Development, 2006).

[7] See Ting Xu and Alison Clarke (eds), *Legal Strategies for the Development and Protection of Communal Property* (OUP, 2017); Lee Godden and Maureen Tehan (eds), *Comparative Perspectives on Communal Lands and Individual Ownership: Sustainable Futures* (Routledge, 2010).

2.1 Eminent domain, property rights, and natural resources

Property rights over land and natural resources have an important historical pedigree that is linked to the emergence of liberal individual rights as well as to colonialism.[8] The institution of property has been central to the development of political rights.[9] In terms of natural resources, an important element relates to the political importance given to property rights to land. For many centuries property ownership has been the determining factor for the right to political participation, and thus for the exercise of political rights, for example, the democracies of ancient Greece and ancient Rome.[10] Additionally, in England, France, and the United States, political rights were also granted based on (white, male) land ownership for many centuries.[11] Many philosophers and political writers influential in the development of political theories during Europe's Age of Enlightenment emphasized the importance of the institution of property as a central aspect of personal liberties that should be guaranteed by the State. For example, both Locke and Smith described the individual ownership of private property as being crucial to the overall well-being of society.[12] Rousseau situated the origin of civil society with the establishment of private individual ownership of property in land, famously saying that 'the first man who, having enclosed a piece of ground, thought of saying "this is mine" and found people simple enough to believe him, was the real founder of civil society'.[13] The guarantee of property rights in land was one of the central issues that triggered the development of an emergent human rights system. In the UK, the protection of property rights was a key issue in the proclamation of the *Magna Carta* in 1215, as well as the Bill of Right in 1689.[14] Both the eighteenth-century US Bill of Rights and French Declaration of Human Rights gave the protection of property rights the same gravitas as the right to life.

---

[8] See Andro Linklater, *Owning the Earth: The Transforming History of Land Ownership* (Bloomsbury, 2013).

[9] See Richard Schlatter, *Private Property: The History of an Idea* (Allen & Unwin, 1951); Lawrence Becker, *Property Rights: Philosophical Foundations* (Routledge & Kegan Paul, 1977); James Penner, *The Idea of Property in Law* (OUP, 2000); Theo R. G. van Banning, *The Human Right to Property* (Intersentia, 2002).

[10] See Moses Finely, *The Legacy of Greece: A New Appraisal* (OUP, 1981); Richard Saller, *Patriarchy, Property and Death in the Roman Family* (CUP, 1994); Christopher Rowe and Malcolm Scofield (eds), *The Cambridge History of Greek and Roman Political Thought* (CUP, 2000).

[11] In England, it was only with the Reform Acts of 1830 that males without property were given franchise on a limited basis. See Chilton Williamson, *American Suffrage: From Property to Democracy* (Princeton University Press, 1960); Alexander Keyssar, *The Right to Vote: The Contested History of Democracy in the United States* (Basic Books, 2000); Alain Garrigou, *Histoire Sociale du Suffrage Universel en France: 1848–2000* (Seuil, 2002).

[12] See Edwin West, 'Property Rights in the History of Economic Thought'. In: Terry L. Anderson and Fred S. McChesney (eds), *Property Rights: Cooperation, Conflict, and Law* (Princeton University Press, 2003).

[13] Jean-Jacques Rousseau, *Discourse on the Origin and Basis of Inequality among Men* (*Discours sur l'origine et les fondements de l'inégalité parmi les hommes*), also commonly known as the 'Second Discourse', was published in 1754. Donald A. Cress (trans), *Discourse on the Origin of Inequality* (Hackett Publishing, 2011), p. 66.

[14] See Bernard Siegan, *Property Rights: From Magna Carta to the 14th Amendment* (Transaction Publishers, 2001).

The gradual protection of property has been developed with the parallel affirmation of the public authorities' right of 'eminent domain', or of 'compulsory acquisition'. The concept of eminent domain, i.e. a taking of private property by the State in the general interest, is common to most legal systems.[15] The notion of eminent domain, from the Latin *dominium eminens*, refers to the ultimate power of the State to acquire all lands and resources.[16] In contemporary legal parlance, whether it is called eminent domain, compulsory purchase, compulsory acquisition, or public expropriation, it refers to the overall power of the State to expropriate any private property in land without the owner's consent, even if such a right is legally and constitutionally protected. In terms of international law, in his 1625 treatises *De Jure Belli et Pacis* Grotius integrated the notion of eminent domain within the power of the State when it comes to property of the land:

> The property of subjects is under the eminent domain of the state, so that the state or he who acts for it may use and even alienate and destroy such property, not only in the case of extreme necessity, in which even private persons have a right over the property of others, but for ends of public utility, to which ends those who founded civil society must be supposed to have intended that private ends should give way.[17]

This power of eminent domain is connected to the ultimate sovereign power of the State in controlling land and natural resources allocation. According to Ederington, 'the protection of private property from state interference has been one of the most pronounced themes throughout the history of modern international law since its inception in the seventeenth century.'[18] This tension between eminent domain and individual rights to property is reflected in the international contemporary system of human rights protection.[19] The right to property is affirmed in several international human rights instruments, including the Universal Declaration of Human Rights (UDHR),[20] the International Convention on the Elimination of All Forms of Racial Discrimination,[21] and the Convention on the Elimination of All Forms of Discrimination against Women.[22] Most regional human rights instruments also include a specific protection for property rights.[23] Under this generic approach,

[15] See Richard A. Epstein, *Takings: Private Property and the Power of Eminent Domain* (Harvard University Press, 1985); Ellen Frankel Paul, *Property Rights and Eminent Domain* (Transaction Publishers, 2008).

[16] See William D. McNulty, 'Eminent Domain in Continental Europe', 21(7) *The Yale Law Journal*, 1912, 555.

[17] Hugo Grotius, *De Jure et pacis*. F. Kelsey (trans), (Clarendon Press, 1925), p. 807.

[18] Benjamin Ederington, 'Property as a Natural Institution: The Separation of Property from Sovereignty in International Law', 13(2) *American University International Law Review*, 1997, 263–331, 263.

[19] See Christophe Golay and Ioana Cismas, *Legal Opinion: The Right to Property from a Human Rights Perspective* (Geneva Academy of International Humanitarian Law and Human Rights, 2010).

[20] See Catarina Krause, 'The Right to Property'. In: Asbjørn Eide, Catarina Krause, and Allan Rosas (eds), *Economic, Social and Cultural Rights: A Textbook*, 2nd revised edition (Martinus Nijhoff, 2011), pp. 192–3; William Schabas, 'The Omission of the Right to Property in the International Covenants', 4 *Hague Yearbook of International Law*, 1991, pp. 135–60.

[21] Article 5(d) (v), 1966, 660 UNTS 195.   [22] Article 15(2), 1979, 1249 UNTS 13.

[23] See Ali Riza Çoban, *The Protection of Property Rights within the European Convention on Human Rights* (Gower Publishing, 2004); see also Christophe Golay and Ioana Cismas, *Legal Opinion: The Right to Property from a Human Rights Perspective* (Droits & Democratie, 2010).

property rights covers a wide range of both movable and immovable type of property such as contractual rights, tenancy rights, or pension rights, but none of these human rights instruments include specific references to property on natural resources.

Nonetheless, despite this lack of specific inclusion of natural resources as a form of property in the treaties, the connection between the human rights to property and natural resources can be found in the jurisprudence of regional human rights bodies. For example, in *Case of Doğan and Others v Turkey*, the European Court of Human Rights (ECtHR) examined whether the forced eviction of the concerned villagers constituted a violation of the right to property. Relevantly, the connection of the applicants with the common land in the village, such as pasture, grazing, and forest land, was an important element to define their right to property as they earned their living from stockbreeding and tree felling.[24] The ECtHR recognized that these resources qualified as 'possessions' for the purposes of Article 1 of Protocol No. 1 to the European Convention, which guarantees the right to peaceful enjoyment of possessions.[25] Crucially, the ECtHR also recognized that in *Case of Doğan and Others*, the applicants had property rights over the common lands, and implicitly, the natural resources they contained, despite the applicants' lack of a formal land title. Likewise, in *Ucci v Italy* regarding the forced expropriation of agricultural land in Italy, the ECtHR also connected the right to property and usage of land and natural resources, highlighting that that the term 'possessions' covers housing and real property as well as land possession.[26] This approach is not limited to the European Court; for example, in a case concerning attacks on civilian populations in Darfur, the African Commission on Human and Peoples' Rights (ACoHPR) found violations of the right to property in connection to the forced eviction from land used for agricultural or herding purposes.[27] The ACoHPR noted that 'the fact that the victims cannot derive their livelihood from what they possessed for generations means they have been deprived of the use of their property under conditions which are not permitted by Article 14'.[28] These cases are an indication that the right to property can include possession of land allowing people to enjoy essential economic activities such as agriculture or grazing.[29] However, it should be noted that in this context the connection between the right to property and natural resources is only incidental as it concerns the loss of economic opportunities in case of forced dispossession. Usually the cases have focused on establishing whether the individuals had received adequate compensation notably when States authorities have reduced access and

[24] See European Court of Human Rights, *Case of Dogan and Others v Turkey*, Application Nos 8803-8811/02, 8813/02, and 8815-8819/02 (2004), paras 138–9.
[25] Ibid.
[26] European Court of Human Rights, *Ucci v Italy*, Application No. 213/04 (2006).
[27] African Commission on Human and Peoples' Rights, Sudan Human Rights Organisation & Centre on Housing Rights and Evictions (COHRE)/Sudan (2009).
[28] Ibid., para. 205.
[29] For a compilation of human rights cases concerning land rights, see Office of the High Commissioner for Human Rights, *Land and Human Rights, Annotated Compilation of Case Law* (2015). Available at: http://www.ohchr.org/Documents/Publications/Land_HR-CaseLaw.pdf.

use of natural resources for the public interest of protecting the environment.[30] The human rights approach to property usually serves as a weighing scale between, on the one hand, the rights of private owners and, on the other, the right of the public authorities to exercise expropriation in the public interest. Under this approach the fundamental power of eminent domain of the State over natural resources has not been fully challenged. The approach is to ensure that the public authorities offered a fair compensation for 'economic loss', but there are very few cases that specifically affirm a human right to property over natural resources in a non-incidental manner not connected with loss of economic opportunities. However, as examined further on, there has been some very progressive development to establish a more direct correlation between property rights and natural resources under the specific framework of indigenous peoples' rights.

2.2 Indigenous peoples' property rights to land and natural resources

The Inter-American Court of Human Rights (IACtHR) has developed a very substantive jurisprudence linking the right to property and indigenous peoples' rights to lands and natural resources.[31] This connection was clearly established in the 2001 landmark decision concerning the Awas Tingni community of Nicaragua.[32] Until this decision there was a slow evolution towards the affirmation that property rights should cover the collective rights to land and natural resources of indigenous peoples; *Awas Tingni* was one of the first clear legal rulings on the issue.[33] The IACtHR recognized that possession of the land should suffice for indigenous peoples lacking formal title to obtain official recognition of their rights to property to land and natural resources.[34] This marks an important step in the interpretation of property rights when it comes to land and natural resources. The IACtHR placed its interpretation of property rights within the natural evolution of international law, highlighting that it was part of 'an evolutionary interpretation of international instruments for the protection of human rights'.[35] This gave a clear international perspective to the issue grounding the connection between property rights, land rights, and natural resources. Since then the case has been used as a benchmark by

---

[30] For examples, see European Court of Human Rights, *Banér v Sweden* (1989) 60 DR 128; *Fredin v Sweden* (18 February 1991); *Almeida Garrett, Mascarenhas Falcão and others v Portugal* (11 January 2000).

[31] See Inter-American Commission on Human Rights, *Indigenous and Tribal Peoples' Rights over Their Ancestral Lands and Natural Resources: Norms and Jurisprudence of the Inter-American Human Rights System*, OEA/Ser.L/V/II. Doc. 56/09 (2009); Enzamaria Tramontana, 'The Contribution of the Inter-American Human Rights Bodies to Evolving International Law on Indigenous Rights over Lands and Natural Resources', 17(2) *International Journal on Minority and Group Rights*, 2010, 241–63.

[32] *The Mayagna (Sumo) Awas Tingni Community v Nicaragua*, Judgment. Series C No. 79 (2001).

[33] See James Anaya and Claudio Grossman, 'The Case of *Awas Tingni v Nicaragua*: A Step in the International Law of Indigenous Peoples', 19 *Arizona Journal of International and Comparative Law*, 2002, 1.

[34] *The Mayagna (Sumo) Awas Tingni Community* (n 32).

[35] Ibid., para. 148.

several UN monitoring bodies and intergovernmental organizations, as well as in several national cases, not only in the Americas but worldwide.[36]

In its ensuing jurisprudence, the IACtHR highlighted that property rights to land are intrinsically connected to resource rights. For example, in *Yakye Axa* and *Sawhoyamaxa*, the IACtHR highlighted that members of tribal and indigenous communities have a right to the natural resources they have traditionally used within their territory, as it is a right attached to their right to own the land they have traditionally used and occupied for centuries.[37] This constitutes an important recognition that property rights to land ought to include rights over natural resources. The precise content of indigenous peoples' land rights and its connection to natural resources was a central element of 2007 ruling against Suriname in *Saramaka*. Here, both the government and the members of the Saramaka people were claiming rights to the natural resources found on indigenous territory. On the one hand, the Saramaka highlighted that their right to use and enjoy their natural resources was a necessary condition for the enjoyment of their right to property to land. On the other hand, the government argued that all the rights to the natural resources, particularly the subsoil resources, are vested in the State, which can freely dispose of these resources through concessions to third parties. Hence, the Court was stuck between the traditional sovereign discourse equating State power with ownership rights over natural resources, and the human rights-based claim to natural resources made by the indigenous community. Referring to its own previous jurisprudence, the IACtHR highlighted that 'members of tribal and indigenous communities have the right to own the natural resources they have traditionally used within their territory for the same reasons that they have a right to own the land they have traditionally used and occupied for centuries'.[38] The IACtHR stated that:

due to the inextricable connection members of indigenous and tribal peoples have with their territory, the protection of their right to property over such territory ... is necessary to guarantee their very survival. Accordingly, the right to use and enjoy their territory would be meaningless in the context of indigenous and tribal communities if said right were not connected to the natural resources that lie on and within the land.[39]

However, as noted by the Court, the natural resources that fall under the protection of the right to property to land 'are those natural resources traditionally used and necessary for the very survival, development and continuation of such people's way

---

[36] See Jonathan P. Vuotto, '*Awas Tingni v. Nicaragua*: International Precedent for Indigenous Land Rights', 22 *Boston University International Law Journal*, 2004, 219; Alexandra Xanthaki, 'Indigenous Rights in International Law over the Last 10 Years and Future Developments', 10 *Melbourne Journal of International Law*, 2009, 27; Leonardo J. Alvardo, 'Prospects and Challenges in the Implementation of Indigenous Peoples' Human Rights in International Law: Lessons from the Case of *Awas Tingni v. Nicaragua*', 24 *Arizona Journal of International and Comparative Law*, 2007, 609; Tramontana (n 31).

[37] *Case of the Yakye Axa Indigenous Community v Paraguay*, Merits, Reparations and Costs, Judgment. Series C No. 125 (2005), paras 124, 137; *Case of the Sawhoyamaxa Indigenous Community v Paraguay*. Merits, Reparations and Costs, Judgment. Series C No. 146 (2006), paras 118, 121.

[38] *Saramaka People v Suriname*, Preliminary Objections, Merits, Reparations, and Costs, Judgment. Series C No. 172 (2007), para. 121.

[39] Ibid., para. 122.

of life'.[40] In terms of IHRL, this statement limits the rights over natural resources to resources that are 'traditionally' used by indigenous peoples. It also limits the potential infringement on these rights to activities that could affect the 'traditional' use of the resources that are essential to the survival of indigenous peoples. For example, this means that most sub-soil resources would not usually be included as these do not qualify as resources 'traditionally' used by indigenous peoples, and which might not be essential to their survival.[41] Hence, the approach of the IACtHR is based on a right to property over the 'traditionally used resources' that are essential for survival, and that not all resources might classify as such.

The recognition of the connection between the right to property and land and natural resources is not limited to the IACtHR. It was also an important element in the 2010 decision from the ACoHPR in the case concerning the Endorois community in Kenya. This case concerned the forced displacement of the Endorois from their ancestral land in the heart of the Great Rift Valley. A central aspect of the case revolved around defining whether the Endorois' traditional occupation of the land, including many activities connected to the use of natural resources, could constitute property as protected under Article 14 of the African Charter.[42] Relying on international and comparative law, the ACoHPR concluded that for indigenous peoples, traditional possession of land 'has the equivalent effect as that of a state-granted full property title' and 'entitles indigenous people to demand official recognition and registration of property title',[43] which meant that the rights of the Endorois over their ancestral territory were protected under Article 14 of the African Charter. More generally, the Commission highlighted that 'the first step in the protection of traditional African communities is the acknowledgement that the rights, interests and benefits of such communities in their traditional lands constitute "property" under the Charter and that special measures may have to be taken to secure such "property rights"'.[44] Adopting a similar line of reasoning, the African Court of Human Rights also established a connection between the right to property and land and natural resources in the case of the Ogiek community.[45] In relation to the right to property the Court noted it should not be only interpreted in 'its classical conception' since for indigenous peoples it also means rights of possession, occupation, and use of their ancestral land and natural resources.[46]

---

[40] Ibid.

[41] This is confirmed by several cases at the national level; see Stefania Errico, 'The Controversial Issue of Natural Resources: Balancing States' Sovereignty with Indigenous Peoples' Rights'. In: Stephen Allen and Alexandra Xanthaki (eds), *Reflections on the UN Declaration on the Rights of Indigenous Peoples* (Hart Publishing, 2011).

[42] The other connected issue was to determine if Article 21 concerning natural resources was violated. This aspect is examined in Chapter 1 as it relates to the issue of self-determination over natural resources.

[43] *Centre for Minority Rights Development (Kenya) and Minority Rights Group International on behalf of Endorois Welfare Council v Kenya*, Communication 276/2003, para. 209.

[44] Ibid., para. 187.

[45] African Court of Human and Peoples' Rights, *ACHPR v Kenya*, Application No. 006/2012 (2017) (the '*Ogiek* Judgment').

[46] Ibid., paras 123–6.

These developments connecting the human rights to property, land, and natural resources are integrated in the specific legal instruments on indigenous peoples' rights. The 2007 UN Declaration on the Rights of Indigenous Peoples (UNDRIP) dedicates several of its articles to the right to land for indigenous peoples. Article 25 of the Declaration affirms that:

Indigenous peoples have the right to maintain and strengthen their distinctive spiritual relationship with their traditionally owned or otherwise occupied and used lands, territories, waters and coastal seas and other resources and to uphold their responsibilities to future generations in this regard.

The International Labour Convention No. 169 on the Rights of Indigenous and Tribal Peoples (ILO 169) also integrates a human rights-based approach to land and natural resources. The Convention specifically states that 'the rights of ownership and possession of the peoples concerned over the lands which they traditionally occupy shall be recognised', and that 'the rights of the peoples concerned to the natural resources pertaining to their lands shall be specially safeguarded'.[47] International human rights treaty bodies have also embraced a similar approach. For example, the UN Committee on the Elimination of Racial Discrimination (CERD) in its General Recommendation on indigenous peoples invites States to 'recognize and protect the rights of indigenous peoples to own, develop, control and use their communal lands, territories and resources'.[48] This is only an example of the very significant number of recommendations and decisions from international human rights bodies regarding the connection between property rights to land and natural resources for indigenous peoples.[49] The development of this strong corpus of IHRL establishing a correlation between the right to property and natural resources is extremely significant as it challenges the assumption that the State has underlying title to the land and the natural resources it contains. In highlighting that land and natural resources are intrinsically connected to the property rights over their ancestral territories, indigenous peoples' rights also challenge the dichotomy often created between property in land and property over natural resources.[50]

3. Community Property Resources: Forests and Fishing Rights

Most legal systems rarely formally recognize collective or communal forms of ownership over natural resources.[51] In general, the inwards trend has been towards the

[47] International Labour Organization, 'Convention concerning Indigenous and Tribal Peoples in Independent Countries', Arts 14 and 15.

[48] CERD, General Recommendation 23 on Indigenous Peoples, UN Doc. A/52/18, Annex 8 (1997), para. 5.

[49] For a detailed analysis, see Jérémie Gilbert, *Indigenous Peoples' Land Rights under International Law: From Victims to Actors*, 2nd edition (Brill, 2016).

[50] Ibid., Ch. 3.

[51] See Ting Xu and Alison Clarke (eds), *Legal Strategies for the Development and Protection of Communal Property* (OUP, 2017).

individualization of property rights over common resources,[52] and an increasing proportion of the common resources upon which rural communities depend, such as grazing lands, wetlands, and woodlands, are being individualized.[53] In many situations, collective customary resource tenure systems have been undermined or replaced by public management, or eroded by internal divisions or market forces. However, there has been a recent shift towards the recognition of some forms of collective or communal resource ownership. The past decades have witnessed an increased recognition of the need to devolve and decentralize control to local communities over natural resources.[54] Development agencies are increasingly acknowledging that common and collective property rights over natural resources can play an important role as a catalyst for local communities' development.[55] Access to resources through common property regimes often sustains and enhances the livelihoods of rural families and communities.[56]

Community-based property regimes often involve property rights vested in a community.[57] According to Tumushabe, to qualify as community property, 'the rights must have three basic characteristics: common or collective ownership of a given natural resource—often a common pool resource; sharing rights to access and use of the resource in accordance with established traditions or regulations; and a right to regulate access to the resource by outsiders or non-members of the community'.[58] Community property regimes need to be differentiated from the several forms of community conservation and development projects promoted by international organizations, as the latter usually do not include property rights but are restricted to limited management rights over the resources. Many governments and developmental and environmental agencies promote these forms of co-management of natural resources as a way to promote the participation of the local communities. However, these administrations and organizations often do not recognize the fundamental rights to property of the concerned communities over these resources,

---

[52] See Elinor Ostrom and Charlotte Hess, 'Private and Common Property Rights', *Encyclopedia of Law & Economics*, 2008; Glenn G. Stevenson, *Common Property Economics: A General Theory and Land Use Application* (CUP, 1991);

[53] See High Level Panel of Experts on Food Security and Nutrition, *Land Tenure and International Investments in Agriculture* (HLPE, 2011), pp. 26–8.

[54] See Sheona Shackleton, Bruce Campbell, Eva Wollenberg, and David Edmunds, 'Devolution and Community-Based Natural Resource Management: Creating Space for Local People to Participate and Benefit', 76 *Natural Resource Perspectives*, 2002, 1–6; Jesse C. Ribot and Anne M. Larson (eds), *Democratic Decentralisation through a Natural Resource Lens: Cases from Africa, Asia and Latin America* (Routledge, 2013); David Stuart Edmunds and Eva Karoline Wollenberg (eds), *Local Forest Management: The Impacts of Devolution Policies* (Routledge, 2013).

[55] See Jonathan D. Ostry, Andrew Berg, and Charalambos G. Tsangarides, *Redistribution, Inequality, and Growth* (IMF, 2014); Christophe Lakner, Mario Negre, and Espen Beer Prydz, *Twinning the Goals: How Can Promoting Shared Prosperity Help to Reduce Global Poverty?* (World Bank, 2014).

[56] See Andrew Fuys, Esther Mwangi, and Stephan Dohrn, *Securing Common Property Regimes in a Globalizing World: Synthesis of 41 Case Studies on Common Property Regimes from Asia, Africa, Europe and Latin America* (International Land Coalition, 2008).

[57] Ostrom and Hess (n 52).

[58] Godber W. Tumushabe, *The Theoretical and Legal Foundations of Community-Based Property Rights in East Africa* (Advocates Coalition for Development and Environment, Policy Research Series, No. 12, 2005), p. 13.

which remain with the former.[59] Generally, there is a global lack of recognition of the fundamental collective tenure rights of the local communities over their natural resources, with most States favouring individualized property rights.[60]

From this perspective, IHRL may play a positive role in supporting the legal recognition of these localized and customary collective regimes of tenure over natural resources. However, as mentioned earlier, apart from the situation of indigenous peoples, IHRL still remains underdeveloped when it comes to collective rights over natural resources. Collective rights are still controversial, with many States still supporting the idea that IHRL is mainly about protecting the rights of individuals.[61] This position has been challenged with many local communities increasingly referring to IHRL as a vehicle to claim their fundamental right to the recognition of their common property rights over some of their natural resources. As examined further on, this is notably the case regarding forest and fishing rights, which are issues at the forefront of a push towards the recognition of collective property rights for local communities.

3.1 Community forest rights

Under most legal systems, States own forests; most legal systems proclaim forests as an integral part of the domanial asset of the government. This legal entitlement of States over its forests has roots in medieval Europe, and extended globally when colonial powers took ownership of the forests in their colonies.[62] This State-centric approach to ownership of the forests remains the dominant legal approach. Under this overall domanial approach, the rights of the local forest communities who are living in, and often depending on, those forests for their livelihoods have often been restricted or denied.[63] The extent of the rights recognized in favour of the local forest-dependent communities is an important issue, especially when the external threats on the use of the forest are constantly intensifying. Threats to the rights of local communities include forest classification as protected areas, concessions to extractive industries, or invasion by farmers or ranchers. In these contexts of 'external' takeover of the forests, the content of the tenure rights of the communities is

---

[59] More analysis on these co-management regimes appears in Chapter 3, Chapter 5, and Chapter 6.

[60] See Liz Alden Wily, ' "The Law is to Blame": The Vulnerable Status of Common Property Rights in Sub-Saharan Africa', 42(3) *Development and Change*, 2011, 733–57; Fuys, Mwangi, and Dohrn (n 56); Owen James Lynch and Emily Harwell, *Whose Resources? Whose Common Good? Towards a New Paradigm of Environmental Justice and the National Interest in Indonesia* (Center for International Environment Law, 2002).

[61] See Dwight Newman, *Community and Collective Rights: A Theoretical Framework for Rights Held by Groups* (Hart Publishing, 2011); Miodrag A. Jovanović, *Collective Rights* (CUP, 2012); Koen de Feyter and George Pavlakos (eds), *The Tension between Group Rights and Human Rights: A Multidisciplinary Approach* (Hart Publishing, 2008).

[62] The few exceptions being Papua New Guinea, the US, and Mexico. See Andy White and Alejandra Martin, *Who Owns the World's Forests?* (Centre for International Environmental Law, 2002).

[63] See Marcus Colchester; Forest Peoples Programme, 'Forest Peoples, Customary Use and State Forests: The Case for Reform'. In: *Paper to 11th Biennial Congress of the International Association for the Study of Common Property.* Bali, 19–23 June 2006. pp. 19–22.

of fundamental importance to ensure their right to remain in the forest and use the forest's natural resources.

At the local levels, most forest communities suffer from very restricted and un-protected tenure rights over their forests. Nonetheless, in the last few decades there has been a shift in international policies to support the development of 'community forests' or other forms of transfer of ownership and usage rights to local communities. The move is part of the increased acknowledgment that conservation of the forests might be better supported with the involvement of the local forest communities. For example, the 2006 International Tropical Timber Agreement encourages members to 'recognise the role of the forest-dependent indigenous and local communities . . .'.[64] The last few years have also witnessed a surge of research, studies, and advocacy work from civil society organizations working on forestry to support and document the emergence of community forms of forest managements and tenure systems.[65] Despite these recent changes, figures still indicate that by far the largest proportion of the world's forests are owned by governments, with an increasing number of forests assigned to communities.[66] The international trend has been to support community-based forest management schemes, where the rights of the local communities are usually constrained to participatory and consultative rights, with local communities not exercising tenure rights but limited usufructuary rights, or customary right to use the forest. Moreover, governments often limit the kinds of forests available for communities, restricting them to wastelands or degraded forests. It is within these overall changes to the legal landscape governing forest rights that IHRL has increasingly been seen as a potential relevant vehicle to support the rights of local forest communities.[67]

There is no specific mention of any rights to the forests in the main human rights legal instruments, but some of the international monitoring bodies have mentioned communities' right of tenure over the forests as an important element of IHRL. The UN Committee on Economic, Social and Cultural Rights (CESCR) has high-lighted the need for States to recognize and protect the customary property rights of indigenous peoples over the forests. For example, in its 2014 report on the situation in Indonesia, the Committee criticized the adoption of a new national law which did not respect the property rights of an indigenous community over its forest,[68] and called on the government to identify and demarcate the customary lands and forests belonging to the concerned community.[69] There are several other examples of this

---

[64] International Tropical Timber Agreement, 2006, preamble at (r).

[65] See Anne M. Larson, *Forests for People: Community Rights and Forest Tenure Reform* (Earthscan, 2010).

[66] Recent figures indicated that a large percentage of forests are publicly owned, e.g. Africa (98 per cent), Asia (95 per cent), Europe (including Russia) (90 per cent), Oceania (76 per cent), North and Central America (70 per cent), and South America (82 per cent). See Anne Larson, Deborah Barry, and Ganga Ram Dahal, 'Tenure Change in the Global South'. In: *Forests for People: Community Rights and Forest Tenure Reform* (Earthscan, 2010), pp. 5–11.

[67] See Thomas Sikor and Johannes Stahl (eds), *Forests and People: Property, Governance, and Human Rights* (Routledge, 2012).

[68] Concluding Observations on the Initial Report of Indonesia, UN Doc. E/C.12/IDN/CO/1 (2014), para. 39.

[69] The concerned community are the Masyarakat Hukum Adat. See Yance Arizona and Erasmus Cahyadi, 'The Revival of Indigenous Peoples: Contestations over a Special Legislation on *Masyarakat*

increased focus on forest rights for indigenous peoples in many of the concluding observations of the committee.[70] The CERD has also touched on the connection between property rights over the forest and indigenous peoples' rights. In its 2009 concluding observations on the situation in Congo, CERD has specifically called for the recognition of forest rights for indigenous peoples. CERD recommended that the government 'establish the forest rights of indigenous peoples in domestic legislation'.[71]

The rights of indigenous women have also been put into perspective by the UN Committee on the Elimination of Discrimination against Women (CEDAW). For example, its 2013 concluding observations concerning the situation in the Democratic Republic of Congo (DRC), CEDAW noted that women belonging to the Pygmy community have become unable to make a livelihood for themselves in the forest, notably due to the extensive discrimination they face. CEDAW invited the government to 'ensure that Pygmy women have access, without discrimination, to basic services, including health care and education, and to land, ensure that they have access to self-sufficient livelihoods in the forest and provide compensation when they have been displaced from the forest'.[72] Another angle of focus on forest tenure rights comes under the banner of children rights. The UN Committee on the Rights of the Child (CRC) has paid particular attention to the rights of children belonging to forest communities, especially indigenous forest communities. In its 2013 report regarding the situation in the Rwanda it noted that the 'Batwa communities, including children, have been forcibly displaced from their ancestral forest lands without consent or compensation and deprived of their traditional livelihoods, which has resulted in serious damage to their distinct lifestyles, livelihoods and culture'.[73] The CRC invited the government to 'grant Batwa children and families recognition of their special status, recognize their rights to the natural resources of the forests ... '.[74]

All these statements from international human rights treaty bodies indicate the emergence of a human rights-based approach to forest rights. However, it seems that there is a lack of clarity on the distinction between rights of usage and property rights. Human rights monitoring bodies have usually referred broadly to forest rights, with little indication on whether these constitute property or usage rights.

Adat'. In: Brigitta Hauser-Schäublin (ed.), *Adat and Indigeneity in Indonesia: Culture and Entitlements between Heteronomy and Self-Ascription* (Göttingen University Press, 2013), pp. 43–62; Tanya Murray Li, 'Masyarakat Adat, Difference, and the Limits of Recognition in Indonesia's Forest Zone'. 35(3) *Modern Asian Studies*, 2001, 645–76.

[70] See Concluding Observations on the Russian Federation, UN Doc. E/C.12/RUS/CO/5 (2011); Fergus Mackay, *Indigenous Peoples and United Nations Human Rights Bodies—A Compilation of UN Treaty Body Jurisprudence and the Recommendations of the Human Rights Council. Volume V: 2011–2012* (Forest Peoples Programme, 2013).

[71] Concluding Observations of the Committee on the Elimination of Racial Discrimination, Congo, UN Doc. CERD/C/COG/CO/9 (2009), para. 14.

[72] Concluding Observations on the Combined Sixth and Seventh Periodic Reports of the Democratic Republic of the Congo, UN Doc. CEDAW/C/COD/CO/6-7 (2013), para. 36.

[73] Committee on the Rights of the Child, Concluding Observations on the Third and Fourth Periodic Reports of Rwanda, UN Doc. CRC/C/RWA/CO/3-4 (2013), para. 56.

[74] Ibid., para. 57.

This issue was specifically addressed in a case examined by the IACtHR concerning the Saramaka peoples in Suriname. In this case, the IACtHR noted the shortcomings of the national legislation regarding the right to property of the concerned communities, markedly engaging on the restriction existing under the notion of 'community forest'. The government claimed that the national Forest Management Act gave legal effect to the community members to the use and enjoyment of property in conformity with their communal property system. The IACtHR disputed this analysis, highlighting that 'the "community forests" permits are essentially revocable forestry concessions that convey limited and restricted use rights, and are therefore an inadequate recognition of the Saramakas' property rights'.[75] The IACtHR stated that:

[i]n sum, the State's legal framework merely grants the members of the Saramaka people a privilege to use land, which does not guarantee the right to effectively control their territory without outside interference. The Court has previously held that, rather than a privilege to use the land, which can be taken away by the State or trumped by real property rights of third parties, members of indigenous and tribal peoples must obtain title to their territory in order to guarantee its permanent use and enjoyment.[76]

This represents an important statement in a global context where community usufructuary rights are increasingly proposed as a solution to protect the rights of the local forest communities. Extending from the IACtHR reasoning, this approach falls short of guaranteeing a 'proper' right over the forest to the local communities, instead only providing them with mere restrictive and abrogable usage rights. The legal reasoning of the IACtHR offers a much more advanced analysis on the content of collective forestry rights by putting the emphasis on the need for States to recognize 'real' property rights rather than limited privileges to use the forest. The focus on tenure rights over the forest rather than rights of usage could become an important contribution of IHRL.

The other promising development comes from the extension of forest rights to other non-indigenous communities. While indigenous peoples constitute one of the most discriminated groups in terms of access to their forests, other local non-indigenous forest communities are also lacking protection of their right of tenure. More recently references to broader categories such as 'forest-dependent communities' have started to emerge in the language of the international human rights institutions. For example, in its 2012 report on the situation in Thailand, CERD has focused on the category of 'ethnic groups living in forests', noting its concerns 'that the various forestry and environment protection laws may have a discriminatory effect on ethnic groups living in forests'.[77] CERD urged the government 'to review the relevant forestry laws in order to ensure respect for ethnic groups' way of living, livelihood and culture, and their right to free and prior informed consent in decisions affecting them, while protecting the environment'.[78]

---

[75] Ibid., para. 113.   [76] Ibid., para. 115.
[77] Committee on the Elimination of Racial Discrimination, Concluding Observations on the First to Third Periodic Reports of Thailand, UN Doc. CERD/C/THA/CO/1-3 (2012), para. 16.
[78] Ibid.

While these statements linking IHRL to community forest rights are still scarce, the increasing focus on community tenure rights over their forest needs to be placed within the overall changing legal landscape governing conservation and climate change.[79] The recent focus of international human rights institutions with community forest rights needs to be examined within the rapidly expanding international environmental framework, which is also emphasizing the need to recognize the rights of the local communities over their forest.[80] With the increased pressure to act against the rapidly degrading state of the forests, the rights of the local communities over the forests are very often on the front line between environmental concerns and the human rights of local communities. The place of IHRL within the emerging legal frameworks on community forestry and forest conservation needs to be strengthened, as there is still a lack of recognition of the fundamental right to property of the local communities over their own forests. In this context, the development of a more systematic and comprehensive human rights-based approach to property rights of the communities over their forests is increasingly becoming urgent for many communities. Overall, the model of State ownership is still predominant across the globe, leaving forest communities with limited rights over the forests when they are forcefully displaced to benefit other interests.

3.2 Community fishing rights

The colossal expansion of commercial fishing, increased industrialization and its impact on the resources, the expansion of tourism leading to the privatization of access to the shorelines, ports and other nautical areas, and other similar factors have increasingly led to depriving traditional fishing communities of their access to the sea and maritime resources. The legal regime governing fishing rights is complex and stretches between different areas of international law. Most States exercise exclusive power to control all activities in their territorial waters from the coastline to their internationally recognized territorial sea and seabed.[81] Over the last decades, most fishing rights have undergone drastic changes as quotas were introduced as a consequence of necessary reductions of the total allowable catch. It is within this larger framework that the issue of community fishing rights has emerged. Many social economists have argued that better-defined and guaranteed fishing property rights for small-scale fishing communities would guarantee longer term stability and responsibilities over fishing.[82] Part of the rationale here is that insecure resource

[79] See Frances Seymour, 'Forests, Climate Change and Human Rights: Managing Risks and Trade-Offs'. In: Stephen Humphreys , *Human Rights and Climate Change* (CUP, 2009).

[80] This is examined in detail in Chapter 6 which focuses on the connection between these conservation policies and local communities' rights.

[81] Under international law, national fisheries legislation extends up to 200 nautical miles from the coast and, in limited form, further beyond into the high seas. See Yoshifumi Tanaka, *The International Law of the Sea* (CUP, 2015); Donald Rothwell and Tim Stephens, *The International Law of the Sea* (Bloomsbury Publishing, 2016).

[82] See Neil Andrew and Louisa Evans, *Approaches and Frameworks for Management and Research in Small-Scale Fisheries in the Developing World* (The WorldFish Center, 2009); Robert S. Pomeroy and Neil L. Andrew (eds), *Small-Scale Fisheries Management: Frameworks and Approaches for the Developing World* (CABI Publishing, 2011); Ross Shotton (ed.), *Use of Property Rights in Fisheries Management: Proceedings*

access and inadequate legal and operational frameworks for fishery management led to more resource degradation and poor management of the fishing resources. This approach, which finds it source in Harding's theory of the tragedy of commons, had strong echoes in some of the most recent policies that have shifted towards more individualistic fishing rights.[83] Nonetheless, fishing communities have asked increasingly for collective group-based quotas rather than individual quotas, which tend to favour the richer and more corporate fishing enterprises. These are 'community property rights, i.e. the rights to a particular fishing ground for a community rather than a number of individual actors'.[84] In terms of their content, community fishing rights include different types of rights including access, management, and ownership. These fishing rights can also include the right to a preferred position, either as an exclusive right in certain areas or as a priority in decision making, for instance, when stipulating fishing quotas in sea fisheries. These rights are not limited to inshore coastal and inland fisheries, but also concern both the seas and waters adjoining them, such as bays, estuaries, and fjords. Property fishing rights also directly relate to issues of participation in the State regulation of public and commercial fisheries.[85] The interests of the local communities have been acknowledged in some of the international policy documents. For example, Article 5(i) of the United Nations Fish Stocks Agreement requires States to take into account the interests of artisanal and subsistence fishers.[86] However, in most situations, the right to property of the communities are not well protected or recognized, pushing many small-scale local fishing communities to turn to human rights to claim their collective fishing rights as a fundamental right.[87] As Allison and colleagues note, '... when compared with the more conventional approach to fisheries management focused on fishing rights and economic efficiency, a human-rights-based approach allows

---

of the FishRights Conference. Fremantle, Western Australia, 1999, Volume 2 (FAO Fisheries Technical Paper, 2000).

[83] Despite the fact that Hardin's theory is based on open access resources and not common property, see O.J. Lynch, 'From Land to Coasts and Shining Seas? Reflections on Community-Based Property Rights Concepts and Marine and Coastal Tenure'. In: Teresita Gimenez-Maceda, Rosario M. Espino, Shivani Chaudhry (eds), *Marine and Coastal Resources and Community-Based Property Rights.* Workshop proceedings, Anilao, Mabini, Batangas, Philippines, 12–15 June 2001, pp. 4–15; Fikret Berkes, 'Fishermen and "the Tragedy of the Commons"', 12(3) *Environmental Conservation,* 1985, 199–206.

[84] Edward H. Allison, Blake D. Ratner, Bjørn Åsgård, Rolf Willmann, Robert Pomeroy, and John Kurien, 'Rights-Based Fisheries Governance: From Fishing Rights to Human Rights', 13(1) *Fish and Fisheries,* 2012, 14–29, 17. However, labelling these as 'property rights' is in fact a misnomer because they relate to the catch as opposed to exclusive control of the underlying resource, see Seth Macinko and Daniel W. Bromley, 'Property and Fisheries for the Twenty-First Century: Seeking Coherence from Legal and Economic Doctrine', 28 *Vermont Law Review,* 2003, 623.

[85] For an enlightening analysis of the different tenure rights, see Anthony Charles, 'Governance of Tenure in Small-Scale Fisheries: Key Considerations', 1 *Land Tenure Journal,* 2013, 9–37.

[86] The United Nations Agreement for the Implementation of the Provisions of the United Nations Convention on the Law of the Sea of 10 December 1982 relating to the Conservation and Management of Straddling Fish Stocks and Highly Migratory Fish Stocks (in force as from 11 December 2001).

[87] See Civil Society Preparatory Workshop. 2008. Statement from the Civil Society Preparatory Workshop to the Global Conference on Small-Scale Fisheries (4SSF), Bangkok, Thailand. SAMUDRA Report No. 51: 7–9; Chandrika Sharma, 2008. 'Securing Economic, Social and Cultural Rights of Fishworkers and Fishing Communities. International Collective in Support of Fishworkers'. Paper prepared for the FAO Global Conference on Small-Scale Fisheries. Bangkok, 11–13 October 2008.

fisheries departments and fishing communities to develop or broker novel links to strengthen fishery governance and address poverty reduction.'[88]

In terms of IHRL, there is no specific mention of fishing rights under the main international human rights treaties. Instead, the main connection between fishing and human rights has appeared in situations of exploitation, notably as part of part the increased exposure of child labour, slavery practices, and gender abuses in the fishing industry.[89] Outside these situations of exploitation, the other connection between IHRL and the fisheries is part of the emergence of an international jurisprudence recognizing the importance of collective fishing rights for indigenous peoples.[90] Regarding property rights, the most direct connection between fishing rights and IHRL concerns mostly small-scale fisherfolk and fishery-dependent indigenous peoples. For example, in its 2011 review of the situation in Norway, CERD called the government to ensure fishing rights of the Sea Sami.[91] In its 2001 concluding observations regarding Sweden, CERD had highlighted its concerns with the rights of the Sami peoples over their lands and territories, 'in particular hunting and fishing rights which are threatened by, inter alia, the privatization of traditional Sami lands'.[92] The Committee has also engaged with the government of New Zealand when it enacted a legislation vesting areas of the foreshore and seabed where Māori might have an interest.[93] In general, CERD has increasingly paid attention to the rights of indigenous peoples over their traditional fishing grounds, with fishing being part of the right to land and natural resources.[94] The Human Rights Committee in its 2009 review of the situation in Russia has also highlighted the danger posed to indigenous peoples regarding the loss of their fishing grounds.[95] The CESCR has also linked indigenous peoples' rights with fishing rights.[96] UN

---

[88] Allison, Ratner, Åsgård, Willmann, Pomeroy, and Kurien (n 84) 25. See also Edward H. Allison, Bjørn Åsgård, and Rolf Willmann, 'Human Rights Approaches to Governing Fisheries', 10 *Maritime Studies*, 2011, 5–13.

[89] See Alastair Couper, Hance D. Smith, and Bruno Ciceri. *Fishers and Plunderers: Theft, Slavery and Violence at Sea* (Pluto Press, 2015); Axel Marx and Jan Wouters, 'Combating Slavery, Forced Labour and Human Trafficking. Are Current International, European and National Instruments Working?' 8(4) *Global Policy Journal*, 2017, 495–7; Louise Shelley, 'Human Trafficking at Sea' 45(1) *Women's Studies Quarterly*, 2017, 305–9.

[90] See Robert Charles G. Capistrano, 'Reclaiming the Ancestral Waters of Indigenous Peoples in the Philippines: The Tagbanua Experience with Fishing Rights and Indigenous Rights' 34 *Marine Policy*, 2010, 453–60; see also Allison, Åsgård, and Willmann (n 88).

[91] Concluding Observations of the Committee on the Elimination of Racial Discrimination, Norway, UN Doc. CERD/C/NOR/CO/19–20 (2011), para. 18.

[92] Concluding observations of the Committee on the Elimination of Racial Discrimination: Sweden, UN Doc. CERD/C/304/Add.103 (2001), para. 13.

[93] See Claire Charters and Andrew Erueti, 'Report from the Inside: The CERD Committee's Review of the Foreshore and Seabed Act 2004', 36(2) *Victoria University of Wellington Law Review*, 2005, 257–90.

[94] See 'Concluding Observations of the Committee on the Elimination of Racial Discrimination: Russian Federation', CERD/C/RUS/CO/20-22 (2013), para. 20; Early Warning and Urgent Action Procedure: United States of America, UN Doc. CERD/C/USA/DEC/1 (CERD, 2006); Colombia: UN Doc. CERD/C/COL/CO/15-16 (2015).

[95] Concluding Observations of the Human Rights Committee, Russian Federation, UN Doc. CCPR/C/RUS/CO/6 (2009), para. 28.

[96] See, for example: Committee on Economic, Social and Cultural Rights, Norway, UN Doc. E/C.12/NOR/CO/5 (2013), para. 26.

Charter bodies have also paid specific attention to the fishing rights of indigenous peoples. For example, the UN Special Rapporteur on the rights of indigenous peoples have very often highlighted the connection between land, natural resources, and fishing rights.[97] This approach to indigenous peoples' right to fishing is part of the larger right to land and natural resources that was examined at the start of this chapter. However, it is worth noting that this approach is still very limited, as apart from the few examples listed herein, there is no comprehensive doctrine or jurisprudence defining the exact legal content of what community fishing rights might be. So far, the approach has been vague with broad references to 'fishing rights' but no analysis as to whether these constitute property rights or whether these are 'only' rights to fish within States' imposed regulations. As part of their right to self-determination and collective property rights over their natural resources, indigenous peoples want to see a much more encompassing and clearer legal right to collective forms of property similar to their rights to land.

The other noticeable legal development concerning the connection between fishing and IHRL relates to the increased reference to fishing rights to other non-indigenous communities. The CESCR has extended its concerns over fishing rights beyond indigenous peoples and started to refer to 'small-scale fishing communities'. For example, in its 2013 concluding observations on the situation in Djibouti, the CESCR urged 'the State party to protect the fish stocks in its territorial waters, which are a source of livelihood for small-scale fishing communities'.[98] This is part of Article 11 of the ICESCR, which affirms 'the right of everyone to an adequate standard of living for himself and his family, including adequate food, clothing and housing, and to the continuous improvement of living conditions'. This approach is based on the right to food rather than the right to property; hence, it is not entirely clear if it concerns 'only' the management of the fisheries, or whether it encapsulates a right to property. In short, there is scope for a much more comprehensive and analytical approach to what might be the content of collective fishing rights.

On this front, there are some lessons to be learned from the development of fishing rights under the leadership of the Food and Agriculture Organization (FAO). The 2012 FAO *Voluntary Guidelines on the Responsible Governance of Tenure of Land, Fisheries and Forests* recognizes tenure rights as an essential element of promoting the livelihood and right to food of most vulnerable rural poor to secure tenure in land, fisheries, and forests.[99] The *Guidelines* highlight that 'the livelihoods of many, particularly the rural poor, are based on secure and equitable access to and control over these resources'. This marks an important turning point recognizing that tenure rights are essential, and that participation, consultation, or other forms

---

[97] See Report of the Special Rapporteur on the Rights of Indigenous Peoples on the Situation of the Sami People in the Sápmi Region of Norway, Sweden, and Finland, UN Doc. A/HRC/18/35/ADD.2 (2011); Situation of Indigenous Peoples in the Russian Federation: UN Doc. A/HRC/15/37/Add.5 (2010).

[98] Committee on Economic, Social and Cultural Rights, Concluding Observations on the Initial and Second Periodic Reports of Djibouti, UN Doc. E/C.12/DJI/CO/1-2 (2013), para. 29.

[99] *Voluntary Guidelines on the Responsible Governance of Tenure of Land, Fisheries and Forests in the Context of National Food Security* (FAO, 2012).

of participatory management rights are not enough to ensure the protection of the rights of the local communities. The guidelines make specific references to human rights, noting that they 'are complementary to, and support, national, regional and international initiatives that address human rights'. The guidelines specifically connect tenure rights with IHRL, observing that:

States should strive to ensure responsible governance of tenure because land, fisheries and forests are central for the realization of human rights, food security, poverty eradication, sustainable livelihoods, social stability, housing security, rural development, and social and economic growth.[100]

The quintessential importance of tenure rights put forward by these guidelines should serve as a benchmark for the guarantee of other rights connected to use of lands, fisheries, and forests for local communities. This focus on tenure rights offers a very promising development which encapsulates in a much better way the different forms of customary and collective fishing rights exercised by local communities. As Palmer and colleagues note, 'the Guidelines do not focus on property and property rights, which are usually associated with rights of ownership. Instead, they refer to tenure rights in recognition that many of the poor gain access to land and other natural resources through tenure rights other than ownership.'[101]

Overall, there is an emergent and burgeoning human rights-based approach to collective fishing and forestry rights, but it is not yet precisely defined and embedded into the legal doctrine and jurisprudence. Collective community rights are still a new emerging focus within the work of the international human rights institutions. While IHRL has started to engage with property rights over land and natural resources, it needs to follow the FAO approach in highlighting that tenure rights are an essential and fundamental part of local communities. The important benefit of IHRL would be to move from a voluntary approach to a legally binding one. From this perspective, the recent inclusion of local forest communities and small-scale fishing communities as potential rights-holders by some international human rights institutions offers some promising avenues. This represents a significant development since the international legal regime on fishing and forestry rights are usually very top-down, focusing on the rights of the States and the private individuals (usually corporations), rather than local communities. Without a doubt, the other important element of the development of a more systematic and comprehensive jurisprudence concerning collective tenure rights for local communities is connected to the increasing encroachment of private actors, notably investors and multinational corporations, over local communities' rights over their natural resources.

---

[100] Ibid., para. 4.1.
[101] David Palmer, Mika-Petteri Törhönen, Paul Munro-Faure, and Anni Arial, 'Fostering a New Global Consensus. The Voluntary Guidelines on the Governance of Tenure', 1 *Land Tenure Journal*, 2012, 19–36.

4. Corporate Property Rights, Natural Resources, and Local Communities

This section focuses on the impact of the transfer of propriety rights to private corporations in the context of contracts or agreements of concession over natural resources.[102] Agreements or contracts of concessions can take several forms, but broadly speaking when it comes to natural resources, these can be described as agreements between a State and a private corporation under which the public authorities transfer rights in minerals, oil, gas, forests, water, or other natural resources to the concessionaire for exploitation.[103] These concessions do not necessarily entail the full transfer of property rights over the concerned natural resources, as public authorities usually maintain some form of ownership over the resources. However, concessions rights often provide for the rights to explore, extract, exploit, manage, and use the resources. This transfer to private corporations raises some serious issues about the power of the State to regulate the use of the concerned resources as well as the impact on the right to property of the local communities over the resources.[104] Contracts of concessions often overlap with land and natural resources that local communities use to gather food, obtain drinking water, graze and water livestock, hunt and trap, or other essential uses that can be undermined by the property rights of the concessionaires.

The following discussion examines the impact that these transfers of property rights to corporations can have on the human rights of the local communities. Section 4.1 examines how the privatization of the management, use, and delivery of natural resources such as water can affect the rights of the public authorities and the local communities over these resources. Section 4.2 focuses on the relationship between public authorities, investors, and local communities in situations of concessionary transfers to investors. These situations of concessionary rights have given rise to a very large volume of cases of investment arbitration regarding the nature and extent of the private rights of the investors, often leading to a negative impact on the human rights of the local communities.

4.1 Corporate property rights, privatization, and the right to water

An important area of transfer of property rights to corporations comes under the expanding privatization of natural resources management. Many resource economists have long argued that privatization of the management and ownership of natural

---

[102] There are many titles used to identify the different types of contracts of concessions over natural resources, but the term 'natural resource contract' is often used to capture all these varieties; see Liz Mitchell, *Natural Resource Contracts: A Practical Guide* (Environmental Law Alliance Worldwide, 2013).

[103] See Emmanuel Laryea, 'Contractual Arrangements for Resource Investment'. In: Francis N. Botchway (ed.), *Natural Resource Investment and Africa's Development* (Edward Elgar, 2011), pp. 109–ss.

[104] Cotula (n 2).

resources like forests, fisheries, and rangelands promotes economic efficiency.[105] This privatization is usually guided by market principles promoted as a key to support growth and development, most notably by international organizations, which have been advocating for the privatization of the ownership of natural resources as a means of improving developmental goals.[106] This has led to the development of legal frameworks supporting the transfer of use and management of natural resources to the private sector. While this does not necessarily result in the full transfer of property rights to corporations, it usually entails the transfer of some use, management, and exclusion rights attached to property rights. This transfer of rights to private corporations over natural resources has consequences regarding the rights of the citizens to access, use, and own these resources.

Generally, IHRL does not take a particular stand in favour or against privatization of services connected to the use and management of natural resources.[107] As Kok notes, 'States are allowed to use a variety of means in realising socio-economic rights (which would presumably include privatisation), and a particular economic system is not prescribed in realising socio-economic rights.'[108] In his in-depth study on the relationship between privatization and IHRL, Hallo de Wolf notes that, while human rights treaty bodies have examined the consequences of privatization on IHRL, this examination has been ad hoc, rather than systematic,[109] but this does not mean that the connection between privatization and human rights has not been examined.[110] For example, many studies have highlighted that privatization of resources, especially land, water, and forest, have detrimental consequences on women's rights.[111] Human rights treaty bodies have also noted the negative impact that privatization of public lands can have on the rights of indigenous peoples. For example, in its concluding observations, CERD was concerned, '[o]ver the issue of land rights of the Sami people, in particular hunting and fishing rights which are threatened by, inter alia, the privatization of traditional Sami lands. The Committee recommends that the Government introduce legislation recognizing traditional Sami land rights and reflecting the centrality of reindeer husbandry to the way of life of Sweden's indigenous people.'[112] CERD raised similar concerns over the privatization of land

[105] See Thomas H. Tietenberg and Lynn Lewis, *Environmental and Natural Resource Economics*, 10th edition (Routledge, 2016); Nicolas Spulber and Asghar Sabbaghi, *Economics of Water Resources: From Regulation to Privatization* (Springer, 2012); John Vickers and George Yarrow, 'Economic Perspectives on Privatization', 5(2) *The Journal of Economic Perspectives*, 1991, 111–32.
[106] See the *Highly Indebted Poor Countries (HIPC) Initiative: A Human Rights Assessment of the Poverty Reduction Strategy Papers* (PRSP), UN Doc. E/CN.4/2001/56 (2001).
[107] See Koen De Feyter and Felipe Gómez Isa (eds), *Privatisation and Human Rights in the Age of Globalisation* (Intersentia, 2005).
[108] Anton Kok, 'Privatisation and the Right to Access to Water'. In: De Feyter and Gómez Isa (n 107) 263.
[109] Antenor Hallo de Wolf, *Reconciling Privatization with Human Rights* (Intersentia, 2011), p. 127.
[110] See notably Manfred Nowak, *Human Rights or Global Capitalism: The Limits of Privatization* (University of Pennsylvania Press, 2016).
[111] See Ruth S. Meinzen-Dick, Lynn R. Brown, Hilary Sims Feldstein, and Agnes R. Quisumbing, 'Gender, Property Rights, and Natural Resources', 25(8) *World Development*, 2009, 1303–15; Margreet Zwarteveen and Ruth S. Meinzen-Dick, 'Gender and Property Rights in the Commons: Examples of Water Rights in South Asia', 18(1) *Agriculture and Human Values*, 2001, 11–25.
[112] UN Doc. CERD/C/304/Add.103 (2001), para. 13.

and natural resources and its impact on indigenous peoples' rights in the Russian Federation.[113] Likewise, CERD pointed to reports that showed that the privatization of land held by collective farms of the Soviet era had led to landlessness among persons belonging to some minorities in Moldova.[114]

The main issue that has been at the forefront of the engagement of human rights bodies with the privatization of the management of natural resources concerns the privatization of the delivery and management of water resources.[115] In recent years, this privatization, driven by the neo-liberal ideology that private companies can ensure better delivery of drinking and wastewater services, has drastically increased.[116] Nonetheless, many studies focusing on privatization have highlighted that, in most situations, instead of bringing more investments and improvement of water services, privatization has often resulted in pricing hikes leading to loss of access for the most vulnerable segment of society as well as increased inequality in access.[117] It is specifically around these issues of access to water that international human rights bodies have examined the consequences of the privatization of water supplies and infrastructure for the delivery of water. In its General Comment No. 15 on the right to water, the CESCR highlighted that water should not be primarily treated as an economic asset, but should also be regarded as a social and cultural good.[118] Regarding privatization, the CESCR specifically stated that:

[w]here water services (such as piped water networks, water tankers, access to rivers and wells) are operated or controlled by third parties, States parties must prevent them from compromising equal, affordable, and physical access to sufficient, safe and acceptable water.[119]

The main message of General Comment No. 15 is that water should be available, of sufficient quality, and physically as well as economically accessible on a non-discriminatory basis to everyone. This approach is echoed in the CESCR review of States' activities. For example, in the light of a water legislation and the privatization of water services in Kenya, the CESCR requested more detailed information on the measures taken to ensure affordable access to adequate water and sanitation and to reduce waiting times for collecting water, particularly in rural areas and in informal settlements in some of the cities.[120] However, the committee does not specifically

---

[113] Committee on The Elimination of Racial Discrimination, Russian Republic, UN Doc. CERD/C/RUS/19 (2008).

[114] Committee on the Elimination of Racial Discrimination, Republic of Moldova, UN Doc. CERD/C/60/CO/9 (2002), para. 13.

[115] See De Feyter and Gómez Isa (n 107).

[116] See World Bank, Operational Policy OP 8.60: Adjustment Lending Policy (11 August 2004) and 'Approaches to Private Participation in Water Services: A Toolkit' (2006); Susan Spronk and Jeffery R. Webber, 'Struggles Against Accumulation by Dispossession in Bolivia: The Political Economy of Natural Resource Contention', 34(2) *Latin American Perspectives*, 2007, 38.

[117] See Violeta Petrova, 'All the Frontiers of the Rush for Blue Gold: Water Privatization and the Human Right to Water', 31(2) *Brooklyn Journal of International Law*, 2006. Available at: https://brooklynworks.brooklaw.edu/bjil/vol31/iss2/6.

[118] General Comment No. 15: The Right to Water (Arts 11 and 12 of the International Covenant on Economic, Social and Cultural Rights), UN Doc. E/C.12/2002/11 (2003).

[119] Ibid., para. 24.

[120] Concluding Observations of the Committee on Economic, Social and Cultural Rights, Kenya, UN Doc. E/C.12/KEN/CO/1 (2008), para. 30.

challenge the privatization of water resources, although it does nonetheless issue serious warnings about the potential consequences on the rights of the citizens to access these resources.

Relatedly, the Human Rights Council in its resolution on 'Human Rights and Access to Safe Drinking Water and Sanitation' has recalled that States should ensure that non-State service providers '[c]ontribute to the provision of a regular supply of safe, acceptable, accessible and affordable drinking water and sanitation services of good quality and sufficient quantity'.[121] The UN General Assembly resolution adopted in 2010 declaring that access to clean water and sanitation is an essential human right does not specifically challenge the privatization of water services but calls for the absolute guarantee of access and affordability and quality.[122] Overall, a clear human rights approach to the privatization of water service putting the emphasis on States' obligations to maintain access to existing water supplies as a fundamental human rights is emerging.[123] While this approach does not prohibit privatization, it does put some limitations on the way privatization is conducted. The right to water includes the right to be free from arbitrary disconnections or contamination of water supplies and entitlements to a system of water supply and management that provides equality of opportunity for people to enjoy the right to water.

One of the main legal battles on these issues of transfer of the management of water distribution to private corporations is taking place under investor–state arbitration tribunals. There have been several cases of arbitration focusing on the privatization of water services and its connection to IHRL.[124] For example, in 2010, in *Suez, Sociedad General de Aguas de Barcelona S.A., and Vivendi Universal S.A. v Argentine Republic* regarding the concession for water distribution in the city of Buenos Aires, the government of Argentina justified its termination of the water concession as part of its obligation to safeguard the human right to water of its citizens.[125] Regarding the property rights over the water, the arbitral tribunal noted that under the concession contract, neither the privatized water utility nor the consortium '... owned or had property rights in the physical assets of the water and sewage system of Buenos Aires'.[126] On this point, the tribunal concluded that no

[121] Resolution adopted by the Human Rights Council, 'Human Rights and Access to Safe Drinking Water and Sanitation', UN Doc. A/HRC/RES/15/9 (2010), para. 9.

[122] The Human Right to Water and Sanitation, Resolution adopted by the General Assembly, UN Doc. A/RES/64/292 (3 August 2010).

[123] On the application of the right to water at the national level, see The Rt Hon Lady Justice Arden, 'Water for All? Developing a Human Rights to Water in National and International Law', 65(4) *International and Comparative Law Quarterly*, 2016, 771–89.

[124] See *Biwater Gauff (Tanzania) Ltd. v United Republic of Tanzania*, ICSID Case No. ARB/05/22 (2008); *Compañia de Aguas del Aconquija, SA & Vivendi Universal v Argentine Republic*, ICSID Case No. ARB/97/3; *Aguas del Tunari SA v Republic of Bolivia*, ICSID Case No. ARB/02/03; *Waste Management Inc. v Mexico*, ICSID Case No. ARB(AF)/98/2. For analysis, see Tamar Meshel, 'Human Rights in Investor-State Arbitration: The Human Right to Water and Beyond', 6(2) *Journal of International Dispute Settlement*, 2015, 277–307; Emma Truswell, 'Thirst for Profit: Water Privatisation, Investment Law and a Human Right to Water'. In: Chester Brown and Kate Miles (eds), *Evolution in Investment Treaty Law and Arbitration* (CUP, 2011), pp. 570–85.

[125] *Suez, Sociedad General de Aguas de Barcelona S.A., and Vivendi Universal S.A. v Argentine Republic*, Decision on Liability, ICSID Case No. ARB/03/19 (2010).

[126] Ibid., para. 148.

expropriation had taken place, but ultimately rejected the human rights-based argument ruling that the government could have acted to protect the right to water of its citizens in a way which was not in violations of its investment treaties. A similar approach was affirmed in a 2016 case of arbitration as the government had raised a similar defence to justify the termination of a private contract alleging that the concessionaire's failure to provide the necessary level of investment in the concession led to violations of the human right to water of its citizens.[127] These examples of arbitration are only an illustration of a larger issue highlighting the restriction put on States in their right to manage, use, and dispose of natural resources when these resources have been transferred under investment treaties or agreements. Thus, the consequences of the privatization of the management of natural resources that are essential to the realization of fundamental human rights, e.g. the right to water or food, are increasingly at the juncture between investment law and IHRL.[128]

4.2 Concessionary rights, investors, and arbitration

The exploitation and extraction of natural resources is usually extremely capital intensive, and as a result, many resource-rich developing countries are not able to exploit their natural resources without the help of foreign direct investment (FDI).[129] In this exchange the investors usually receive some concessionary rights, which could extend to some forms of proprietary rights over the concerned resources.[130] The role of international law regarding these concessionary rights is extremely significant as these are usually protected under international investment treaties. Typically, these investments treaties protect foreign investors against expropriation, and provide protection and security for the investors. Broadly speaking, the international rules on foreign investment are concerned with both ensuring adequate security and non-discrimination of investors and allowing the host State some rights to control the actions of the foreign investors.[131] The protection of investors regarding the exploitation of natural resources has played a central role in the development of

---

[127] *Urbaser S.A. and Consorcio de Aguas Bilbao Bizkaia, Bilbao Biskaia Ur Partzuergoa v The Argentine Republic*, Award, ICSID Case No. ARB/07/26 (2016).

[128] See Kaitlin Y. Cordes and Anna Bulman, 'Corporate Agriculture Investment and the Right to Food: Addressing Disparate Protections and Promoting Rights-Consistent Outcomes', 20 *UCLA Journal of International Law and Foreign Affairs*, 2016, 87.

[129] See Jose De Gregorio, 'The Role of Foreign Direct Investment and Natural Resources in Economic Development'. In: Edward M. Graham (ed.), *Multinationals and Foreign Investment in Economic Development* (Palgrave Macmillan, 2005), pp. 179–97; Steven Poelhekke and Frederick van der Ploeg, 'Do Natural Resources Attract FDI? Evidence from Non-Stationary Sector Level Data', De Nederlandsche Bank, Working Paper No. 266, November 2010; Frederick van der Ploeg, 'Rapacious Resource Depletion, Excessive Investment and Insecure Property Rights: A Puzzle', 48(1) *Environmental and Resource Economics*, 2011, 105–28.

[130] See Aileen McHarg (ed.), *Property and the Law in Energy and Natural Resources* (OUP, 2010).

[131] At national, bilateral, regional, and multilateral level; see Americo Beviglia Zampetti and Pierre Sauvé, 'International Investment'. In: Andrew Guzman and Alan Sykes (eds), *Research Handbook in International Economic Law* (Edward Elgar, 2007), pp. 211–70.

international law on foreign investment.[132] While the correlation between control over natural resources and foreign investment is not new, it has gained prominence in recent years. Numerous countries have profoundly reformed their national legislations to create more harmonization and stability in their economic sector via in-depth remodelling of their regulatory framework on FDIs concerning the exploitation of their natural resources. This remodelling has resulted in a large increase of FDIs in the extractive industries sector. By and large, these legal frameworks have benefited industries and investors involved in the exploitation of natural resources, but rarely the peoples living in the countries where these resources are exploited.[133]

The relationship between the interests of the investors, the rights of the States to regulate these investments, and the respect for the human rights of the local populations is increasingly a topic of arbitration. In the last few years, the recourse to arbitration over investments has dramatically increased, and several of these cases directly concern rights over natural resources.[134] The connection to IHRL is usually extremely tenuous as these arbitral tribunals operate on the basis of the law defined in the investment treaties. As Kriebaum and Schreuer note, 'the protection of private owner property has developed independently in human rights law and in international investment law.'[135]

Nonetheless, despite the divide which exists between international investment law and IHRL, human rights institutions are increasingly examining the impact that investment treaties can have on human rights. A good example of this interaction between concessionary rights of investors, investment protection, and human rights comes from the ruling of the IACtHR concerning the Sawhoyamaxa community of Paraguay[136] regarding the rights of the indigenous community to the restitution of their ancestral territory, which was owned by cattle ranchers. The land had been acquired by private cattle ranchers, but also foreign investors, notably a German

---

[132] See Muthucumaraswamy Sornarajah, *The International Law on Foreign Investment*, 3rd edition (CUP, 2010); Kate Miles, *The Origins of International Investment Law: Empire, Environment and the Safeguarding of Capital* (CUP, 2013).

[133] See notably Bonnie K. Campbell (ed.), *Regulating Mining in Africa: For Whose Benefit?* (Nordic African Institute, 2004); Lorenzo Cotula, 'The New Enclosures? Polanyi, International Investment Law and the Global Land Rush', 34(9) *Third World Quarterly*, 2013, 1605–29; Sonja Vermeulen and Lorenzo Cotula, 'Over the Heads of Local People: Consultation, Consent, and Recompense in Large-Scale Land Deals for Biofuels Projects in Africa', 37(4) *The Journal of Peasant Studies*, 2010, 899–916; Francesca Romanin Jacur, Angelica Bonfanti, and Francesco Seatzu (eds), *Natural Resources Grabbing: An International Law Perspective* (Brill, 2015); Lauge N. Skovgaard Poulsen, *Bounded Rationality and Economic Diplomacy: The Politics of Investment Treaties in Developing Countries* (CUP, 2015); Jorge E. Viñuales, *International Investment Law and Natural Resource Governance* (International Centre for Trade and Sustainable Development, 2015).

[134] See the ICSID Figures for the last ten years which reveal an ever-increasing number of cases: seven of 12 cases launched in 2000, 12 of 14 in 2001, and 16 of 19 in 2002. See http://icsid.worldbank.org/ICSID/Index.jsp. In 2016, the natural resource sector (extractives and agriculture) continues to account for 30 per cent of ICSID cases.

[135] Ursula Kriebaum and Christoph Schreuer, 'The Concept of Property in Human Rights Law and International Investment Law'. In: Stephan Breitenmoser, Bernhard Ehrenzeller, and Marco Sassoli (eds), *Human Rights, Democracy and the Rule of Law: Liber Amicorum Luzius Wildhaber* (Dike, 2007), p. 743.

[136] *Sawhoyamaxa Indigenous Community v Paraguay*, Judgment. 29 March 2006. Series C No. 146.

investor who was protected under an investment treaty between Paraguay and Germany.[137] The government had specifically raised this point to support its legal argumentation against the restitution of the concerned land. Hence, the IACtHR had examined the connection between investment protection and property rights of the concerned community. On this issue, the Court noted that the investment treaty allowed 'for capital investments made by a contracting party to be condemned or nationalized for a "public purpose or interest", which could justify land restitution to indigenous people'.[138] Concerning more generally the relationship between IHRL and investment protection, the IACtHR stated that:

the enforcement of bilateral commercial treaties negates vindication of non-compliance with state obligations under the American Convention; on the contrary, their enforcement should always be compatible with the American Convention, which is a multilateral treaty on human rights that stands in a class of its own and that generates rights for individual human beings and does not depend entirely on reciprocity among States.[139]

This approach was confirmed in the 2012 case of the Kichwa indigenous people of Sarayaku against Ecuador,[140] which concerned oil operations in the Amazon region where investment plans had been designed to approved oil exploration and exploitation on some parts of the traditional territory of the indigenous communities. Looking at the development of the investment plans, the IACtHR ruled that by approving the investment without consulting the indigenous community, the State had violated their collective right to property. The IACtHR also highlighted that before the design of any investment plans, public authorities have the obligation to consult the community 'in an active and informed manner, in accordance with its customs and traditions, within the framework of continuing communication between the parties'.[141]

Interestingly the same situation was also examined in a separate arbitral proceeding as one of the oil companies concerned filed an investment arbitration claim against the government under an applicable bilateral investment treaty.[142] The claim was that authorities had failed to protect the investment from disruption caused by opposition from local communities, thereby violating the full protection and security clause included in the treaty. Ultimately, the tribunal rejected the jurisdiction, but this case highlights an interesting but not so unusual point of contact between international investment arbitration and IHRL. Investors are increasingly bringing international arbitral claims against public authorities relating to investments in natural resource-related projects, and these claims often directly concern the rights and interests of local communities. International arbitral awards are increasingly integrating some human rights concerns, notably when the public authorities include human rights-based argument to justify the expropriation of the investors.[143] The

---

[137] Ibid., para. 115.   [138] Ibid., para. 140   [139] Ibid.
[140] *Kichwa Indigenous People of Sarayaku v Ecuador*, Judgment. Series C No. 4 (2012).
[141] Ibid., para. 177.
[142] *Burlington Resources Inc. v Republic of Ecuador*, Decision on Jurisdiction, ICSID Case No. ARB/08/5, 342(E)(2) (2010).
[143] See *Álvarez y Marín Corporación S.A. and others v Republic of Panama*, ICSID Case No. ARB/15/14 (2016); *South American Silver Limited v Bolivia*, UNCITRAL, PCA Case No. 2013–15 (2016).

approach in these examples of arbitration is very different as the focus is on ensuring that the investors are treated fairly and equitably, but there is very little concern for the human rights to property over the concerned land natural resources of the local populations. The relationship between IHRL and international investment arbitration is a rapidly expanding area of international law, and while it was until recently little concerned with the integration of human rights issues, there is increasing pressure to ensure that the human rights of local communities are respected.[144] This should include the right to property, to land, and to natural resources of indigenous peoples and local communities.

However, one of the challenges is that public authorities often disregard the rights to property over land and natural resources of the local populations living in places where concessions over natural resources are granted. This represents a significant challenge since the access to international investment arbitration remains extremely restrictive, being usually limited to the concerned investors and the public authorities. In this triangular relationship between public authorities, investors, and local communities, the human rights arguments must be presented by the State. This leaves the defence of the right to property over the concerned resources to the public authorities in situations where often these same public authorities have denied the recognition of the property to the concerned local populations. While recently there has been a more sustained use of *amicus curiae* by civil society and representatives of indigenous peoples' organizations to get these arguments to the tribunals, there is still a lack of access to these arbitral forums for local communities.[145] There is still very little evidence of the integration of human rights arguments and the respect of local communities' rights over the natural resources in the existing corpus of international arbitral awards.[146] Nonetheless, this discussion needs to be placed in the larger expansion of IHRL, as well as the environmental and public health concerns in the field of international arbitration. As part of the overall 'legitimacy crisis' of investment arbitration, there is a serious push to reform the legal framework governing arbitration.[147] A promising development concerning the increase

[144] See Lorenzo Cotula, 'Human Rights and Investor Obligations in Investor-State Arbitration', 17(1) *Journal of World Investment and Trade*, 2016, 148–57; Jorge Taillant and Jonathan Bonnitcha, 'International Investment Law and Human Rights'. In: Marie-Claire Cordonier Segger, Markus W. Gehring, and Andrew Newcombe (eds), *Sustainable Development in World Investment Law* (Kluwer Law International, 2011), pp. 53–80.

[145] See *Glamis Gold Ltd. v United States of America*, Application for Leave to File a Non-Party Submission and Submission of the Quechan Indian Nation, UNCITRAL (19 August 2005); *Pac Rim Cayman LLC v The Republic of El Salvador*, Application for Permission to Proceed as Amici Curiae, 2 (2 March 2011); and for analysis, see Eugenia Levine, 'Amicus Curiae in International Investment Arbitration: The Implications of an Increase in Third-Party Participation', 29 *Berkeley Journal of International Law*, 2011, 200–24; Sarah Schadendorf, 'Human Rights Arguments in Amicus Curiae Submissions: Analysis of ICSID and NAFTA Investor-State Arbitrations', 10(1) *Transnational Dispute Management*, 2013, 1–23.

[146] As an illustration, see *Bear Creek Mining Corporation v Republic of Peru*, ICSID Case No. ARB/14/2 (2017).

[147] See Charles N. Brower and Stephan W. Schill, 'Is Arbitration a Threat or a Boon to the Legitimacy of International Investment Law?' 9 *Chicago Journal of International Law*, 2009, 471–98; Susan D. Franck, 'The Legitimacy Crisis in Investment Treaty Arbitration. Privatizing Public International Law through Inconsistent Decisions', 73 *Fordham Law Review*, 2005, 1521–5; Andreas Kulick, 'Investment Arbitration, Investment Treaty Interpretation, and Democracy', 4(2) *Cambridge Journal of*

in direct integration of regulations relating to human health, the environment, and public safety in some of the most recent investment treaties, this push for reform could support a better integration of IHRL in arbitration cases.[148] However, there is still a long way to go before the right to property over land and natural resources of the local communities can take priority over commercial interests protected under investments arbitrations mechanisms.

5. Conclusion

The issue of property rights over natural resources creates tensions between the rights of the States, the local communities, and corporations. Under their power of eminent domain over most natural resources, States still exercise their paramount property rights over many of the natural resources located in their territories. However, public authorities increasingly have transferred some of these proprietary interests to corporations and investors. In this context, the human right to property over natural resources for the local communities is only in its nascent stages, and the advances have been sporadic and often limited to very specific issues or to specific communities. In terms of the issues, land rights have received the greatest attention, but there is an increasing focus on tenure rights over forests and fisheries. It is worth noting that other natural resources, especially mineral resources such as oil and gas, are not part of the development of a human rights-based approach to property rights over natural resources. These mineral resources are still considered as national property by most States, and IHRL has not yet interfered directly with this approach.[149]

In terms of the concerned communities, indigenous peoples have been leading the push for a better integration and consideration of property rights over their lands, waters, and forests. There are also indications that other communities, including small-scale fishing, rural, forest, and local communities, might also be covered. In terms of human rights legal theory, these claims to a right to collective ownership are touching on a very controversial issue as many governments still defend the idea that human rights only support individual claims. While in the last few years, IHRL has clearly evolved to become more universal by encompassing a broader approach to collective rights, there is still a general reluctance towards the recognition of collective rights to property. Outside the situation of common property rights to land for indigenous peoples, IHRL has not yet fundamentally extended its reach to other forms of collective property rights. To date, the approach to forestry and fishing rights is still based on use rights, rather than full property rights. There is nonetheless an increased connection made in terms of advocacy between IHRL and claims for

---

International and Comparative Law, 2015, 441–60; Michael Waibel, Asha Kaushal, Kyo-Hwa Chung, and Claire Balchin (eds), *The Backlash Against Investment Arbitration: Perceptions and Reality* (Wolters Kluwer, 2010).

[148] See Pierre-Marie Dupuy, Ernst-Ulrich Petersmann, and Francesco Francioni (eds), *Human Rights in International Investment Law and Arbitration* (OUP, 2009).

[149] Chapter 3 examines governance over these resources.

collective forms of property over natural resources. The approach is based on the rationale that tenure rights and the security of property rights supports and enhances the livelihood of the local communities. Having secure, long-term, and opposable tenure rights allows communities to project and sustain their continuing development and ensure a better realization of their human rights.

Another point concerning the importance of having a human rights-based approach to property over natural resources involves the underlying tensions that exist between different fields of international law when it comes to rights to use, dispose of, and manage some of the natural resources, especially between international investment law and IHRL. With increased investments over natural resources, greater tension between investment law and IHRL is unavoidable. In this context a stronger international human rights framework protecting and guaranteeing the fundamental right to property of the local communities would constitute an important element to counterbalance the dominant rights of public authorities, investors, and corporations. An important element of the human rights-based approach is to highlight that property rights should not only be measured and protected based on their market and financial value, but also based on their cultural, livelihood, and collective dimensions for local communities.[150]

---

[150] See also Chapter 5.

3

Governance of Natural Resources and Human Rights

From Development to Benefit-Sharing

The human person is the central subject of development and should be the active participant and beneficiary of the right to development.

Declaration on the Right to Development, Article 2

1. Introduction

After examining issues of sovereignty and property in the first two chapters, in Chapter 3 attention is focused on the issue of governance of natural resources and its relationship with international human rights law (IHRL). Governance of natural resources, or natural resource governance, is a broad term referring to the norms, mechanisms, and decision-making processes concerning the exploration, licensing, contracting, extraction, allocation, and revenue generation of natural resources. The governance of natural resources also concerns the distribution of the benefits emerging from the use and exploitation of the resources that often represent an important source of income in many countries across the globe. There are no direct treaty-based connections to the governance of natural resources in human rights treaties, but there are several entry points to support the development of human rights-based approach to the governance of natural resources. Governance, and more precisely 'good governance', has increasingly been included as an important concept within IHRL. The UN Human Rights Council has associated good governance to sustainable human development, putting the emphasis on principles such as accountability, participation, and the enjoyment of human rights.[1]

The key anchor to support a human rights-based approach to good governance over natural resources is probably the right to development. The Office of the High

---

[1] Human Rights Council: Resolution 7/11: 'The role of good governance in the promotion and protection of human rights'; see also (Former) Commission on Human Rights, Resolution 2005/68 of 20 April 2005.

Natural Resources and Human Rights: An Appraisal. Jérémie Gilbert. © J. Gilbert 2018. Published 2018 by Oxford University Press.

Commissioner for Human Rights noted that 'there is a significant degree of con-sensus that good governance relates to political and institutional processes and out-comes that are deemed necessary to achieve the goals of development'.[2] Much ink has been spilled in trying to define the very elusive and paradigmatic right to de-velopment, but increasingly it is recognized that a human rights-based approach to development includes important procedural rights—notably the right to partici-pate and benefit from development. This chapter is placed within this connection between governance of natural resources and the evolution of the right to develop-ment. Using the compass of the right to development, this chapter explores how IHRL supports the emergence of a right to participation, to consent, and to benefit from the exploitation of natural resources. It analyses how the right to development, despite its flaws and controversies, has become an important anchor to support the right of local communities to the governance over the natural resources located on their territories (Section 2). It then explores the increased references made by human rights institutions to the principle of benefit-sharing (Section 3), and finally examines the correlation between IHRL and fiscal regimes over natural resources (Section 4).

2. The Right to Development and Natural Resources: From Participation to Consent

The right to development has often been labelled as one of the 'shallowest' human rights, as well as one of the most controversial human rights.[3] There is a very exten-sive literature engaging on the shortcomings and drawbacks of a normative human rights-based approach to development.[4] However, there little analysis on the con-nection between the right to development and the governance of natural resources as the debates have usually focused on issues relating to the duty bearers of the right to development (notably between 'developed' and 'developing' States) and its lack of possible legal enforcement mechanisms.[5] This chapter does not focus on

---

[2] Office of the High Commissioner for Human Rights, 'Good Governance and Human Rights', at: http://www.ohchr.org/EN/Issues/Development/GoodGovernance/Pages/GoodGovernanceIndex. aspx.

[3] See Arne Vandenbogaerde, 'The Right to Development in International Human Rights Law: A Call for Its Dissolution', 31 *Netherlands Quarterly of Human Rights*, 2013, 187; Peter Uvin, 'From the Right to Development to the Rights-Based Approach: How Human Rights Entered Development', 17 *Development Practice*, 2007, 597–606.

[4] See Jack Donnelly, 'In Search of the Unicorn: The Jurisprudence and Politics of the Right to Development,' 15 *California Western International Law Journal*, 1985, 473, 507; Philip Alston, 'Making Space for New Human Rights: The Case of the Right to Development', 1 *Harvard Human Rights Yearbook*, 1988, 3, 7; Brigitte I. Hamm, 'A Human Rights Approach to Development', 23 *Human Rights Quarterly*, 2001, 1005, 1030; Arjun Sengupta, 'On the Theory and Practice of the Right to Development,' 24 *Human Rights Quarterly*, 2002, 837, 889; Daniel Aguire, *Human Right to Development in a Globalized Context* (Ashgate Publishing, 2008).

[5] See (n 4) as well as: Olajumoke O. Oduwole, *International Law and the Right to Development: A Pragmatic Approach for Africa* (International Institute of Social Studies, 2014); S Marks (ed.), *Implementing the Right to Development—The Role of International Law* (Friedrich Ebert Stiftung, 2008).

these specific aspects, but rather on whether the right to development, as expressed under IHRL, could support the participation of local communities to the governance of natural resources. More precisely, the following discussion focuses on the evolutionary interpretation of the right to development as a right to participate, be consulted, and consent to natural resources governance. Taking a chronological approach regarding the interpretation of the right to development, it examines how there has been a slow and gradual evolution in interpreting the right to development as a right to participate in, and sometimes to consent to, developmental projects connected with natural resources exploitation.

2.1 A human rights-based approach to development: from rhetoric to participation

The right to development has a long and controversial historical pedigree, and has not always been connected to IHRL.[6] One of the big pushes to connect development and IHRL has emerged following a drive by many international organizations to adopt a 'rights-based approach' to development. [7] The rationale been that successful development leads to respect for human rights, and that alternatively, respect for IHRL contributes to longer term and sustainable development.[8] Instead of mainly focusing on economic indicators for development, the human rights-based approach puts the emphasis on the direct participation and benefit for the local populations. It is within this paradigm that the human rights-based approach to development gained momentum and put more emphasis on the *process* of development, rather than the *outcomes* of development.

Legally, the United Nations Declaration on the Right to Development (UNDRTD) clearly grounds development within IHRL.[9] Its Article 1 states that 'the right to development is an inalienable human right by virtue of which every human person and all peoples are entitled to participate in, contribute to, and enjoy economic, social, cultural and political development, in which all human rights and fundamental freedoms can be fully realized'. There are only two direct mentions of natural resources in the whole declaration. The preamble recalls 'the right of peoples to exercise, subject to the relevant provisions of both International Covenants on Human Rights, full and complete sovereignty over all their natural wealth and resources'. Additionally, Article 1(2) states that:

[t]he human right to development also implies the full realization of the right of peoples to self-determination, which includes, subject to the relevant provisions of both International

---

[6] See Isabella D. Bunn, *The Right to Development and International Economic Law: Legal and Moral Dimensions* (Hart Publishing, 2012).

[7] See Paul Gready and Jonathan Ensor (eds), *Reinventing Development? Translating Rights-based Approaches from Theory into Practice* (Zed Books, 2005).

[8] This was notably institutionalized by the United Nations Development Programme (UNDP) in 1990 with the launch of its Human Development Reports.

[9] Declaration on the Right to Development, GA Res. 41/128, UN Doc. A/RES/41/128 (1986).

Covenants on Human Rights, the exercise of their inalienable right to full sovereignty over all their natural wealth and resources.[10]

Therefore, the main connection between natural resources and development is via self-determination and sovereignty. Chapter 1 examines the limitations to this approach, notably based on the ambiguous language of stewardship that is embedded in the language of sovereignty and self-determination.[11] Instead of engaging with the importance of governance of natural resources for development, the declaration kicks back towards the two international covenants and their reference to self-determination and sovereignty, leaving the connection between natural resources and development nearly untouched. However, despite what—on the surface—could seem extremely generic, the declaration offers some relevant and innovative approaches via its participatory approach to development. The spirit of the declaration is expressed in its Article 2, which states that 'the human person is the central subject of development and should be the active participant and beneficiary of the right to development'. This focus on participation and benefit provides the basis for a human rights-based approach to development, highlighting the importance of meaningful and active participation of all individuals and groups in the design, implementation, and monitoring of development policies.

It is mainly at the regional level that the meaning of this participatory approach to development has been examined. Indeed, there has been more positive engagement regarding the justiciability of the right to development, notably in Africa.[12] Article 22 of the African Charter on Human and Peoples' Rights states that 'all peoples shall have the right to their economic, social and cultural development with due regard to their freedom and identity and in the equal enjoyment of the common heritage of mankind' and that all States 'shall have the duty, individually or collectively, to ensure the exercise of the right to development'. The connection between the right to development and natural resources was at the heart of the 2010 decision of the African Commission on Human and Peoples' Rights (ACHPR) in the case concerning the Endorois community of Kenya,[13] which was extremely significant as it led to one of the first human rights decisions on the justiciability of the right to development in the context of natural resources development.[14] The case concerned a pastoralist community that had been expelled from their ancestral territories,

---

[10] Ibid.   [11] See Chapter 1.

[12] See Serges Djoyou Kamga, *The Right to Development in the African Human Rights System* (Routledge, 2018); Serges Alain Djoyou Kamga and Charles Manga Fombad, 'A Critical Review of the Jurisprudence of the African Commission on the Right to Development,' 57(2) *Journal of African Law*, 2013, 196.

[13] African Commission on Human and Peoples' Rights, *Centre for Minority Rights Development (Kenya) and Minority Rights Group International on behalf of Endorois Welfare Council v Kenya*, Communication 276/2003 (2010) (*Endorois* Case).

[14] See Jérémie Gilbert, 'Indigenous Peoples' Human Rights in Africa: The Pragmatic Revolution of the African Commission on Human and Peoples' Rights', 60(1) *International & Comparative Law Quarterly*, 2011, 245–70; Serges Alain Djoyou Kamga, 'The Right to Development in the African Human Rights System: The Endorois Case', 44(2) *De Jure*, 2011, 381–91; Wilmien Wicomb and Henk Smith, 'Customary Communities as "Peoples" and Their Customary Tenure as "Culture": What We Can Do with the Endorois Decision', 11(2) *African Human Rights Law Journal*, 2011, 422–46.

notably to make way for national development projects. At the heart of the dispute were two conflicting approaches to the right to development. A central argument put forward by the government was the need to support national development, as the territory was to be used for both tourism and mining purposes. The government argued that tourism and the exploitation of natural resources (the mining of ruby) would bring significant resources to the region and the country. The government highlighted that other communities, and the country as a whole, was to benefit from these developments. In contrast, the advocates for the Endorois community argued that such developmental projects were taking place in violation of the Endorois right to development as they were not involved in the development process and were not benefiting from it. They highlighted that the Endorois had 'suffered a loss of well-being through the limitations on their choice and capacities, including effective and meaningful participation in projects that will affect them'.[15] Finally, they underlined that the government 'did not embrace a rights-based approach to economic growth, which insists on development in a manner consistent with, and instrumental to, the realisation of human rights and the right to development through adequate and prior consultation'.[16]

The African Commission was asked to balance the two competing claims on the scope of the right to development: the governmental argumentation that exploitation of natural resources was done to benefit national development, and the community's claim that this was done in violation of their own right to development. It is worth noting that the argumentation put forward by the government of Kenya is not unusual and isolated. When it comes to development and exploitation of natural resources governments often put forward the argument that they cannot stop these types of large-scale developments which will allegedly bring significant wealth to the whole country to protect just a few 'marginalized' local indigenous communities.[17] Regarding the scope of the right to development, the African Commission adopted a pragmatic approach, noting that the right to development is constitutive of two elements: one procedural and one substantive.[18] Regarding the procedural aspect of the right to development, it found that the consultations undertaken with the community were inadequate and could not be considered to constitute effective participation. The Commission observed that the 'community members were informed of the impending project as a *fait accompli*, and not given an opportunity to shape the policies or their role in the Game Reserve'.[19] Moreover the forced eviction of the community from its territory took away any possible form of participation in the project. Importantly, regarding the content of such participation, the Commission stated that:

even though the Respondent State says that it has consulted with the Endorois community, the African Commission is of the view that this consultation was not sufficient. It is

---

[15] *Endorois* Case (n 13) para. 129.   [16] Ibid., para. 135.
[17] See Mario Blaser, Harvey A. Feit, and Glenn McRae, *In the Way of Development: Indigenous Peoples, Life Projects and Globalization* (Zed Books, 2004).
[18] *Endorois* Case (n 13) para. 277.   [19] Ibid., para. 281.

convinced that the Respondent State did not obtain the prior, informed consent of all the Endorois before designating their land as a Game Reserve and commencing their eviction.[20]

On the second aspect, regarding the substantive element of the right to development, the Commission put the emphasis on the fact that the result of development should be the empowerment of the Endorois community. The failure to provide adequate compensation and benefits emerging from these developments meant that the concerned community was left out of the development process. The Commission added that it supported the view that 'the Endorois, as beneficiaries of the development process, were entitled to an equitable distribution of the benefits derived from the Game Reserve'.[21]

The decision from the African Commission highlights two interrelated and complementarily elements of the right to development: first, it is a right to participate directly in the process of development; second, it should translate into direct and tangible benefits for the concerned communities. These two aspects, participation and benefit, probably constitute one of the most significant practical applications of human rights to development in terms of the governance of natural resources. This puts forward the potential of the right to development as a process right, supporting the participation as well as a right to benefit from development.[22] From a global legal perspective, this decision is extremely significant as there are few legal human rights cases which have specifically focused on the right to development in the context of natural resources governance. It gives a much more justiciable meaning to the right to development, which until then had remained quite rhetorical, and highlights the meaning and precise content of the principles of participation in a developmental project over natural resources. It also highlights how indigenous peoples have managed to motivate human rights institutions to develop a more comprehensive approach to the right to development in connecting it to the right to FPIC.

2.2 From consultation to a right to free, prior, and informed consent (FPIC): indigenous peoples and beyond?

In the evolution of IHRL, the emergence of right to FPIC probably constitutes one of the most important contributions of IHRL to the governance of natural resources. It has moved the debate from a quite rhetorical basis regarding the human rights-based approach to development to a right to consent to development in situations of exploitation of natural resources located on indigenous peoples' territories. This evolution is based on years of advocacy from indigenous peoples and supporting advocates for an increased right to be consulted when decisions concerning the exploitation of natural resources are undertaken. The aim of the following discussion is not to provide a comprehensive analysis of FPIC, as a very significant body of analysis

---

[20] Ibid., para. 290.   [21] Ibid., para. 297.
[22] On these aspects, see Arjun Sengupta, 'On the Theory and Practice of the Right to Development', 24(4) *Human Rights Quarterly*, 2002, 837–89.

already exists on the issue, [23] but rather to analyse how FPIC is intimately connected to issues of governance of the natural resources located on indigenous territories.

The right to FPIC is usually understood to be a 'composite' right emerging from the evolution of several internationally recognized human rights.[24] As noted in Chapter 1, international human rights treaty bodies have strongly connected the right to self-determination, the right to freely dispose of natural resources, and indigenous peoples' right to FPIC. The other important foundational rights of FPIC are the rights to participation and consultation, both of which are specific rights of indigenous peoples concerning indigenous territory. The ILO Convention 169 put great emphasis on the obligation of consultation and participation to the management of natural resources. As a general principle, Article 6 requires that consultation must be undertaken in good faith, in a form appropriate to the circumstances, and with the objective of achieving consent.[25] Article 7 affirms the 'right to decide their own priorities for the process of development' and 'to exercise control, to the extent possible, over their own economic, social and cultural development'. More specifically on natural resources, Article 15 states that:

[t]he rights of the peoples concerned to the natural resources pertaining to their lands shall be specially safeguarded. These rights include the *right of these peoples to participate in the use, management and conservation of these resources*. In cases in which the State retains the ownership of mineral or sub-surface resources or rights to other resources pertaining to lands, governments shall establish or maintain procedures through which they *shall consult* these peoples, with a view to ascertaining whether and to what degree their interests would be prejudiced, *before* undertaking or permitting any programmes for the exploration or exploitation of such resources pertaining to their lands.[26]

These rights to participation and consultation in the context of natural resources governance have been at the heart of many recommendations of the ILO's Committee of Experts on the Application of Conventions and Recommendations (CEACR). For example, when examining Ecuador's non-compliance with the Convention, the CECAR stated that 'the spirit of consultation and participation constitutes the cornerstone of ILO Convention No. 169 on which all its provisions are based'.[27] The Committee added: 'The concept of consulting the indigenous communities

[23] See Cathal Doyle, *Indigenous Peoples, Title to Territory, Rights and Resources: The Transformative Role of Free Prior and Informed Consent* (Routledge, 2014); Joji Cariño, ' "Indigenous Peoples" Right to Free, Prior, Informed Consent: Reflections on Concepts and Practice', 22 *Arizona Journal of International and Comparative Law*, 2005, 19; Tara Ward, 'The Right to Free, Prior, and Informed Consent: Indigenous Peoples' Participation Rights within International Law' 10 *Northwestern University Journal of International Human Rights*, 2011, 54.

[24] See (Former) Working Group on Indigenous Populations, Legal Commentary on the Concept of Free, Prior and Informed Consent, UN Doc. E/CN.4/Sub.2/AC.4/2005/WP.1 (2005).

[25] Convention Concerning Indigenous and Tribal Peoples in Independent Countries (ILO No. 169), 72 *ILO Official Bulletin* 59 (1989), reprinted in 28 *International Legal Materials*, 1989, 1382.

[26] Convention Concerning Indigenous and Tribal Peoples in Independent Countries (ILO No. 169), Art. 15 (emphasis added).

[27] Report of the Committee Set Up to Examine the Representation Alleging Non-Observance by Ecuador of the Indigenous and Tribal Peoples Convention, 1989 (ILO No. 169), made under Article 24 of the ILO Constitution by the Confederación Ecuatoriana de Organizaciones Sindicales Libres (CEOSL), ILO Doc. GB.282/14/2, 14 November 2001.

that could be affected by the exploration or exploitation of natural resources includes establishing a genuine dialogue between both parties characterized by communication and understanding, mutual respect, good faith and the sincere wish to reach a common accord.'[28] The CEACR has repeatedly called on State parties to respect their obligations to consult with indigenous peoples *prior* to exploration and exploitation of natural resources within their traditional territories, and has required the adoption and implementation of domestic legislation in order to facilitate such consultations.[29] While the ILO Convention does not directly refer to a right to FPIC as such, the requirements of prior consultation and the good faith negotiations to obtain agreement or consent form the basis of a similar requirement.[30]

The United Nations Declaration on the Rights of Indigenous Peoples (UNDRIP) also strongly insists on the duty of States to consult indigenous peoples in any decisions that may affect them, and on the duty to ensure indigenous peoples' participation in decision making.[31] The duty to consult indigenous peoples is reflected in several provisions of the Declaration.[32] Specifically, Articles 19 and 32 require States to consult indigenous peoples in good faith, through appropriate procedures, with the objective of obtaining their agreement or consent when measures that may affect indigenous peoples are considered. Regarding the content of consultation, Article 32 affirms that:

States shall consult and cooperate in good faith with the indigenous peoples concerned through their own representative institutions in order to obtain their free and informed consent prior to the approval of any project affecting their lands or territories and other resources, particularly in connection with the development, utilization or exploitation of their mineral, water or other resources.

The Declaration makes a distinction in situations where planned developmental projects might result in the forced relocation of indigenous peoples, and that, in these situations, indigenous peoples have a right to FPIC (Art. 10). Article 29 concerning the storage of hazardous materials on their lands adds that the consent of indigenous peoples should actually be obtained if it results in their relocation. The reference to consent opens a whole new approach to the meaning of development.

---

[28] Ibid., para. 38. See also Report of the Committee Set Up to Examine the Representation Alleging Non-Observance by Argentina of the Indigenous and Tribal Peoples Convention, 1989 (No. 169), made under Article 24 of the ILO Constitution by the Education Workers Union of Río Negro (UNTER), local section affiliated to the Confederation of Education Workers of Argentina (CTERA).

[29] CEACR, Individual Observations Concerning Indigenous and Tribal Peoples Convention, 1989 (No. 169) Ecuador, ILO Doc. 062010ECU 169 (2010), para. 4; CEACR, Individual Observation Concerning Indigenous and Tribal Peoples Convention, 1989 (No. 169) Guatemala, ILO Doc. 062006GTM169 (2006), paras 10, 13, and 15; CEACR, Individual Observation Concerning Indigenous and Tribal Peoples Convention, 1989 (No. 169) Mexico, ILO Doc. 062006MEX169 (2006), para. 10.

[30] For further evidence and analysis, see 'Contribution by the ILO', International Workshop on Free, Prior and Informed Consent and Indigenous Peoples, Permanent Forum on Indigenous Issues, UN Doc. PFII/2005/WS.2/4 (17–19 January 2005).

[31] See Mauro Barelli, 'Free, Prior and Informed Consent in the Aftermath of the UN Declaration on the Rights of Indigenous Peoples: Developments and Challenges Ahead', 16(1) *The International Journal of Human Rights*, 2012, 1–24.

[32] Arts 10, 11, 15, 17, 19, 28, 29, 30, 32, 36, 37, and 38.

The right to development, as operationalized via the right to FPIC, should ensure that indigenous territories are included in developmental projects only with the consent of the concerned indigenous peoples. This has important consequences on any potential project of exploitation of natural resources. One of the main emerging debates relates to whether this right gives indigenous peoples veto power regarding such projects. It has been highlighted that FPIC is not meant to be a veto right, but rather a way of ensuring that indigenous peoples meaningfully participate in decisions directly impacting their lands, territories, and resources.[33] It also requires that States should aim at obtaining the consent of indigenous peoples, although it is an objective rather than a threat.

The connection between development, consultation, effective participation, and consent is not only limited to specialized instruments on indigenous peoples' rights, but is also part of the wider practice of the international human rights monitoring bodies. In its General Comment 23, the Human Rights Committee (HRC) pointed out that, as part of State obligations under Article 27 of the ICCPR, 'Indigenous communities must have effective participation in decisions that affect the community'. The HRC has also affirmed that when taking action that might infringe indigenous peoples' rights, States have a duty to consult indigenous peoples.[34] In recent years, the HRC has increasingly referred to consent rather than just consultation. For example, in 2014, in relation to the United States, the HRC urged the State party to 'ensure that consultations are held with the indigenous communities that might be adversely affected by the State party's development projects and exploitation of natural resources *with a view to obtaining their free, prior and informed consent* for proposed project activities'.[35] This approach based on consent rather than mere consultation is also reflected in the individual opinions of the HRC. In the *Poma Poma* decision, relating to a dispute over the exploitation of natural water resources in Peru, the HRC endorsed the right to FPIC.[36] The case concerned the rerouting of water supplies which led to loss of water access for the indigenous Aymara people traditionally living in the highlands. Going back to the process of development adopted by the government, the HRC highlighted that 'participation in the decision-making process must be effective, which requires not mere consultation but the free, prior and informed consent of the members of the community'.[37] Due to the lack of consultation and consent, the HRC concluded that the government had violated the rights of the applicants, endorsing the right to free, prior, and informed consent as part of its interpretation of Article 27 of the Covenant.

---

[33] See Special Rapporteur James Anaya on the Rights of Indigenous Peoples, Report of the Special Rapporteur on the Situation of Human Rights and Fundamental Freedoms of Indigenous People, UN Doc. A/HRC/13/34, 15 July 2009, para. 48.

[34] *Länsman et al v Finland* (Communication No. 511/1992), UN Doc. CCPR/C/52/D/511/1992, 9(5).

[35] Human Rights Committee, Concluding Observations on the United States, 23 August 2014 CCPR/C/USA/CO/4, para. 25, Art. 27 (emphasis added).

[36] Human Rights Committee, *Ángela Poma Poma v Peru*, Communication No. 1457/2006, Doc. CCPR/C/95/D/1457/2006 of 27 March 2009.

[37] Ibid.

The Committee on Economic, Social and Cultural Rights (CESCR) has adopted a similar approach in systematically putting forward the obligation to respect and seek indigenous peoples' FPIC before undertaking projects exploiting natural resources within their ancestral territories. For example, in the 2013 report concerning Gabon, the CESCR picked on 'the absence of any specific regulatory or legislative framework that would make it possible to systematize practice in implementing the right to prior informed consultation of indigenous peoples in decision-making processes concerning the exploitation of natural resources in traditional territories'.[38] Likewise, in its 2016 report concerning Canada, the CESCR expressed its concern that 'the right to free, prior and informed consent of indigenous peoples to any change to their lands and territories is not adequately incorporated in domestic legislation and not consistently applied by the State party'.[39] The Committee on the Elimination of Racial Discrimination (CERD) has also engaged with the connection between development, consultation, and consent. In its General Recommendation 23 on indigenous peoples, CERD pointed out that States have to 'ensure that members of indigenous peoples have equal rights in respect of effective participation in public life and that no decisions directly relating to their rights and interests are taken without their informed consent'.[40] CERD urged States to make sure 'that no decisions directly relating to [indigenous] rights and interests are taken without their informed consent'.[41] CERD has also made reference to indigenous peoples' right to consent to decisions directly affecting them in many of its concluding observations.[42]

The right to FPIC has also been integrated in the jurisprudence of regional human rights institutions. As noted by the Inter-American Court of Human Rights (IACtHR) in the case of the Saramaka community, 'regarding large-scale development or investment projects that would have a major impact within Saramaka territory, the State has a duty, not only to consult with the Saramaka, but also to obtain their FPIC, according to their customs and traditions'.[43] The IACtHR acknowledged that the State may grant concessions for the exploration and extraction of natural resources, but highlighted that it must do so with adequate participatory safeguards to 'ensure their survival as a tribal people'. In the words of the IACtHR, effective participation means the carrying out of 'good faith' consultations 'with the objective of reaching an agreement'. Getting into the details of the process that is necessary to ensure such effective participation, the IACtHR highlighted several obligations for the State, including:

---

[38] E/C.12/GAB/CO/1 (CESCR, 2013), para. 6.

[39] Committee on Economic, Social and Cultural Rights, Concluding Observations on the Sixth Periodic Report of Canada, UN Doc. E/C.12/CAN/CO/6 (23 March 2016).

[40] CERD, General Comment XXIII (51st Session), para. 4(d) (1997).

[41] General Recommendation XXIII (51), UN Doc. CERD/C/365, in A/52/18, Annex V, para. 3 (1997).

[42] For a compilation of these recommendations, see UN-REDD, 'Legal Companion to the UN-REDD Programme—Guidelines on Free, Prior and Informed Consent (FPIC), International Law and Jurisprudence Affirming the Requirement of FPIC (2013)' (Geneva: UN-REDD Programme Secretariat).

[43] *Saramaka Peoples v Suriname*, Judgment, Series C No. 172 (2007), para. 134.

(1) actively consult with said community according to their customs and traditions and guarantee that consultations 'should take account of the [indigenous] ... people's traditional methods of decision-making';

(2) conduct consultations in 'in good faith' and commence consultations at the 'the early stages of a development or investment plan, not only when the need arises to obtain approval from the community';

(3) disseminate proper and relevant information to ensure that consultations make communities 'aware of possible risks, including environmental and health risks';

(4) carry out consultations 'with the objective of reaching an agreement' to guarantee that 'proposed development or investment plan' must be 'accepted knowingly and voluntarily'.[44]

Crucially, the IACtHR added that States have a duty to obtain FPIC where 'large-scale development or investment projects ... would have a major impact within [indigenous peoples] territory'.[45] This requirement to obtain consent is based on the fact that the exploitation of natural resources would deprive indigenous peoples of the capacity to use and enjoy their lands and other natural resources necessary for their subsistence. It means that there is a duty to consult with indigenous peoples to reach an informed agreement for any developmental project which might affect them, and that there is a requirement to obtain their FPIC when such developmental projects will affect the resources located on their territories. Since then, several other rulings of the IACtHR have included the right to FPIC in the context of natural resources exploitation taking place on indigenous territories.[46] The aforementioned case of the Endorois community against Kenya examined by the African Commission is another illustration of the integration of the right to FPIC by regional human rights institutions. This was also affirmed in the 2017 ruling of the African Court on Human and Peoples' Rights regarding the Ogiek community in Kenya.[47] Former UN Special Rapporteur on the rights of indigenous peoples James Anaya has highlighted that, overall, based on its central importance in both the instruments and the jurisprudence, the requirement to conduct 'meaningful consultation' should be regarded as representing a norm of customary international law.[48] If such process leads to an eventual relocation, then consent is mandatory. In order to ensure that consultations are 'meaningful', certain procedural rights have also evolved. Consultations must be free from manipulations and coercion, respect traditional decision-making processes, be held in sufficient time in advance of project

[44] *Saramaka People v Suriname*, Preliminary Objections, Merits, Reparations, and Costs, Judgment. Series C No. 172 (2007), para. 133.

[45] Ibid., para. 134.

[46] See *Kichwa Indigenous People of Sarayaku v Ecuador*, Merits and Reparations, Judgment. Series C No. 245 (2012); *Kaliña and Lokono Peoples v Suriname*, Merits, Reparations and Costs. Series C No. 309 (2015), para. 61; for references to other cases, see IACHR, *Indigenous and Tribal Peoples' Rights over their Ancestral Lands and Natural Resources: Norms and Jurisprudence of the Inter-American Human Rights System*, OEA/Ser.L/V/II. Doc. 56/09 (2010), section IX.

[47] *African Commission on Human and Peoples' Rights v Republic of Kenya*, Application No. 006/2012 (2017).

[48] James Anaya, 'Indigenous Peoples' Participatory Rights in Relation to Decisions about Natural Resource Extraction: The More Fundamental Issues of What Rights Indigenous Peoples Have in Lands and Resources', 22(8) *Arizona Journal of International and Comparative Law*, 2005, 7–17.

execution, and with adequate information provided to enable informed decisions to be taken. This evolution is not limited to human rights institutions, as a number of international financial institutions have recently included safeguard policies to reflect the evolutions in the recognition of indigenous peoples' rights to FPIC within their policies.[49] Another example of the recognition of FPIC in the management of natural resources is the guidelines provided by the Forest Stewardship Council.[50]

One of the questions regarding the evolution of the right to FPIC relates to its eventual application to non-indigenous communities. As examined earlier, the right to FPIC has clearly emerged within the specific rights of indigenous peoples. Questions have started to surface on its potential application to non-indigenous communities, notably based on the fact that the right to FPIC is based on a composite of several universal human rights, such as the right to self-determination, the right to development, the right to property, and the right to participation.[51] Rights that have been positively interpreted in the context of indigenous peoples' rights, but which, in theory, are not restricted to indigenous peoples only, form part of the universal human rights legal framework. As an illustration of this potential extension of the right to FPIC to non-indigenous communities, the ACHPR in its 2012 resolution on a Human Rights-Based Approach to Natural Resources Governance states that 'all necessary measures must be taken by the State to ensure participation, including the free, prior and informed consent of communities, in decision making related to natural resources governance'.[52] The text refers to all local communities, not just specifically indigenous peoples. There is also the indication that the right to FPIC has been extended to Afro-Descendant communities in Latin America, and nomadic communities in central Asia. For example, in its review of the implementation of the International Covenant on Economic, Social and Cultural Rights (ICESCR) in China, the CESCR noted its concerns 'about the resettlement of nomadic herdsmen in the "new socialist villages" carried out in the State party without proper consultation and in most cases without *free, prior and informed* consent, particularly in the western provinces and autonomous regions (Arts 1 and 11)'.[53] In its 2012 review on the situation in Mauritania, the CESCR called on the authorities

---

[49] See European Bank for Reconstruction and Development (EBRD) *Environmental and Social Policy* (May 2008); Operational Policy on Indigenous Peoples and Strategy for Indigenous Development Inter-American Development Bank (Sustainable Development Department Sector Policy and Strategy Series OP-765 July 2006); IFC Performance Standard No. 7, World Bank Operational Policy on Indigenous Peoples No. 4.1; Office of the Compliance Advisor/Ombudsman (CAO) IFC and MIGA; Asian Development Bank, The Safeguard Policy Statement (Second Draft) October 2008, 11, 19.

[50] Forest Stewardship Council, Guidelines for the Implementation of the Right to Free, Prior and Informed Consent (FPIC), Forest Stewardship Council Technical Series No. 2012-2, Version 1, 30 October 2012, https://ic.fsc.org/download.fsc-fpic-guidelines-version-1.a-1243.pdf.

[51] See Brant McGee, 'The Community Referendum: Participatory Democracy and the Right to Free, Prior and Informed Consent to Development', 27 *Berkeley Journal of International Law*, 2009, 570.

[52] African Commission on Human and Peoples' Rights, Resolution on a Human Rights-Based Approach to Natural Resources Governance, adopted at its 51st Ordinary Session held from 18 April to 2 May 2012.

[53] Committee on Economic, Social and Cultural Rights: Concluding Observations on the Second Periodic Report of China, including Hong Kong, China, and Macao, China, UN Doc. E/C.12/CHN/CO/2 (2014), para. 31 (emphasis added).

to 'ensure that the free, prior and informed consent of the population is obtained in decision-making processes on extractive and mining projects affecting them'.[54] This is in the context of mining activities taking place across the country, not specifically concerning indigenous peoples. These are only illustrations of the application of FPIC to non-indigenous peoples rather than a comprehensive review of all statements that make explicit the application of FPIC to other local communities. At the time of writing it might be too early to affirm that this constitutes a definitive application of FPIC to non-indigenous peoples, although it is certain that IHRL is increasingly concerned with the lack of participation and consultation of local communities in the governance of natural resources, which often leads to the mention of FPIC as a right to be respected. Whether it is an approach that will extend to other non-indigenous communities remains an open issue, but it seems clear that human rights institutions have fully embraced the importance of the right to FPIC, and more generally participation and consultation when natural resources development projects are taking place.[55] The overall trajectory has been a (slow) progression from a rhetorical right to development to a more concrete right to participation, then a right to consultation, and finally to a right to consent. This evolution offers a new perspective on the potential role of IHRL when it comes to the governance of large-scale developmental projects involving the exploitation of natural resources, although it might take some time before its practical implementation is felt at the local level.

3. Development, Participation, and Benefit-Sharing

The progressive integration of the principle of benefit-sharing in IHRL is another promising development regarding the governance of natural resources. The exploitation of natural resources, and especially extractives industries, often lead to impoverishment rather than development for the local communities. While in general the exploitation of minerals, particularly high-priced minerals such as oil, gas, and diamonds, is generating enormous profits for the corporations and the investors involved, in most situations little is shown regarding the economic development of the local populations who live in the vicinity of the extractive industries. Across the globe, the absence of expected direct benefits to the local communities is causing tension between them and the concerned industries. This is not limited to extractive industries, as more generally the exploitation and use of natural resources does not bring much benefit to the local communities as most of the profits are seen by external actors, notably investors and corporations. In this overall context of lack of local community benefit, the principle of benefit-sharing has gained momentum as an important way to minimize the negative impact of extractive projects. Legally, benefit-sharing is a recurrent theme in international debates, but little analysis exists

[54] Committee on Economic, Social and Cultural Rights: Concluding Observations on the Initial Report of Mauritania, UN Doc. E/C.12/MRT/CO/1 (2012), para. 8.
[55] McGee (n 51) 572.

regarding its potential application within the sphere of IHRL and its connection to the governance of natural resources.[56] The following discussion examines how the emergence of a right to benefit-sharing could offer an important legal platform to ensure a fairer and more equitable distribution of the benefits emerging from the exploitation of natural resources at the local level.

3.1 Fair and equitable benefits: from biodiversity to human rights

The principle of fair and equitable benefit-sharing has primarily emerged within the sphere of international environmental law, and more specifically within the field of biodiversity law. The notion of benefit-sharing from natural resources was first formalized in international law in 1992 through the Convention on Biological Diversity (CBD).[57] The CBD requires State parties to ensure 'the equitable sharing of the benefits' that arise from the utilization of indigenous and local communities' traditional knowledge (Art. 8(j)). This was further reinforced with the adoption of the Nagoya Protocol on Access to Genetic Resources and the Fair and Equitable Sharing of Benefits Arising from their Utilization to the Convention on Biological Diversity (Nagoya Protocol) in 2010. The main thrust of the protocol is that governments should provide for the fair and equitable sharing of benefits arising from the utilization of genetic resources, especially for indigenous peoples and local communities. Benefit-sharing has also been affirmed in several other decisions of the governing body of the CBD as an important principle to ensure the protection of biodiversity.[58] This increased connection between the use of biological resources and benefit-sharing has paved the way for the emergence of a human rights-based approach to benefit-sharing.[59]

In terms of IHRL, while the Universal Declaration of Human Rights mentions 'the right of everyone to share in the benefits of scientific advancements as part of the human right to science', it is only recently that the principle of benefit-sharing has developed in the field of IHRL.[60] It is within the field of indigenous peoples' rights that a human rights-based approach to benefit-sharing has germinated. The UN Special Rapporteur on the rights of indigenous peoples (present and former) has supported the development of benefit-sharing processes as an important element of

---

[56] See Elisa Morgera, 'The Need for an International Legal Concept of Fair and Equitable Benefit-Sharing', 27 *European Journal of International Law*, 2016, 353; Doris Schroeder, 'Benefit Sharing: It's Time for a Definition', 33(4) *Journal of Medical Ethics*, 2007, 205–9.

[57] Convention on Biological Diversity, 1992. See Article 1 stating that one of the objectives of the Convention is to ensure 'the fair and equitable sharing of the benefits arising out of the utilization of genetic resources'.

[58] See Bonn Guidelines on Access to Genetic Resources and Fair and Equitable Sharing of the Benefits Arising out of their Utilization (CBD Decision X/1 (2010), Preamble, para. 6.

[59] See Elisa Morgera, 'Against All Odds: The Contribution of the Convention on Biological Diversity to International Human Rights Law'. In: Denis Alland, Vincent Chetail, Olivier de Frouville, and Jorge E. Viñuales (eds), *Unity and Diversity of International Law: Essays in Honour of Professor Pierre-Marie Dupuy* (Brill, 2014), p. 983. See Chapter 6 in this volume for further discussion.

[60] See Elisa Morgera, 'Fair and Equitable Benefit-Sharing at the Cross-Roads of the Human Right to Science and International Biodiversity Law', 4(4) *Laws*, 2015, 803–31.

indigenous peoples' human rights.[61] International human rights monitoring bodies are increasingly integrating specific references to the fact that indigenous peoples should benefit from the exploitation of resources located in their territories. The CESCR has been referring to benefit-sharing in several of its concluding observations concerning the rights of indigenous peoples. For example, regarding New Zealand, the CESCR insisted on the importance of ensuring that indigenous peoples 'enjoy tangible benefits from the exploitation of their resources.'[62] Likewise, in the context of logging concessions in the DRC the CESCR highlighted that the government should adopt a moratorium on concessions to ensure the protection of indigenous peoples' rights to their ancestral lands and natural resources, and their benefits over natural resources exploitation.[63] The CESCR has made similar recommendations in the context of mining in Indonesia, noting 'these projects have not brought about tangible benefits for local communities.'[64] Pertinently, the CESCR recommended that the government ensure 'that tangible benefits and their distribution are not left solely to the voluntary policy of corporate social responsibilities of companies, but are also defined in license agreements, in the form of employment creation and improvement of public services for local communities, among others.'[65] Looking at the legal basis for benefit-sharing, the CESCR has relied on Article 1.2 (the right to self-determination over natural resources), Article 2.2 (non-discrimination), and Article 11 (the right of everyone to an adequate standard of living) of the Covenant.

The work of CERD reflects this approach to benefit-sharing, with several concluding observations making specific references to States' obligation to ensure that indigenous peoples benefit from the exploitation of natural resources located in their territories.[66] For example, it positively noted that the government of Bolivia had put in place processes to ensure '[p]rofit-sharing when natural resources are extracted from the territories of [indigenous peoples],'[67] and in its report on the situation in Ecuador, it mentioned the need to ensure the 'equitable' sharing of benefits, stating that:

As to the exploitation of the subsoil resources of the traditional lands of indigenous communities, the Committee observes that merely consulting these communities prior to exploiting the resources falls short of meeting the requirements set out in the Committee's general recommendation XXIII on the rights of indigenous peoples. The Committee therefore recommends that the prior informed consent of these communities be sought, and that the *equitable sharing of benefits* to be derived from such exploitation be ensured.[68]

---

[61] See The Situation of Indigenous Peoples in Australia, UN Doc. A/HRC/15/37/Add.4 (2010), paras 27, 86; The Situation of the Sami People in the Sápmi Region of Norway, Sweden and Finland, UN Doc. A/HRC/18/35/Add.2 (2011), paras 56, 85; The Situation of Indigenous Peoples in the Russian Federation: UN Doc. A/HRC/15/37/Add.5 (2011), para. 46; Report of the Special Rapporteur on the Situation of Human Rights and Fundamental Freedoms of Indigenous People, James Anaya, UN Doc. A/HRC/15/37 (2010), para. 77.

[62] New Zealand, UN Doc. E/C.12/NZL/CO/3 (2012), para. 11.

[63] Democratic Republic of Congo, UN Doc. E/C.12/COD/CO/4 (2009), para. 14.

[64] Indonesia, UN Doc. E/C.12/IDN/CO/1 (2014), para. 28.   [65] Ibid.

[66] See CERD, Norway, UN Doc. CERD/C/NOR/CO/21-22 (2015), para. 30(d); CERD, Bolivia, UN Doc. CERD/C/BOL/CO/17-20 (2011), para. 7(f).

[67] Ibid., Bolivia (n 66).

[68] Ecuador, UN Doc. CERD/C/62/CO/2 (2003), para. 16 (emphasis added).

This reference to 'equitable benefit-sharing' is grounded in the non-discriminatory and participatory approach adopted by CERD.

Benefit-sharing also forms an important element in the jurisprudence of the regional human rights institutions. The IACtHR has made several references to indigenous peoples' rights to benefit-sharing in the context of natural resources exploitation projects taking place on their lands. In the *Saramaka* case, the IACtHR stated that 'in the event that development or investment plans are carried out within indigenous territories, the benefits arising from those plans must be reasonably shared with the indigenous communities concerned'.[69] In *Garífuna Community of Punta Piedra and its members*, the IACtHR specifically mentioned the right of indigenous peoples to benefit-sharing,[70] saying that:

in the case of any development, investment, exploration or extraction project in traditional territories of indigenous or tribal communities, the State must comply with the following safeguards: (i) conduct an appropriate and participatory process that guarantees their right to consultation; (ii) make a prior social and environmental impact assessment, and (iii) as appropriate, *reasonably share the benefits produced by the exploitation of the natural resources.*[71]

The IACtHR adopted a similar approach in the 2016 case of the Kaliña and Lokono communities of Suriname and reiterated its prior jurisprudence by highlighting that when States are 'considering development plans within the territories of indigenous and tribal peoples, [they] should, within reason, share the benefits of the project in question, as appropriate'.[72] The ACHPR has also mentioned benefit-sharing in the Endorois decision against Kenya noting that 'the failure to guarantee effective participation and to *guarantee a reasonable share in the profits* of the Game Reserve (or other adequate forms of compensation) also extends to a violation of the right to development'.[73] The ACHPR added that it supported the view that 'the Endorois, as beneficiaries of the development process, were entitled to an *equitable* distribution of the benefits derived from the Game Reserve'.[74] Specifically connecting the right to property and benefit-sharing, the ACHPR noted 'that the concept of benefit-sharing also serves as an important indicator of compliance for property rights; failure to duly compensate (even if the other criteria of legitimate aim and proportionality are satisfied) result in a violation of the right to property.'[75] In this context, the ACHPR highlighted that the right to benefit from the exploitation of their lands emerges from the right to obtain 'just compensation' resulting from the deprivation of their right to the use and enjoyment of their traditional lands and of those natural resources necessary for their survival.

As noted, benefit-sharing is not explicitly expressed in human rights treaties; rather, its emergence is based on the interpretation and application of other relevant human rights. Additionally, the CESCR has based itself on a bundle of rights

---

[69] *Saramaka People* (n 43) para. 138 ff.
[70] *Garífuna Community of Punta Piedra and its members v Honduras*, Preliminary Objections, Merits, Reparations and Costs, Judgment. Series C No. 304 (2015), paras 217, 223.
[71] Ibid., para. 215 (emphasis added).   [72] *Kaliña and Peoples* (n 46) para. 227.
[73] *Endorois* Case (n 13) para. 228 (emphasis added).
[74] Ibid., para. 297 (emphasis added).   [75] Ibid., para. 294.

including self-determination, non-discrimination, and the right to an adequate standard of living. CERD instead relies more on a participatory approach, putting forward the need to recognize the fundamental rights of indigenous peoples to participate and benefit in a non-discriminatory manner from development. The Inter-American and African human rights jurisprudence is also grounded on a participatory approach, adding another entry point in putting forward the right to property for indigenous peoples. The importance of benefit-sharing as a right to participate in development is also expressed in the ILO Convention 169, Article 15, which says: 'The peoples concerned shall wherever possible participate in the benefits of such activities, and shall receive fair compensation for any damages which they may sustain as a result of such activities'. While the reference to participation in the benefits is quite vague, the ILO Committee has highlighted that this should be done 'on a case by case basis, taking into account the circumstances of the particular situation of the indigenous peoples concerned'.[76] In its practice, the ILO Committee has consistently highlighted the importance of ensuring the participation of indigenous peoples in the sharing of the benefits emerging form natural resources exploitation.[77] The approach here is that indigenous peoples should not be seen as passively 'receiving' benefits, but rather that their active participation in the identification of benefits and sharing modalities should be an essential element of their right to effective participation.

Overall, all these recommendations from international human rights bodies, regional courts and commissions, and the ILO committee provide a solid legal basis for the principle of benefit-sharing that emerges as a composite right reflecting on the importance of non-discrimination, development, participation, and property rights over natural resources. There is nonetheless a worrying development regarding the human rights approach which equates benefit-sharing with reparations and compensation for loss of lands and territories. This was expressed in *Saramaka*, where the IACtHR suggested that benefit-sharing might be 'inherent to the right of compensation' recognized under Article 21 of the American Convention. In this context, the IACtHR viewed benefit-sharing as a form of compensation for loss of property rights. This is a restrictive approach, as benefit-sharing should not be confused with compensation schemes sometimes paid for loss of access to natural resources. These compensations concern reparations for forced resettlement, or for damages directly faced by the indigenous communities due to loss of access to essential natural resources. Anaya highlights that the duty to share benefits is independent of compensation measures.[78] Benefit-sharing refers to a right to participate in the benefits of

---

[76] ILO, 'Monitoring Indigenous and Tribal Peoples' Rights through ILO Conventions: A Compilation of ILO Supervisory Bodies' Comments 2009-2010', Observation (Norway), CEARC 2009/80th Session, 95.

[77] See ILO, Report of the Committee Set Up to Examine the Representation Alleging Non-Observance by Ecuador of ILO Convention No. 169, Doc. GB.282/14/4 (2001), para. 44(3); ILO, Monitoring Indigenous and Tribal Peoples' Rights through ILO Conventions: A Compilation of ILO Supervisory Bodies' Comments 2009-2010, Observation (Norway), Canadian Environmental Assessment Research Council 2009/80th Session (2009), 95.

[78] Report on the Situation of Human Rights and Fundamental Freedoms of Indigenous People, UN Doc. A/HRC/15/37 (2010), paras 67, 89, and 91.

the project, and is a much more provocative and participatory principle. As noted in a multiple-country study regarding forestry rights, 'Whereas benefit sharing was originally understood as referring to the distribution of financial benefits, the concept has come to encompass broader forms of social accountability and responsibility.'[79] While benefit-sharing could form a part of compensation packages, it should be seen as a standalone principle of good governance over natural resources. It is based on a participatory approach to the right to development grounded in the right to self-determination, the right to the right of everyone to an adequate standard of living, and the principle of non-discrimination.

In terms of the rights-holders, references to benefit-sharing have thus far been primarily within the remits of indigenous peoples' rights. Nonetheless, there are a few rare appearances of benefit-sharing for non-indigenous communities. The report of the UN Special Rapporteur on the situation in the Democratic People's Republic of Korea called for the introduction of 'more extensive food security-related measures, such as sound agricultural practices, environment conservation, disaster preparedness and people's participation and mobilization in planning, programming, and benefit-sharing'.[80] The CESCR has also mentioned the need to recognize the right of local communities of Togo to benefit from the exploitation of natural resources.[81] Legally speaking, there is support for the extension of benefit-sharing to other local communities. The bundle of rights that has been used to support benefit-sharing, namely self-determination, participation, and property rights, are not exclusive to indigenous peoples' rights as these rights form part of the main human rights treaties. Human rights treaty-monitoring bodies and regional human rights institutions have embraced, via influence from indigenous peoples, an interpretation of these norms that lead to the inclusion of benefit-sharing. This does not preclude other non-indigenous communities from doing likewise. Moreover, the Declaration on the Right to Development highlights that States should 'formulate appropriate national development policies that aim at the constant improvement of the well-being of the entire population and of all individuals, on the basis of their active, free and meaningful participation in development and in the fair distribution of the benefits resulting therefrom'. It adds that development should be seen as a process which should benefit 'the entire population and ... all individuals on the basis of their active, free and meaningful participation in development and in the fair distribution of benefits resulting therefrom'. What is important regarding the role of IHRL in the governance of natural resources is that a human rights-based approach to benefit-sharing adds a new legal support for indigenous peoples (and, eventually, other local communities) to benefit directly from the exploitation of natural resources. It is a revolutionary approach as it challenges the current predominant system, which sees

---

[79] Pham Thu Thuy, Maria Brockhaus, Grace Wong, Le Ngoc Dung, Januarti Sinarra Tjajadi, Lasse Loft, Cecilia Luttrell, and Samuel Assembe Mvondo, *Approaches to Benefit Sharing: A Preliminary Comparative Analysis of 13 REDD+ Countries* (Center for International Forestry Research, Working Paper 108, 2013), p. 1.

[80] Report of the Special Rapporteur on the Situation of Human Rights in the Democratic People's Republic of Korea, Vitit Muntarbhorn, UN Doc. A/HRC/10/18 (2009), para. 80(b).

[81] See CESCR, Togo, UN Doc. E/C.12/TGO/CO/1, (2013), para. 27.

most of the benefits being enjoyed by other actors, i.e. public authorities and corporations, with no direct or significant returns to local communities.

3.2 Benefit-sharing agreements and human rights: states, peoples, and industries

States still predominately exercise sovereignty and property rights over natural resources. From this perspective, public authorities are usually the main recipients of the benefits of natural resources exploitation; other beneficiaries are usually the concerned industries. Benefit-sharing places itself in the arena of sovereignty over natural resources by suggesting a new relationship between governments, industries, and local communities, i.e. a conciliatory platform to allow local communities to benefit from the exploitation of the resources without fundamentally challenging States' sovereignty.[82] Morgera suggests that benefit-sharing places itself within 'an evolutionary and systemic understanding of national sovereignty over natural resources calls for accommodating larger society's development and communities' way of life, with the latter being protected by a distinctive bundle of rights to participation, culture and subsistence that does not call into question States' territorial integrity'.[83] This innovative focus on the role of the communities in defining the content of benefit-sharing agreements engages with an area of international law largely dominated by States actors. This is part of a participatory model on the use of natural resources, and

[t]he justification for indigenous peoples to benefit from projects within their territories *within a partnership model* should be self-evident: even if they do not, under domestic law, own the resources to be extracted, they provide access to the resources and give up alternatives for the future development of their territories by agreeing to the projects.[84]

Benefit-sharing is about developing partnership, and unlike compensation or reparation, it is a long-term process. The main principle behind a right to benefit-sharing is about direct access to the benefits generated by natural resources exploitation.

There is no ready-made formula to apply regarding how to establish benefit-sharing agreements, but the main recommendation emerging from human rights bodies is to respect the local decision-making processes. The IACtHR issued clarifications about the content of benefit-sharing in some of its judgments. For example, in the interpretative judgment of the IACtHR in its *Saramaka* decision, the judges explained that the beneficiaries of benefit-sharing must be determined 'in consultation

---

[82] See Lila Barrera-Hernández, Barry Barton, Lee Godden, Alastair Lucas, and Anita Rønne (eds), *Sharing the Costs and Benefits of Energy and Resource Activity: Legal Change and Impact on Communities* (OUP, 2016).

[83] Elisa Morgera, *Under the Radar: Fair and Equitable Benefit-Sharing and the Human Rights of Indigenous Peoples and Local Communities Connected to Natural Resources*, Benelex Working Paper No. 10, January 2017, p. 4.

[84] Report of the Special Rapporteur on the Situation of Human Rights and Fundamental Freedoms of Indigenous People, Extractive Industries and Indigenous Peoples, UN Doc. A/HRC/24/41 (2013), para. 76 (emphasis added).

with the Saramaka people, and not unilaterally by the State'. The IACtHR also added that if there is any internal conflict among the Saramaka regarding who should be beneficiaries, this must be 'resolved by the Saramaka in accordance with their own traditional customs and norms, not by the State or this Court in this particular case'.[85] Likewise, in the case concerning the Kichwa Indigenous Community of Sarayaku in Ecuador, the IACtHR declared that 'the company's actions, by attempting to legitimate its oil exploration activities and justify its intervention in Sarayaku territory, failed to respect the established structures of authority and representation within and outside the communities'.[86] One of the main messages here is that it is not for the State (or the corporations) to decide and establish a process to put in place a benefit-sharing agreement, but to the communities under their own terms and customs. Arguably, this leaves the process of developing benefit-sharing agreements quite vague, but it does establish some fundamental principles for the negotiations of these agreements. Morgera suggests that 'even if treaty law leaves significant leeway to States in determining appropriate forms of sharing benefits with communities, culturally appropriate sharing would be difficult to ensure in the absence of a good-faith, consensus building process with communities'.[87]

This partnership approach is even more significant as regards the rise of direct negotiations between private corporations and indigenous peoples. The last few decades have witnessed an increase in benefit-sharing agreements between indigenous communities, governments, and private actors, notably mining and extractives corporations.[88] There is the emergence of an important body of practice regarding benefit-sharing arrangements across the world.[89] In Canada, several Impact and Benefit Agreements (IBAs) have been established between the federal, or provincial governments, and extractive industries. Increasingly, these agreements are directly negotiated between indigenous peoples and corporations.[90] Typically, these agreements provide indigenous peoples with sharing of project revenues, and preferential indigenous access to employment and business development opportunities.[91] Other forms of benefit-sharing agreements have emerged under the banner of Community Development Agreements (CDA), which have been increasingly used by resources companies and investors to establish mechanisms for ensuring that local communities benefit from large-scale investment projects, such as mines or forestry concessions. In formalizing agreements between investors and project

---

[85] *Saramaka People* (n 43) paras 25–6.

[86] *Kichwa Indigenous People of Sarayaku* (n 46) para. 194.

[87] Elisa Morgera, *An International Legal Concept of Fair and Equitable Benefit-Sharing*, University of Edinburgh School of Law Research Paper 2015/20, Benelex Working Paper No. 6, p. 12.

[88] See Ciaran O'Faircheallaigh, 'Community Development Agreements in the Mining Industry: An Emerging Global Phenomenon', 44 *Community Development*, 2013, 222–38; Svetlana Tulaeva and Maria Tysiachniouk, 'Benefit-Sharing Arrangements between Oil Companies and Indigenous People in Russian Northern Regions', 9(8) *Sustainability*, 2017, 1326.

[89] For analysis notably in terms of energy, see Barrera-Hernández et al. (n 82).

[90] See Ciaran O'Faircheallaigh, 'Aboriginal-Mining Company Contractual Agreements in Australia and Canada: Implications for Political Autonomy and Community Development', 30(1–2) *Canadian Journal of Development Studies*, 2010, 69–86.

[91] See Ciaran O'Faircheallaigh, 'Negotiating Cultural Heritage? Aboriginal–Mining Company Agreements in Australia', 39(1) *Development and Change*, 2008, 25–51.

affected communities, CDAs establish how the benefits will be shared with local communities. These benefit-agreements take various forms, depending on the industry involved, but most agreements are based on the guarantee of a percentage of profits from the extractive operations. In general, one of the dangers of the increased development of benefit-sharing agreements is the lack of proper legal framework to protect indigenous peoples and local communities, who due to the asymmetry of the power relationships could easily find themselves in situations where their interests are not properly integrated and respected.

In this context of power asymmetries, the emerging human rights to benefit-sharing could become extremely significant, notably in respecting the fundamental rights and interests of the concerned communities. While under IHRL the exact nature and content of the direct obligations of the private corporations is still a work in progress (WIP), the UN Framework on Business and Human Rights has clearly indicated that there is a strong obligation within the legal framework for corporations to respect IHRL,[92] and it highlights the fundamental role of governments in making sure that the human rights of indigenous peoples are protected when corporations enter into negotiations. The role of IHRL is not about dictating the exact content and shape of benefit-sharing agreements, but instead to ensure that a fair, participative, and respectful process between the concerned actors is followed to ensure that the concerned communities will receive some forms of benefit-sharing (which should be directly determined and negotiated by them). The exact details of these agreements are mainly left to the parties, but while some fundamental principles have been highlighted, these benefits should be procedural (management) and substantive. Morgera notes that this is still very much a WIP area of international human rights that is based mainly on 'authoritative interpretations, rather than unequivocal treaty provisions'.[93] Nonetheless, the clear increased engagement of human rights institutions, especially at the regional level, supports the affirmation that benefit-sharing has definitively entered the human rights lexicon, which is important not only for ensuring fairer and equitable process, but also to provide a new approach to the construction and content of benefit-sharing agreements.

Inherently, benefit-sharing agreements are part of the constant increase in the marketization of natural resources. Fundamentally it is about 'benefits', and mainly about quantifying the monetary value (present and future) of natural resources. By providing scope for indigenous peoples and local communities to decide and participate directly in these processes, IHRL could support the integration of another vision of benefit-sharing with a focus on other types of benefits that can be relevant to local communities. This is not to say that these benefits should not be material and financial, but rather that communities should be able to define these benefits, both material and immaterial. One of the key messages of IHRL is that such a process should be based on a fundamental respect for the cultural rights

---

[92] See Human Rights Council, 'Guiding Principles on Business and Human Rights: Implementing the United Nations "Protect, Respect and Remedy" Framework', UN Doc. A/HRC/17/31 (21 March 2011).

[93] Morgera (n 83) 44.

of the concerned communities. The integration of cultural, social, and spiritual value of the resources is then an element that is to be integrated in benefit-sharing agreements. [94] From this perspective a stronger and more developed human rights approach to benefit-sharing represents an important expansion of the largely dominant economical definition of benefit regarding natural resources usage and exploitation. It is within these dynamics that, slowly but surely, IHRL is starting to engage with benefit-sharing.

4. Taxation, Fiscal Regimes, and Transparency

This last section explores the connection between fiscal regimes governing natural resources and IHRL. Here, fiscal regime refers to the set of tools, including royalties, production sharing, or taxation, that are used by governments to benefit from the exploitation the resources located in their countries. These fiscal regimes usually constitute an important source of revenues for governments,[95] and the way these regimes are established can have significant impact on the human rights of the concerned citizens.[96] By indirectly re-using these resources for public spending they represent another way for governments to ensure a stewardship role over the natural resources. However, due to the high cost of exploration, exploitation, and the instability of potential returns that are usually attached to natural resources, most countries provide a significant reduction in, or no, taxation when it comes to the exploitation of natural resources, especially when it comes to minerals because of the significant upfront investment costs and the variability of the price of minerals.[97] Taxation tends to be ring-fenced, and in most situations exemptions are offered to corporations and investors in a bid to attract and retain investment.[98] This practice has usually been supported and encouraged by international financial institutions as a way to encourage investments in low-income countries.[99] Another major issue is

---

[94] These cultural aspects and the connection to cultural rights are examined in more detail in Chapter 5.

[95] See Naazneen Barma, Kai Kaiser, Tuan Minh Le, and Lorena Vinuela, *Rents to Riches? The Political Economy of Natural Resource-Led Development* (World Bank, 2012).

[96] The Natural Resources Charter notes that '[n]atural resource development may provide employment and other returns, but its principal benefit is the generation of government revenues to support development and the well-being of citizens. Realizing these revenues requires a well-designed fiscal system that takes into account the nature of extractive resources, the considerable uncertainties inherent in their exploration, and the capacities of the government' (Precept 4).

[97] See Philip Daniel, Michael Keen, and Charles McPherson (eds), *The Taxation of Petroleum and Minerals: Principles, Problems and Practice* (Routledge, 2010); Commonwealth Secretariat and ICMM, 'Mineral Taxation Regimes: A Review of Issues and Challenges in their Design and Application/The Challenge of Mineral Wealth: Using Resource Endowments to Foster Sustainable Development' (February 2009).

[98] See Joseph E. Stiglitz, *The Price of Inequality, How Today's Divided Society Endangers Our Future* (Norton, 2012) and John Quiggin, *Zombie Economics: How Dead Ideas Still Walk Among Us* (Princeton University Press, 2010).

[99] See Philip Daniel, Michael Keen, Artur Swistak, and Victor Thuronyi (eds), *International Taxation and the Extractive Industries: Resources without Borders* (Routledge, 2016); Jack Calder, *Administering Fiscal Regimes for Extractive Industries: A Handbook* (International Monetary Fund, 2014).

that these revenues frequently are exported, resulting in a very low income for many resource-rich countries when compared to the export value,[100] and tax avoidance also makes the list of issues regarding a lack of return to the national economy of the countries where the natural resources are located;[101] thus, while enormous benefits usually emerge from the exploitation of natural resources, very little goes back to the local economy.[102] The countries concerned are usually those with both the highest concentration of raw natural resources and the highest level of poverty. In these contexts, the lack of proper and efficient taxation on natural resources exploitation leads to lack of revenue to support the development of good infrastructure, health, and education facilities. As a result, countries richly endowed with natural resources are often at the bottom of the scale when it comes to redistribution of the resources that could potentially emerge through fair and redistributive taxation systems.

How could IHRL play a role to ensure a fairer and better distribution of the revenues generated by the exploitation of natural resources, and support a return of these benefits to the local populations? To undertake such analysis, it is necessary to focus on the correlation between the notion of 'maximum available resources' and on the issue of transparency and a right to information regarding the fiscal regimes that are put in place.

4.1 Maximum of available resources and natural resources

Although taxation is rarely discussed from a human rights perspective, taxes are essential in generating resources to finance human rights-related expenditure. Saiz notes that taxation has an enormous potential role in redistributing resources in order to mitigate and redress social inequalities.[103] International human rights institutions have highlighted the need to ensure fair and adequate taxation to support governmental obligations to protect human rights. The closest connection between fiscal regimes and IHRL come under States' obligations to devote the 'maximum available resources' to ensure the progressive realization of all economic, social, and cultural rights.[104] Article 2.1 of the ICESCR states that:

---

[100] For illustrations, see *Africa Progress Report 2013: Equity in Extractives* (Africa Progress Panel, 2013), p. 64.

[101] On tax avoidance and its impact on human rights, see *Tax Abuses, Poverty and Human Rights* (International Bar Association, 2013); and Shane Darcy, ' "The Elephant in the Room"; Corporate Tax Avoidance and Business and Human Rights', 2(1) *Business and Human Rights Journal*, 2017, 1–30.

[102] This does not mean that all countries are in this situation. For example, Botswana is often mentioned as a country that has used its diamond wealth to uplift the population in terms of education, social services, and infrastructure. See James Clark Leith, *Why Botswana Prospered* (McGill-Queen's Press, 2005); I. B. Matshediso, 'A Review of Mineral Development and Investment Policies of Botswana', 30(3) *Resources Policy*, 2005, 203–7.

[103] Ignacio Saiz, 'Resourcing Rights: Combating Tax Injustice from a Human Rights Perspective'. In: Aoife Nolan, Rory O'Connell, and Colin Harvey (eds), *Human Rights and Public Finance: Budgets and the Promotion of Economic and Social Rights* (Hart, 2013).

[104] International Covenant on Economic, Social and Cultural Rights (ICESCR), adopted by UN General Assembly Resolution 2200, 16 December 1966, Art. 2(1). See also Convention on the Rights of the Child, Art. 4; and the Convention on the Rights of Persons with Disabilities, Art. 4(2).

[e]ach State Party to the present Covenant undertakes to take steps, individually and through international assistance and co-operation, especially economic and technical, to the maximum of its available resources, with a view to achieving progressively the full realization of the rights recognized in the present Covenant by all appropriate means, including particularly the adoption of legislative measures.[105]

It means that governments must demonstrate that every effort has been made to use all resources at their disposal to satisfy, as a matter of priority, their minimum core human rights obligations,[106] which include making sure that their fiscal regimes are adequate to support such progressive realization of human rights. The CESCR has focused its attention on this obligation with the adoption of a General Comment on 1991,[107] as well as a statement in 2007.[108] The connection between maximum available resources and governments' fiscal regimes has also been part of the expanding jurisprudence of the CESCR,[109] which has notably developed several indicators in assessing governments' compliance with their obligations. However, these indicators mainly focus on government expenditures (and international assistance), with little focus on the need to raise adequate and efficient taxation, and no mention of natural resources. Other international human rights treaty-monitoring bodies have also pushed governments to ensure that they make the best use of their available resources, including taxation, to support the realization and protection of human rights.[110] Skogly suggests that the focus has been mainly on financial resources, rather than other (specifically natural) resources.[111] Although there is an increased focus on the obligation to ensure the maximum use of available resources and taxation, IHRL has not yet systematically addressed the issue of poor and inadequate taxation on natural resources extraction and exploitation.

Some of the UN Special Rapporteurs and Independents Experts have started to examine more specifically the connection between endowment of natural resources and fiscal regimes. As (former) UN Special Rapporteur on extreme poverty and human rights Magdalena Sepúlveda Carmona noted in her 2014 report focusing on taxation, a 'State allowing or directly undertaking exploitation of natural resources without ensuring that a fair share of the proceeds are taxed and/or allocated towards fulfilling human rights could be an indication of a failure to mobilize adequate

---

[105] Ibid.

[106] See Radhika Balakrishnan, Diane Elson, James Heintz, and Nicholas Lusiani, *Maximum Available Resources & Human Rights: Analytical Report* (Center for Women's Global Leadership, 2011).

[107] Committee on Economic, Social and Cultural Rights, General Comment 3, The Nature of States Parties' Obligations (Fifth Session, 1990), UN Doc. E/1991/23, Annex III at 86 (1991).

[108] 'An Evaluation of the Obligation to Take Steps to the Maximum of Available Resources under an Optional Protocol to the Covenant', UN Doc E/C.12/2007/1 (2007).

[109] See for example 'Concluding Observations: Hong Kong', UN Doc E/C.12/1/Add. 58 (2001), para. 14; 'Concluding Observations: Spain', UN Doc E/C.12/ESP/CO/5 (2012).

[110] This notably includes the Committee on the Rights of the Child and the Committee on the Elimination of Discrimination against Women, for analysis and references see: Radhika Balakrishnan, Diane Elson, James Heintz, and Nicholas Lusiani, *Maximum Available Resources & Human Rights: Analytical Report* (Centre for Women Global Leadership, 2011).

[111] Sigrun Skogly; 'The Requirement of Using the "Maximum of Available Resources" for Human Rights Realisation: A Question of Quality as Well as Quantity?', 12(3) *Human Rights Law Review*, (2012), 393–420.

resources'.[112] Likewise, the (former) Special Rapporteur on the right to food Olivier De Schutter, in his 2012 report on the situation in Cameroon, advised reconsideration of tax policies on concessions of agricultural land and on the exploitation of natural resources (particularly forests and minerals) so as to optimize the revenue earned from the harnessing of these resources and to improve food security for vulnerable groups.[113] These examples display an increased concern by human rights institutions on the potential role of IHRL to push for clearer and efficient fiscal regimes and taxation on the exploitation of natural resources, and represent an important element to support the establishment of more transparent and clearer fiscal regimes on natural resources. This clarity has been lacking as most fiscal regimes governing natural resources are usually extremely opaque and lack transparency in their knowledge and information-sharing processes regarding those citizens who may potentially be affected.[114]

4.2 Transparency on taxation over natural resources

The other significant connection between fiscal regimes and IHRL comes under the larger agenda of increased transparency. The lack of transparency, specifically accessible and reliable information, on fiscal regimes in the area of natural resources is significant.[115] This is not only connected to corruption but also relates to a more general lack of transparency and available information regarding revenue generated by natural resources exploitation.[116] There is usually a lack of publicly reported and progressive fiscal regimes, and incidents of non-published special deals and tax avoidance/evasion of tax declaration when it comes to natural resources. Transparency is not only limited to taxes, but also concerns royalties, production sharing, bonuses, cost recovery provisions, state participation, fiscal pricing, and service agreements, all of which are common forms of revenue. There is growing consensus on the importance of transparency in this area, but it has not yet been translated into the development of any international effective regulatory frameworks and institutions. Recently, there has been a large international initiative to push for transparency led mainly by private non-governmental organizations (NGO) and multi-stakeholder initiatives; one of the latter is the Extractive Industries Transparency Initiative (EITI), a global civil society platform advocating for a transparency and accountability in

---

[112] Report of the Special Rapporteur on Extreme Poverty and Human Rights, Magdalena Sepúlveda Carmona, UN Doc. A/HRC/26/28 (2014), para. 72.

[113] Report of the Special Rapporteur on the Right to Food, Olivier De Schutter, Mission to Cameroon, Un Doc. A/HRC/22/50/Add.2 (2012), paras 55–67.

[114] See International Bar Association, *Tax Abuses, Poverty and Human Rights* (International Bar Association, 2013), pp. 44–50.

[115] For references and analysis, see *International Monetary Fund, Guide on Resource Revenue Transparency* (IMF, 2005); Andreanna Truelove, 'Oil, Diamonds, and Sunlight: Fostering Human Rights through Transparency in Revenues from Natural Resources', 35(1) *Georgetown Journal of International Law*, 2003, 207, 238.

[116] On the link between corruption and IHRL, see Ndiva Kofele-Kale, 'The Right to a Corruption-Free Society as an Individual and Collective Human Right: Elevating Official Corruption to a Crime under International Law,' 34 *International Lawyer*, 2000, 149–78.

the extractives sector through the disclosure of government revenues. The initiative relies primarily on a multi-stakeholder process whereby governments, corporate actors, civil society, and NGOs contribute to a scheme of disclosure for payments issued to governments in relation to oil, gas, and mining revenues. Further initiatives exist regarding transparency, for example, the Kimberly Process Certification Scheme (KPCS) and the Publish What You Pay Coalition (PWYP). There are also national-level legislative initiatives concerning extractive industries, e.g. the adoption of specific regulations under section 1504 of the US Dodd–Frank Act and the EU Accounting and Transparency Directive.[117] However, there is still a dominant lack of transparency when it comes to revenues generated from natural resources, with most initiatives still predominately based on a voluntary approach, rather than a legal one. From this perspective, a human rights-based approach to taxation could provide a relevant platform to support a normative approach to a more transparent and redistributive approach to the revenues emerging from natural resources exploitation.

IHRL does not offer a great deal when it comes to transparency, as legally speaking no treaty or instrument directly tackles the issue. Nonetheless, there is a human rights push for transparency regarding revenue emerging from natural resources exploitation,[118] specifically, the Joint Declaration on Natural Resources Governance and Human Rights adopted by the Inter-American Commission on Human Rights and the ACHPR in 2012. This declaration sits within a larger call by civil society and human rights NGOs to ensure better transparency in the way fiscal regimes over natural resources are put in place. It links the human right to freedom of information with transparency in terms of revenue emerging from natural resources. On this issue, the joint declaration states that:

[s]tates should place natural resources governance under transparency, including through open budgeting and certification processes and protection of the freedoms of the press, information and expression. The right of access to information and to documents generated by the government, or to which the government is a party, that are necessary for citizens to understand the extent and value of their natural resources and the payments for those resources received and disbursed by their governments, in order to bring their legislation in line with Article 1 of the African Charter and Article 1 of the American Convention must be ensured.[119]

This call for more transparency and accessible information is enshrined in Article 1 of these two instruments, with both referring to the generic obligations to respect the rights enshrined in the human rights treaties. This places the obligation to ensure more transparency and access to information within the broad spectrum of IHRL

---

[117] See also the declaration made at the G8 meeting in Lough Erne, Northern Ireland in June 2013, where G8 leaders pledged in the Lough Erne Declaration that '[e]xtractive companies should report payments to all governments—and governments should publish income from such companies'.

[118] See, for example, US Congress Commission on Security and Cooperation in Europe, 'The Link between Revenue Transparency and Human Rights', *The Helsinki Accords and the United States: Selected Executive and Congressional Documents* (22 April 2010), p. 45: I–[xxxiv].

[119] Inter-American Commission on Human Rights and the African Commission on Human and People's Rights, 'Declaration on a Human Rights-Based Approach to Natural Resources Management'. Adopted in preparation to the Rio+20 Summit, March 2012.

(rather than focusing on any specific human rights, e.g. freedom of information). However, despite this declaration, the connection between transparency, information, and taxation on natural resources is still a very underdeveloped area of IHRL. There have only been a few comments made by international human rights treaty-monitoring bodies on the issue. The main connection between transparency and natural resources has emerged under the obligation for States to use the maximum available resources to progressively achieve the full realization of the rights recognized in the CESCR covenant. For example, in its concluding observations on the situation in Romania, the CESCR highlighted the need to 'increase transparency and consultations at all levels of decision-making concerning the distribution and use of structural funds and the ongoing evaluation of their impact on the realization of economic, social and cultural rights'.[120] Under its review of the situation in the DRC, one of the most developed statements from the CESCR declared that the

Committee urges the State party to take all appropriate measures to ensure that its natural resources are not subjected to illegal exploitation and mismanagement; to review without delay the mining contracts in a transparent and participatory way; repeal all contracts which are detrimental to the Congolese people; and ensure that future contracts are concluded in a transparent and public way.... The Committee further calls upon the State party to ensure that revenues derived from the mining sector are allocated for the development of the province of Katanga and that its inhabitants are provided with basic social services and infrastructure so that their living conditions may be improved.[121]

The Committee on the Rights of the Child (CRC) has also highlighted the need for States to ensure a transparent process of budget allocation to ensure the respect of the obligations under the Convention on the Rights of the Child. For example, the CRC highlighted its concerns about the absence of transparency in the budgetary process in Myanmar leading to lack of funding for education, health, and the severe lack of financial resources for the protection and promotion of children's rights.[122]

However, despite these few connections made between revenues emerging from natural resources exploitation and IHRL, there is a lack of clear and sustained focus on transparency as a potential significant human rights issue. More generally, there is not yet a proper international legal framework to address the issue. Most of the focus has been in relation to a right to information in relation to international environmental regimes.[123] This is part of several initiatives that have been undertaken within the field of environmental law, notably that led by the Aarhus Convention on access to environmental information.[124] While such developments are relevant

---

[120] Committee on Economic, Social and Cultural Rights, Concluding Observations on the Combined Third to Fifth Periodic Reports of Romania, UN Doc. E/C.12/ROU/CO/3-5 (2014), para. 7. See also Concluding Observations: Tajikistan, UN Doc. E/C.12/TJK/CO/2-3 (2015)

[121] Concluding Observations of the Committee on Economic, Social and Cultural Rights: Democratic Republic of the Congo, UN Doc. E/C.12/COD/CO/4 (2009), para. 13.

[122] Committee on the Rights of the Child, Concluding Observations: Myanmar, UN Doc. CRC/C/MMR/CO/3-4 (2012), para. 17. See also: Concluding Observations: Montenegro, UN Doc. CRC/C/MNE/CO/1 (2010), para. 22.

[123] This is examined in Chapter 6.

[124] Convention on Access to Information, Public Participation in Decision-Making and Access to Justice in Environmental Matters (June 1998).

when pushing for more transparency regarding revenue from natural resources exploitation, they do not directly tackle the issue of revenue redistribution and its connection with the obligations to ensure the progressive realization of human rights.

5. Conclusion

IHRL is playing an increasingly important role in the governance of natural resources. In terms of the norms, the approach to governance is not based on a single and specific human right, but on an enlarged and renewed consideration of the connection between development and human rights. It is under the larger umbrella of a human rights-based approach to development that a very practical legal framework on governance over natural resources is emerging. One of the main criticisms of the right to development is that it remains too rhetorical and lacks proper meaningful implementation. The connection with natural resources participation, consultation, consent, and benefit-sharing gives it a much more practical focus. It supports a much more proactive and direct role to be played by the people most directly affected by the exploitation of natural resources, but also supports a much more redistributive approach to the benefits emerging from natural resources exploitation. This evolution puts a solid foundation for human rights to play a more active and dominant role when it comes to governance of natural resources. This is an important development as it puts communities and populations back at the heart of governance of natural resources. Over the last century the management of natural resources has been dominated by very top-down approaches, with States, international organizations, and corporations dominating the governance of natural resources. A human rights-based approach to governance clearly supports a renewed focus on the rights of the citizens to have a say in the process, but also to benefit from it.

Indigenous peoples have been the main actors who have managed to push IHRL towards engaging more directly on the issue. The right to development earned its practical application expression with the emergence of a right to free, prior, and informed consent, as well as the recognition of the principle of benefit-sharing. This development is at the forefront of the global indigenous peoples' movement, which has urged IHRL to become much more grounded in the governance of natural resources. While there are still serious issues concerning implementation at local levels, nonetheless this very significant shift in the potential role that IHRL can play regarding the governance of natural resources is noteworthy. Undoubtedly, these advances were made based on the specific relationship that most indigenous peoples have with their territories and natural resources. However, other local communities might also be able to push for such recognition. In terms of the international legal argument, there is scope for such extension, e.g. the fundamental right to development and participation are proclaimed for all peoples. From this perspective, the long and drawn-out battle that indigenous peoples have won to impel IHRL to change its stance on the governance of natural resources could serve as an example to other local communities who live and rely on the use and control of their natural resources. As Pring and Noé suggest, '[w]hile arguably not imbued with the same human rights moral force as "indigenous peoples", other local people are increasingly recognized as having been excluded from participation in development decision-making, negatively impacted on by it, and worthy of inclusion.'[125]

Lastly, IHRL can play an important role in the future regarding the allocation, use, and distribution of the fiscal resources emerging from the exploitation of natural resources. The emergence of a human rights-based approach to benefit-sharing offers a promising legal development to support the interests of indigenous peoples and local communities, but benefit-sharing should not be confused with compensation and reparation. Likewise, benefit-sharing is different from the taxes, royalties, and other payment schemes that may exist. The role that IHRL could play regarding a more redistributive taxation system is still very much in its infancy. However, there is great potential for IHRL to support a new international legal framework regarding taxation over natural resources. Warris aptly notes that 'not only may the utilisation of human rights as a policy in taxation solve the issue of legitimacy of the fiscal state through improved fiscal accountability, but it may also possibly answer the dilemma of the realisation of human rights'.[126]

---

[125] George (Rock) Pring and Susan Y. Noé, 'The Emerging International Law of Public Participation Affecting Global Mining, Energy, and Resources Development'. In: Donald Zillman, Alastair Lucas, and George (Rock) Pring (eds), *Human Rights in Natural Resource Development: Public Participation in the Sustainable Development of Mining and Energy Resources* (OUP, 2002), p. 65.

[126] Attiya Warris, *Tax & Development: Solving Kenya's Fiscal Crisis through Human Rights: A Case Study of Kenya's Constituency Development Fund* (Law Africa, 2013), p. 124.

4

Life and Natural Resources

Livelihood, Conflicts, and Personal Integrity

I am a human rights fighter and I will not give up this fight.

Berta Cáceres[1]

1. Introduction

This chapter focuses on when exploitation of natural resources becomes associated with conflicts and loss of life, including murder. The quest to control areas rich in natural resources is often a major cause of conflict and instability, and such control has been a root cause of some of the most violent conflicts across the globe; in these cases, natural resources either triggered, supported the financing, and/or fuelled the conflicts.[2] The relationship between natural resources and conflicts has led to the classification of many conflicts as 'resources wars' or 'conflicts resources'.[3] These conflicts around natural resources usually lead to serious human rights violations and loss of life. Outside these situations, the connection between the right to life and natural resources is also connected to access to essential sources of livelihoods.

This chapter analyses the potential role that international human rights law (IHRL) can play when control over natural resources is associated with loss of life. It examines three different approaches. The first focuses on livelihood and examines situations where the lack of access to natural resources puts life in danger. It explores how the right to life can be interpreted to include access to essential natural resources such as water and food. The second approach focuses on accountability for

---

[1] Berta Cáceres was a Honduran environmental activist who was assassinated in 2016 for her vocal opposition to projects of exploitation of natural resources. Cited in Nina Lakhani, 'Remembering Berta Cáceres: "I'm a human rights fighter and I won't give up"', The Guardian (UK), 3 March 2016.

[2] Examples include Angola, Sierra Leone, Liberia, Cote d'Ivoire, and the Democratic Republic of the Congo (DRC). See Philippe Le Billon, *Fuelling War: Natural Resources and Armed Conflicts* (OUP, 2013); Susanne Hartard and Wolfgang Liebert (eds), *Competition and Conflicts on Resource Use* (Springer, 2014).

[3] See Daniëlla Dam-de Jong, *International Law and Governance of Natural Resources in Conflict and Post-Conflict Situations* (CUP, 2015), p. 27, where the term 'conflict resources' is defined as 'natural resources whose systematic exploitation and trade finance or fuel armed conflicts'.

Natural Resources and Human Rights: An Appraisal. Jérémie Gilbert. © J. Gilbert 2018. Published 2018 by Oxford University Press.

crimes during 'resources conflicts', and examines the relationship between IHRL, international humanitarian law (IHL), and international criminal law (ICL) with the objective of analysing the criminal approach to armed conflicts connected to natural resources. The third approach relates to the protection of individuals who have lost their lives, or whose physical integrity is in jeopardy, as a result of their personal engagement to protect natural resources. It focuses on the rights of 'environmental defenders' and 'land and natural resources defenders'—those who have become human rights defenders as a result of their actions taken to protect natural resources.[4]

2. The Right to Life and Natural Resources: The Livelihood Approach

The right to life, which is affirmed in all the main human rights instruments, is undoubtedly one of the most fundamental human rights, being a prerequisite for the enjoyment of all other human rights.[5] Traditionally, the right to life has been associated with the protection against extrajudicial killing and other unjustified uses of lethal force.[6] However, there is another element of the right to life relating to the obligation to ensure that the minimum conditions to support life are in place, i.e. food, water, air, and all other essential elements. While originally the main human rights jurisprudence on the right to life primarily focuses on the protection against arbitrary killings, a more recent jurisprudence connects the right to life and protection of access to essential means to ensure livelihood. This creates a direct correlation between the right to life and access to natural resources, or at least natural resources essential to ensure life, including access to basic necessities such as food and water.

2.1 Famine, food, and water: a right to human dignity

One of the first connections between the right to life and access to sources of livelihood is via the right to food.[7] The right to food requires that no one is deprived of their access to adequate food. The right to adequate food and its connection with food sovereignty are examined in Chapter 1, where here the analysis focuses

---

[4] This analysis uses the generic terms of 'natural resources defenders' to include all the different categories of persons who are putting their life at risk to protect the environment, their lands, and their natural resources. This includes 'environmental defenders', 'land and resources defenders', or 'environmental and natural resources defenders', terms often used in the literature. See the Report of the Special Rapporteur on the Situation of Human Rights Defenders, 'Situation of Human Rights Defenders', UN Doc. A/71/281 (2016).

[5] See UDHR Art. 3; ECHR Art. 2; ICCPR Art. 6; AFCHPR Art. 4; ACHR Art. 4; CIS Art. 5; AL Art. 5.

[6] See Bertrand G. Ramcharan, *The Right to Life in International Law* (Martinus Nijhoff, 1985); Christian Tomuschat, Evelyne Lagrange, and Stefan Oeter (eds), *The Right to Life* (Martinus Nijhoff, 2010).

[7] See Christophe Golay, 'The Right to Food and the Right to Life'. In: David Fraser and Graça Almeida Rodrigues (eds), *Disrespect Today, Conflict Tomorrow* (Critical, Cultural and Communications Press, 2009).

on another aspect of the right to food, which relates to 'the fundamental right of everyone to be free from hunger', as expressed in Article 11 of the ICESCR.[8] The right to food invites States to take a proactive approach to realize food security for all, and places legal obligations on States to overcome hunger and malnutrition. In terms of treaty rights, only the Convention on the Rights of the Child specifically connects the right to life and survival of children with access to food.[9] However, other treaty-monitoring bodies have adopted an enlarged approach to the right to life connecting to access to food and water.

According to the Human Rights Committee (HRC), the protection of the right to life requires States to adopt positive measures, such as measures to eliminate malnutrition. Its General Comment No. 6 on the right to life states that:

[t]he Committee considers that it would be desirable for States parties to take all possible measures to reduce infant mortality and to increase life expectancy, especially in adopting measures to eliminate malnutrition and epidemics.[10]

The HRC also highlights that measures restricting the 'access to all basic and life-saving services such as food, health, electricity, water and sanitation' are contrary to Article 6.[11] The connection between access to food and life has also been examined by the Committee on Economic, Social and Cultural Rights (CESCR). In its General Comment on the right to health, the CESCR also highlights the strong correlation between life and access to essential resources, noting that:

the right to health embraces a wide range of socio-economic factors that promote conditions in which people can lead a healthy life, and extends to the underlying determinants of health, such as food and nutrition, housing, access to safe and potable water and adequate sanitation, safe and healthy working conditions, and a healthy environment.[12]

The CESCR also highlighted that the right to health is not limited to the delivery of appropriate health care but also to the underlying determinants of health, such as access to safe and potable water and an adequate supply of safe food.

Probably the strongest connection between the right to life and access to food is in time of extreme hunger and famine. Famines are due to a number of factors, e.g. natural disasters and extreme droughts, and often not controlled by human acts. Nonetheless, there are usually some significant human causes, at least in the

---

[8] 'The States Parties to the present Covenant recognize the right of everyone to an adequate standard of living for himself and his family, including adequate food, clothing and housing, and to the continuous improvement of living conditions' (para. 1) and 'The States Parties to the present Covenant recognize the fundamental right of everyone to be free from hunger' (para. 2). International Covenant on Economic, Social and Cultural Rights, General Assembly Resolution 2200A (XXI) of 16 December 1966.

[9] Convention on the Rights of the Child, Art. 24.

[10] Human Rights Committee, General Comment No. 6, Art. 6 (Sixteenth Session, 1982), Compilation of General Comments and General Recommendations Adopted by Human Rights Treaty Bodies, UN Doc. HRI/GEN/1/Rev.1, 6 (1994), para. 5. At the time of writing, the HRC is working on a draft of a new forthcoming General Comment No. 36 on the Right to Life.

[11] UN Doc. CCPR/C/ISR/CO/4 (2014), para. 12.

[12] CESCR General Comment No. 14: The Right to the Highest Attainable Standard of Health (Art. 12), UN Doc. E/C.12/2000/4 (2000), para. 4.

conditions leading to situations of famine, or in the efforts to remedy the consequences of natural disasters.[13] The reaction of the authorities to the lack of essential
nutrition usually dictates the level of loss of life that will follow. For example, massive
historical famine in the late nineteenth century striking many Asian and African
countries caused extraordinarily high numbers of deaths resulting from the colonial powers' disruption to the local traditional ways of dealing with access to food
and water in such harsh times.[14] The colonial powers controlled natural resources
in the concerned countries.[15] In general, while natural disasters trigger large-scale
famine, there is an element of the human reaction to such natural disasters that defines the scale of the famine.[16] More generally, outside extreme cases of famine, food
deprivation is not only connected to natural phenomenon and natural disasters,
but also has an important human aspect relating to the distribution of supplies and
their accessibility. On this front, the CESCR noted that 'fundamentally, the roots
of the problem of hunger and malnutrition are not lack of food but lack of access to
available food, inter alia, because of poverty, by large segments of the world's population'.[17] The (present and former) UN Special Rapporteur on the right to food has
highlighted this connection in many annual reports, notably putting forward the
restriction of access for small-scale farmers and the poor to cultivable land as a cause
for famine.[18]

In terms of human rights jurisprudence, the connection between the right to
life and access to natural resources to ensure food was at the heart of the African
Commission on Human and Peoples' Rights (ACHPR) decision regarding the situation faced by the Ogoni people in Nigeria.[19] In its decision, the ACHPR highlighted that the right to life puts some positive obligations on the authorities to
ensure that there is no interference with essential elements of the right to life, including the direct provision of basic needs such as food.[20] The focus was on Article
21 of the African Charter, which affirms that in no case shall a people be deprived
of its means of subsistence. In this case, the ACHPR found that the destruction and
contamination of food sources (water, soil, and crops) by the Nigerian government

[13] See Alexander De Waal, *Famine Crimes: Politics & the Disaster Relief Industry in Africa* (James
Currey Publishers, 1997); Susan George, *How the Other Half Dies* (Rowman & Littlefield Publishers,
1989); Amartya Sen, *Development as Freedom* (OUP, 2001), pp. 160–209; Thomas Keneally, *Three
Famines: Starvation and Politics* (Hachette, 2011).

[14] Mike Davis, *Late Victorian Holocausts: El Niño Famines and the Making of the Third World*
(Verso, 2002).

[15] Ibid. For further analysis on the connection with IHRL, see Susan Marks and Andrew Clapham,
International Human Rights Lexicon (OUP, 2005), pp. 164–8.

[16] See Simone Hutter, *Starvation as a Weapon: Domestic Policies of Deliberate Starvation as a Means to
an end under International Law* (Brill, 2015).

[17] General Comment: The Right to Adequate Food (Art. 11), UN Doc. E/C.12/1999/5. (1999),
para. 5.

[18] For analysis and references see: Jean Ziegler, Christophe Golay, Claire Mahon, and Sally-Anne
Way, *The Fight for the Right to Food: Lessons Learned* (Springer, 2011).

[19] *Social and Economic Rights Action Centre and the Centre for Economic and Social Rights v Nigeria*
(Communication No. 155/96), 15th Annual Activity Report of the ACHPR (2002); 10 IHRR 282
(2003).

[20] Ibid., paras 44–7.

(and by the Nigerian State oil company) violated the right of the Ogoni people to food. This case remains one of the clearest international human rights decisions regarding the connection between the right to food and the right to life, although it finds some strong echoes in the national case law of several States. The Supreme Court of India has interpreted the right to life in the Indian Constitution to encompass a right to livelihood, including the right to food.[21] Cases connected the right to life and access to food were also adjudicated in Argentina, Brazil, South Africa, Colombia, and Nepal.[22]

Another relevant connection between the right to life and access to natural resources relates to the right to water.[23] The 2010 UN General Assembly proclaiming the human right to water and sanitation 'recognizes the right to safe and clean drinking water and sanitation as a human right that is essential for the full enjoyment of life and all human rights'.[24] The Human Rights Council also highlighted that 'the human right to safe drinking water and sanitation is derived from the right to an adequate standard of living and inextricably related to the right to the highest attainable standard of physical and mental health, as well as the right to life and human dignity'.[25] The CESCR also highlights the close connection between access to water and the right to life, noting that 'water is a limited natural resource and a public good fundamental for life and health. The human right to water is indispensable for leading a life in human dignity.'[26] The HRC has also connected the right to life with access to water, highlighting that the destruction of water and sanitary infrastructures may amount to a violation of the right to life.[27] The committee has used interim measures to demand the restoration of access to water supplies as being essential to support life.[28] The connection between the right to life and access to water is also receiving increased attention in litigation at the national level, with several cases of adjudication highlighting that access to water is an essential element of the right to life.[29]

---

[21] See *Maneka Gandhi v Union of India* (1978) 1 SCC 248; *Francis Coralie Mullin v The Administrator, Union Territory of Delhi* (1981) 2 SCR 516; *People's Union for Civil Liberties v Union of India* (2003) Writ Petition (Civil) No. 196 of 2001 and Interim Order of 2 May 2003.

[22] For review and analysis, see International Development Law Organization, *Realizing the Right to Food: Legal Strategies and Approaches* (IDLO, 2015); Lidija Knuth and Margret Vidar, *Constitutional and Legal Protection of the Right to Food Around the World* (FAO, 2011).

[23] See Inga Winkler, *The Human Right to Water: Significance, Legal Status and Implications for Water Allocation* (Hart Publishing, 2012); Pierre Thielbörger, *The Right(s) to Water: The Multi-Level Governance of a Unique Human Right* (Springer, 2013).

[24] Resolution adopted by the General Assembly, The Human Right to Water and Sanitation, UN Doc. A/RES/64/292 (28 July 2010), para. 1.

[25] Human Rights Council Resolution 15/9, Human Rights and Access to Safe Drinking Water and Sanitation, UN Doc. A/HRC/RES/15/9 (6 October 2010), para. 3.

[26] General Comment No. 15 (2002), The Right to Water (Arts 11 and 12 of the International Covenant on Economic, Social and Cultural Rights), UN Doc. E/C.12/2002/11 (2003), para. 1; see also para. 3.

[27] See Concluding Observations of the Human Rights Committee: Israel, UN Doc. CCPR/C/ISR/CO/3 (2010), at para. 18; Concluding Observations of the Human Rights Committee: Israel, UN Doc. CCPR/C/ISR/CO/4 (2014), para. 12.

[28] See, *Liliana Assenova Naidenova et al. v Bulgaria*, Comm No. 2073/2011 (2011), paras 10–11.

[29] See Madeline Baer, 'From Water Wars to Water Rights: Implementing the Human Right to Water in Bolivia', 14(3) *Journal of Human Rights*, 2015, 353–76; Aman Mishra, 'The Right to Water in

Overall, looking at the approach adopted by the different international human rights treaty-monitoring bodies in recent years there is a visible emergence of a juris-prudence connecting the right to life and access to essential natural resources to sus-tain life, notably food and water. This approach is based on an expansive approach to the right to life to safeguard the right to a dignified existence by ensuring access to enough food and water. As noted in the earlier statements from the CESCR, HRC, and Human Rights Council, the fundamental access to natural resources, to food security, and to water has been connected to the right to lead a life in 'human dignity', and as such, it is part of the ongoing contemporary interpretation of the right to a dignified life. As noted by the IACtHR in *Villagrán Morales et al ('Street Children')*, '[in] essence, the fundamental right to life includes, not only the right of every human being not to be deprived of his life arbitrarily, but also the right that he will not be prevented from having access to the conditions that guarantee a digni-fied existence.'[30] This connection between the right to life and a right to a dignified existence is gaining momentum in the international human rights jurisprudence.[31] This could further extend the connection between the right to life and access to food and water.

2.2 Indigenous peoples' right to livelihood

Probably one of the most developed jurisprudence between the right to life and access to essential means of livelihood has been taking place under the banner of indigenous peoples' rights. The CESCR has underlined the connection between life and access to essential natural resources to sustain indigenous peoples' livelihood.[32] Here, the argument is made that in the case of indigenous peoples, access to their ancestral lands, and to the use and enjoyment of the natural resources found on them, is closely linked to obtaining food and access to clean water. In its concluding observations about the situation in Tanzania, the CESCR expressed its concerns

that several vulnerable communities, including pastoralist and hunter-gatherer communi-ties, have been forcibly evicted from their traditional lands for the purposes of large-scale farming, creation of game reserves and expansion of national parks, mining, construction of military barracks, tourism and commercial game-hunting. The Committee is concerned that these practices have resulted in a critical reduction in their access to land and natural re-sources, particularly threatening their livelihoods and their right to food.[33]

India: Changing Perceptions', 4(2) *International Journal of Research in Humanities and Social Studies*, 2015, 1–5; Bonolo Ramadi Dinokopila, 'The Right to Water in Botswana: A Review of the Matsipane Mosetlhanyane Case', 11(1) *African Human Rights Law Journal*, 2011, 282–95.

[30] *Villagrán Morales et al ('Street Children') v Guatemala*, C 63 (1999), para. 144.

[31] See Elizabeth Wicks, 'The Meaning of "Life": Dignity and the Right to Life in International Human Rights Treaties', 12(2) *Human Rights Law Review*, 2012, 199–219.

[32] See UN Doc. E/C.12/1999/5. The Right to Adequate Food (Art. 11), 20th Session, 1999, para. 13, and UN Doc. HRI/GEN/1/Rev.7, 117. The Right to Water (Arts 11 and 12 of the International Covenant on Economic, Social and Cultural Rights), 29th Session 2002, para. 16.

[33] Committee on Economic, Social and Cultural Rights: United Republic of Tanzania, UN Doc. E/C.12/TZA/CO/1-3 (2012), para. 22.

In this context, it is the denial of access to land and traditional means of subsistence which results in the deprivation of access to food, and thus threatened indigenous peoples' right to life. Other international human rights monitoring treaty bodies such as the HRC, CERD, and the Committee on the Rights of the Child (CRC) have adopted a similar approach highlighting the strong correlation between access to natural resources and indigenous peoples' livelihood.[34]

There have been some strong echoes of such an approach connecting the right to life, access to food and water, and livelihood in the jurisprudence of the Inter-American Court of Human Rights (IACtHR),[35] and it was one of the central points examined in *Sawhoyamaxa Indigenous Community*.[36] In its ruling the IACtHR ruled that the government had violated the right to life of members of the community by failing to ensure them access to their ancestral lands, which provided access to the natural resources that are essential to their survival capacity. The reasoning of the IACtHR was based on the lack of action on the part of the authorities to ensure that the concerned community could live on their ancestral land in order for them to have decent access to sources of livelihood, combined with the lack of access to health facilities. The IACtHR adopted a similar approach focusing on the right to life and access to essential sources of livelihood in *Yakye Axa Indigenous Community*.[37] The IACtHR noted that 'members of the Yakye Axa Community live in extremely destitute conditions as a consequence of lack of land and access to natural resources, caused by the facts that are the subject matter of this proceeding, as well as the precariousness of the temporary settlement where they have had to remain, waiting for a solution to their land claim'.[38] The IACtHR acknowledged that:

[the] displacement of the members of the Community from those lands has caused special and grave difficulties to obtain food, primarily because the area where their temporary settlement is located does not have appropriate conditions for cultivation or to practice their traditional subsistence activities, such as hunting, fishing, and gathering.[39]

The court highlighted that these conditions had a very negative impact on the nutrition required by the members of the community. The ACHPR also embraced a similar approach in its decision regarding the Endorois community in Kenya adopting a comparable reasoning connecting access to land and natural resources with loss of access to essential sources of livelihoods.[40] The ACHPR made direct reference to the approach developed by the IACtHR, noting that 'the Court found

---

[34] See Jérémie Gilbert, *Indigenous Peoples' Land Rights under International Law*, 2nd edition (Brill, 2016), pp. 178–85.

[35] See Steven Keener and Javier Vasquez, 'A Life Worth Living: Enforcement of the Right to Health through the Right to Life in the Inter-American Court of Human Rights', 40 *Columbia Human Rights Law Review*, 2008, 595.

[36] *Sawhoyamaxa Indigenous Community v Paraguay*, Merits, Reparations and Costs, Judgment. Series C No. 146 (2006).

[37] *Yakye Axa Indigenous Community v Paraguay*, Merits, Reparations and Costs, Judgment. Series C No. 125 (2005), paras 160–3.

[38] Ibid., para. 154.   [39] Ibid., paras 50–97.

[40] *Centre for Minority Rights Development (Kenya) and Minority Rights Group International on behalf of Endorois Welfare Council v Kenya*, Communication 276/2003 (2010), para. 216.

that the fallout from forcibly dispossessing indigenous peoples from their ancestral land could amount to an Article 4 violation (right to life) if the living conditions of the community are incompatible with the principles of human dignity'.[41]

However, this jurisprudence does not mean that *any* indigenous community that is suffering from loss of access to its ancestral territories could claim a violation of right to life. Indeed, this approach has been rejected in the 2017 case of the Ogiek community against Kenya (*Ogiek* case), which was examined by the African Court on Human and Peoples' Rights (ACtHPR).[42] Despite recognizing the violations of the indigenous communities' rights to land and natural resources, the ACtHPR did not recognize that this amounted to a violation of their right to life. As noted by the ACtHPR, 'the sole fact of eviction and deprivation of economic, social and cultural rights may not necessarily result in the violation of the right to life'.[43] The violation of the right to life was rejected not due to a lack of connection between the right to life and access to essential natural resources but based on the lack of evidence put forward by the applicants on this connection. The *Ogiek* Case shows that loss of access to essential sources of livelihood such as food and water would not automatically amount to a violation of the right to life, but that there needs to be a clear and causal connection between loss of livelihood and loss of life. This is confirmed by the approach adopted by the IACtHR, which has developed a test to examine whether a restriction could constitute a violation of the right to life. Pasqualucci, in his examination of the jurisprudence of the court on the issue, discusses three basic requirements established by the court, including that:

the applicants first must show that they lack the most basic necessities of life, such as access to potable water, sufficient food, sanitary facilities, and basic health care. Second, the applicant must show that the State knew or had reason to know of the vulnerable situation that was jeopardizing the right to life of groups or individuals within its jurisdiction. Third, a causal relationship must exist between the States' action, negligence or omission and the deplorable living conditions of the alleged victims.[44]

In practice, it might be hard to prove this direct connection between loss of life livelihood and lack of access to natural resources without showing that direct and planned restrictions led to said loss, e.g. the *Sawhoyamaxa* and *Yakye Axa* cases, where the onus of proving such connection was on the indigenous claimants. As highlighted in the *Ogiek* Case, there is no automatic casual connection between loss of access to essential sources of livelihood and loss of life; the applicants have to prove such a connection. However, in situations where restrictions to accessing natural resources could be proven to lead to loss of access to sources of livelihood putting life in jeopardy, courts should recognize that said restrictions constitute a violation of the

---

[41] Ibid.

[42] *African Commission on Human and Peoples' Rights v Republic of Kenya*, Application No. 006/2012, (2017) (*Ogiek* case), para. 153.

[43] Ibid., para. 153.

[44] Jo M. Pasqualucci, 'The Right to a Dignified Life (*Vida Digna*): The Integration of Economic and Social Rights with Civil and Political Rights in the Inter-American Human Rights System', 31 *Hastings International & Comparative Law Review*, 2008, 26.

right to life. While it appears that such jurisprudence has emerged under the banner of indigenous peoples' rights, there are no strong legal arguments on why this could not apply to other communities or groups suffering from similar loss of life due to loss of access to fundamental resources.

3. Conflicts and Natural Resources: The Accountability Approach

As noted in the Introduction, many conflicts and wars are rooted in the quest to control or exploit natural resources, and these hostilities are often referred to as 'natural resource conflicts',[45] which usually have serious negative consequences on the human rights of the local populations. According to Global Witness, 'natural resources whose systematic exploitation and trade in a context of conflict contribute to, benefit from or result in the commission of serious violations of human rights, violations of IHL or violations amounting to crimes under international law'.[46] As an illustration, the 2010 UN Office of the High Commissioner for Human Rights report concerning violations that took place in the Democratic Republic of Congo (DRC) identifies several types of human rights violations due to the presence of natural resources. These violations relate to (1) violations of human rights committed within the context of the struggle by parties to an armed conflict in order to gain access to and control over the areas of the country rich in natural resources; (2) human rights abuses committed by parties to an armed conflict as part of a regime of terror and coercion established in resource-rich areas under their control; and (3) the role of natural resources in funding armed conflicts, which are themselves a source and cause of violations of human rights.[47] Many other conflicts have centred around quests for natural resources where the violence has led to serious human rights violations.[48] In these situations, the control for the natural resources can be the incentives for conflicts, or can also furnish the warring parties the necessary resources to finance their war efforts. The United Nations Development Group report on the topic highlights that '(i) natural resources can contribute to conflict outbreak where there are attempts to control or gain access to natural resources, (ii) they can finance and extend the duration of conflict, and (iii) they can spoil prospects of peace,

---

[45] For references and analysis, see the series of UN and EU Toolkit and Guidance for Preventing and Managing Land and Natural resources. Available at: http://www.un.org/en/land-natural-resources-conflict/extractive-industries.shtml.

[46] Global Witness, *The Sinews of War: Eliminating the Trade in Conflict Resources* (Global Witness, November 2006), p. 1.

[47] Report of the Mapping Exercise Documenting the Most Serious Violations of Human Rights and International Humanitarian Law Committed within the Territory of the Democratic Republic of the Congo Between March 1993 and June 2003, Office of the High Commissioner for Human Rights (2010), p. 350.

[48] See Maarten Bavinck, Lorenzo Pellegrini, and Erik Mostert (eds), *Conflicts over Natural Resources in the Global South: Conceptual Approaches* (CRC Press, 2014); Philippe Le Billon, *Fuelling War: Natural Resources and Armed Conflicts* (Routledge, 2013).

undermining efforts to build transparent processes of revenue collection and good governance.'[49]

Legally, the connection between conflicts and IHRL places itself at the junction of three inter-related fields of international law, namely, IHL, ICL, and IHRL. The following analysis examines how IHRL can play a role in these situations of conflicts by becoming a complement to the development of IHL and ICL in connection to resource conflicts.[50] First it focuses on situations of looting, pillage, and destruction of natural resources during armed conflicts, notably by exploring the prohibition and criminalization of pillaging and destruction of enemy properties. It then focuses on the potential role of ICL, notably the role of international criminal tribunals, in prosecuting international crimes that are related to natural resources.

3.1 War crimes, pillage, and destruction of natural resources

The war crime of pillage is probably one of the closest prohibitions of IHL touching on issues of natural resources during times of conflicts. The origins of the crime of pillage can be traced back to ancient practices and customs that tried to ban the looting that usually is treated as a reward for troops.[51] The crime of pillage was included in the statutes of international tribunal following the end of the Second World War.[52] The prohibition of pillage became internationally codified with the adoption of the 1907 Hague Regulations which stipulated that 'pillage is formally forbidden'.[53] The prohibition of pillage was then incorporated in the IVth Geneva Convention of 1949 (Art. 33.2) and in the 1977 Additional Protocol II (Art. 4.2), both of which address pillage during armed conflicts. More recently, with international and national tribunals having included the crime of pillage in their statutes, it can be argued that the prohibition constitutes a rule of customary international law.[54]

Pillage does not concern the looting or theft of natural resources only, but rather *any* forms of property. It concerns appropriation of any properties that are not directly connected with military objectives. This could include natural resources if these constitute a property of one of the belligerents. The connection between pillage and looting of natural resources during conflicts received specific attention during some of the trials that took place after the end of the Second World War,

---

[49] UNDG/ECHA Guidance Note on Natural Resource Management (NRM) in Transition Settings (United Nations Development Group, 2013), p. 4.

[50] The following analysis is not intended to offer a comprehensive review of the connection between IHL and ICL regarding natural resources. For such comprehensive analysis, see Dam-de Jong (n 3).

[51] See Larissa Van den Herik and Daniëlla Dam-de Jong, 'Revitalizing the Antique War Crime of Pillage: The Potential and Pitfalls of Using International Criminal Law to Address Illegal Resource Exploitation during Armed Conflict', 22(3) *Criminal Law Forum*, 2011, 237–73.

[52] See Statute of the Nuremberg Charter, Art. 6(b), which criminalized 'plunder of public or private property'.

[53] Convention (IV) Respecting the Laws and Customs of War on Land and its Annex: Regulations Concerning the Laws and Customs of War on Land, The Hague, 18 October 1907, Regulations Articles 28 and 47.

[54] See Jean-Marie Henckaerts and Louise Doswald-Beck (eds), *Customary International Humanitarian Law* (CUP/International Committee of the Red Cross, 2005), Vol. 1 (see Rule 52).

notably concerning pillage of oil and coal.[55] For example, in *N.V. De Bataafsche Petroleum Maatschappij & ors*, a British Court stated: 'the seizure and subsequent exploitation by the Japanese armed forces of the oil resources of the appellants was economic plunder of private property in violation of the laws and customs of war.'[56] However, since then, there have not been many cases of war crimes concerning pillage of natural resources.[57] Probably one of the most developed cases relates to the claim of pillage of natural resources by troops from Uganda when they intervened in the territory of the DRC between 1998 and 2003. The DRC sought reparation via the International Court of Justice (ICJ) for acts of looting of national resources by Ugandan troops. In its ruling, the ICJ recognized that the looting, plundering, and exploitation of natural resources by Ugandan military forces constituted a violation of IHL, notably the Hague Regulation of 1907 and Geneva Convention IV relating to the protection of civilian in times of armed conflicts.[58] Moreover the ICJ further determined that Uganda had violated its duty of vigilance 'by not taking adequate measures to ensure that its military forces did not engage in the looting, plundering and exploitation of the DRC's natural resources'.[59] However, other than this ICJ case, the prosecution for pillaging of natural resources during armed conflicts has rarely occurred.[60]

Another relevant war crime relates to the prohibition of destruction of or seizing property of a hostile party to the conflict. The difference here is that, unlike pillage where the resources are looted, the resources are deliberately destroyed or seized. The 1907 Hague Regulations prohibit the destruction or seizure of enemy property during an international armed conflict 'unless imperatively demanded by the necessities of war'.[61] The Geneva Convention IV also prohibits the destruction or seizure of enemies' properties during an occupation unless necessary for military operations.[62] The war crime of extensive destruction and appropriation of property is listed under the grave breaches of the Geneva Conventions, and the statute of the International Criminal Court (ICC) criminalizes the destruction and seizure of the

---

[55] See *United States of America v Ernst von Weizsaecker et al.* (Ministries Case), Trials of War Criminals before the Nuremberg Military Tribunals, Vol. 14, p. 741 (US Government Printing Office, 1949); BHO standards for Berg und Huettenwerke Ost. For detailed analysis, see James G. Stewart, *Corporate War Crimes: Prosecuting Pillage of Natural Resources* (Open Society Foundations, 2010).

[56] *N.V. De Bataafsche Petroleum Maatschappij & ors v The War Damage Commission*, Singapore Law Reports (1956), p. 65.

[57] Keenan refers to an 'episodic' approach; see Patrick J. Keenan, 'Conflict Minerals and the Law of Pillage', 14(2) *Chicago Journal of International Law*, 2014, 524–58.

[58] Armed Activities on the Territory of the Congo (*Democratic Republic of the Congo v Uganda*), Judgment, 2005 ICJ, 19 December 2005, paras 245–50.

[59] Ibid., para. 246. For further analysis, see Shelly Whitman, 'Sexual Violence, Coltan and the Democratic Republic of Congo'. In: Matthew A. Schnurr and Larry A. Swatuk (eds), *Natural Resources and Social Conflict Towards Critical Environmental Security* (Palgrave, 2012), pp. 128–51; Miho Taka, 'Coltan Mining and Conflict in the Eastern Democratic Republic of Congo (DRC)'. In: Malcolm McIntosh and Alan Hunter (eds), *New Perspectives on Human Security* (Routledge, 2010), pp. 159–74.

[60] However, see *Prosecutor v Bemba*, ICC-01/05-01/08, Trial Chamber III, Judgment, 21 March 2016, as well as the ongoing trial of Bosco Ntaganda which, at the time of writing, is being adjudicated by the International Criminal Court, as he was charged with pillaging of natural resources. For analysis, see Keenan (n 57).

[61] Hague Regulations, 1907, Art. 23(g).   [62] Geneva Convention IV, Art. 53.

property of an 'adversary'.[63] This prohibition concerns 'property' in a large sense and not specifically natural resources. Nonetheless, it could be relevant to instances of destruction or seizure of natural resources in situations of conflict.[64]

To fully comprehend the relevance of these rules of IHL to the larger human rights approach to natural resources it is important to consider the relationship between IHL and IHRL. Under international law, wars and conflicts are predominately governed by the specialized field of IHL. The relationship between IHL and IHRL is complex and has been subject to intensive analysis and research which are far beyond the scope of this book.[65] Traditionally, the understanding was that IHL would apply in situations of conflict and IHRL in situations of peace. But this theoretical approach has been comprehensively challenged with a more contemporary approach supporting the view that the two regimes could interrelate, overlap, and be complementary, notably with some of the international human rights norms still applying during conflicts.[66] Without ignoring the very complex rules governing the complementarity between the two fields of IHL and IHRL, in the context of this book it suffices to say that the two set of rules could be relevant to situations of natural resources conflicts.

One main limitation to this approach is when the rules of IHL contradict human rights norms. Where this happens, IHL should prevail and the conflict should be solved by recourse to the principle of harmonious interpretation.[67] As Dam-de Jong notes in her in-depth analysis on the issue, 'IHL contains only a few specialised rules that apply to the management of natural resources. In addition, these rules do not directly conflict with relevant rules of international human rights and environmental law.'[68] This means that IHRL could support the development of a stronger and more developed approach to the prohibition of the war crimes of pillage and destruction and seizure of natural resources during conflicts. However, in practice, there is very little engagement by the main international human rights treaty monitoring bodies with the issue. The CRC remains one of the few international human rights monitoring bodies which has systematically paid specific attention on the negative effects on children's rights that the illegal exploitation of natural resources during conflicts can have, e.g. in the context of the DRC, the CRC noted that it is important for State parties to ensure the respect of IHL principles.[69] However, apart from this connection made by the CRC in the context of the DRC, there is still a

---

[63] Rome Statute, Art. 8(2)(e)(xii).

[64] For further and in-depth analysis, see Dam-de Jong (n 3).

[65] See Orna Ben-Naftali (ed.), *International Humanitarian Law and International Human Rights Law* (OUP, 2011); René Provost, *International Human Rights and Humanitarian Law* (CUP, 2002).

[66] See *Case Concerning Armed Activities on the Territory of the Congo (Democratic Republic of the Congo v Uganda)*, Judgment of 19 December 2005, *ICJ Reports*, 2005, 168, para. 216. ICJ, *Legal Consequences of the Construction of a Wall in the Occupied Palestinian Territory (Advisory Opinion)*, *ICJ Reports*, 2004, para. 106.

[67] See ICJ, *The Legality of the Threat or Use of Nuclear Weapons* (Advisory Opinion of 8 July 1996), General List No. 95 (1995–1998).

[68] Dam-de Jong (n 3) 196.

[69] Concluding Observations of the Committee on the Rights of the Child: Democratic Republic of the Congo, UN Doc. CRC/C/15/Add.153 (2001), para. 6.

lack of systematic and specific engagement by international human rights bodies regarding the impact that pillage, destruction, and seizure of natural resources can have on civilian populations during armed conflicts.

3.2 Criminal accountability, international criminal law, and natural resources

ICL is a field of international law that has developed substantially over the last few decades in addressing the 'most unimaginable atrocities'.[70] Since the 1990s, ICL has advanced via a large jurisprudence of special tribunals, special courts, and hybrid tribunals.[71] It has also developed with the 1998 adoption of the Rome Statute, which created the ICC. These developments could also represent an important element to address the human rights violations that occurred during conflicts centred on the control of natural resources. The crimes covered by ICL concern the most serious, systematic, and large-scale situations of mass killings, covering crimes of genocide, crimes against humanity, and war crimes. Hence, the focus is not on protecting natural resources or on prosecuting abuses on the use of natural resources.[72] However, the connection with natural resources could be made when the destruction or looting of natural resources is used as an element of a larger criminal plan. In this context, international crimes could be connected to wilful destruction of natural resources that are essential to the survival of civilian populations, or acts of deprivation of essential natural resources, which could be part of criminal plans of genocide, crimes against humanity, or war crimes.

The crime of genocide concerns the deliberate killing of a large group of people, especially those of a particular ethnic or religious group, with the aim of eradicating the group. Article 2 of the Genocide Convention defines genocide as acts committed with intent to destroy, in whole or in part, a national, ethnical, racial, or religious group. In the list of acts that constitute genocide, it includes deliberately inflicting conditions of life calculated to cause the physical destruction of a specific ethnic group.[73] Likewise, Article 6 of the ICC Statute highlights as an act of genocide the destruction of the conditions of life of a group, in order to physically destroy it.[74] Thus, deliberately inflicting conditions of life calculated to bring about physical destruction of a specific group, i.e. destruction of natural resources that are essential for the survival of the group, might be considered as an element of the crime of genocide. The Text of the Elements of Crimes supports this claim, saying that 'the

---

[70] See William Schabas, *Unimaginable Atrocities: Justice, Politics, and Rights at the War Crimes Tribunals* (OUP, 2012).

[71] See Shane Darcy, *Judges, Law and War: The Judicial Development of International Humanitarian Law* (CUP, 2014).

[72] For analysis on development of ICL regarding natural resources see Aaron Ezekiel, 'The Application of International Criminal Law to Resource Exploitation: Ituri, Democratic Republic of the Congo', 47 *Natural Resources Journal*, 2007, 225–45.

[73] Convention on the Prevention and Punishment of the Crime of Genocide (1948), 78 UNTS 277, Art. II(c).

[74] Rome Statute of the International Criminal Court, UN Doc. A/CONF.138/9, Art. 6.

term "conditions of life" may include, but are not necessarily restricted to, deliberate deprivation of resources indispensable for survival, such as food or medical services, or systematic expulsions from homes'.[75]

Ultimately, regarding the applicability of the crime of genocide in such a context, the test would be based on the notion of 'specific intent' to destroy the group, which is a central component of the crime of genocide.[76] This would mean proving that by destroying essential natural resources the intent was to place the survival of the group in jeopardy with the effect of destroying the group. Additionally, the Text of the Elements of Crimes declares that 'the conditions of life were calculated to bring about the physical destruction of that group, in whole or in part'.[77] Historically, one of the closest illustrations of the connection between deliberately restricting access to essential resources to destroy a group and the crime of genocide comes from Guatemala. The report of the Commission for Historical Clarification, which was established to examine the atrocities committed during the long civil war between 1962 and the late 1990s, highlighted that the destruction of property and the burning of the harvest, as well as the practice of so-called scorched earth operations, amounted to genocide against the Mayan population.[78] The findings of the Commission were based on a combination of mass killings, notably of leaders from the Mayan communities, and the destruction of their environment. Apart from this specific situation, there is scant jurisprudence linking destruction of essential natural resources to ensure survival and genocide. Nonetheless, this case shows that genocide may be established if it is proven that the destruction of the conditions of life was one of the principal mechanisms used to destroy the group.

Crimes against humanity could also potentially entail situations when destruction of natural resources or restriction to access essential natural resources is part of a widespread and systematic attack against a civilian population. Article 7 of the ICC Statute includes crimes of deportation or forcible transfers of population, with the latter specifically done to exploit natural resources. While in practice no such case has yet been ruled by the Court, there is currently a case pending regarding the forced displacement of 60,000 victims of a large-scale governmental land-grabbing policy in Cambodia that started in January 2014.[79] Also relevant is the prohibition against starving the civilian population as a method of combat during armed conflicts.[80]

---

[75] See Assembly of States Parties to the Rome Statute of the International Criminal Court, First Session, September 2002 ICC-ASP/1/3, at 114, n 4; see also Report of the Preparatory Commission for the International Criminal Court, *Finalized Draft Text of the Elements of Crimes*, PCNI.C.C./2000/INF/3/Add.2, 7 (6 July 2000).

[76] On this issue, see William Schabas, *Genocide in International Law: The Crime of Crimes*, 2nd edition (CUP, 2009).

[77] International Criminal Court, *Finalized Draft Text* (n 75), Art. 6.

[78] Report of the Commission for Historical Clarification, *Guatemala: Memory of Silence* (1999). Available at: http://www.shr.aaas.org/guatemala/ceh/report/english/toc.html.

[79] See the communication sent to the ICC Prosecutor by Global Diligence LLP and FIDH—International Federation for Human Rights; for more information see https://www.fidh.org/IMG/pdf/executive_summary-2.pdf. For analysis, see Franziska Maria Oehm, 'Land Grabbing in Cambodia as a Crime Against Humanity—Approaches in International Criminal Law', 48 *Verfassung und Recht in Übersee/Law and Politics in Africa/Asia/Latin America*, 2015, 469–91.

[80] Article 54(2) of Additional Protocol I, and Article 14 of Additional Protocol II.

This is part of the larger IHL prohibition of attack, destruction, removal, or rendering useless objects indispensable to the survival of the civilian population by parties to an armed conflict. In theory, this could include the destruction of water and food sources essential to the survival of civilian population. This approach is supported by the human rights Covenants stating in their common Article 1 that 'in no case, may a people be deprived of its own means of subsistence'.[81]

Although there is a lack of jurisprudence to support the connection between ICL and the destruction of natural resources, there are some indications about the willingness of the ICC to engage more specifically with the illegal exploitation of natural resources as a source of crime.[82] The Policy Paper on Case Selection and Prioritisation released in 2016 by the Office of the Prosecutor aims to set out considerations which guide on case selection and prioritization by the prosecutor, and specifically mentions illegal exploitation of natural resources.[83] It highlights that the

impact of the crimes may be assessed in light of, inter alia, the increased vulnerability of victims, the terror subsequently instilled, or the social, economic and environmental damage inflicted on the affected communities. In this context, the Office will give particular consideration to prosecuting Rome Statute crimes that are committed by means of, or that result in, inter alia, the destruction of the environment, the illegal exploitation of natural resources or the illegal dispossession of land.[84]

Although this is a policy paper, it is nonetheless a good indication that the Office of the Prosecutor has become aware of the importance of looking at the connection between natural resources and criminal acts. In the near future, this awareness might result in the ICC prosecuting crimes connected with illegal natural resources exploitation.

Overall, looking at both the IHL and ICL approach to natural resources and their role in conflict situations, there are some relevant norms of IHL about pillage, destruction, and seizure of natural resources that could lead to prosecution and accountability. Likewise, in terms of crimes prosecutable by the ICC, pillage, destruction, and seizure of property are potential crimes that could be prosecuted. What is lacking is a developed jurisprudence examining these connections between international crimes and natural resources, as there is currently no systematic jurisprudence regarding pillage of natural resources; what exists instead is what Keenan has labelled an 'episodic' approach to the issue by the ICJ,[85] which is an inter-State mechanism rather than a criminal process. The ability of international law to prosecute individuals in such situations is crucial since in most contemporary acts of pillage, wilful destruction and seizure of natural resources are usually conducted by private actors, e.g. paramilitaries and mercenaries. From this perspective recent ICL

[81] ICCPR and ICESCR, Art. 1(2).

[82] See, for example, the case of Bosco Ntaganda, who is accused of 13 counts of war crimes, including pillaging and destroying the enemy's property. The trial opened on 2 September 2015. Available at: https://www.icc-cpi.int/drc/ntaganda.

[83] The Office of the Prosecutor, 'Policy Paper on Case Selection and Prioritisation, International Criminal Court', International Criminal Court, September 2016.

[84] Ibid., para. 41.   [85] Keenan (n 57).

developments, notably the recognition by the ICC Prosecutor's Office of the importance played by the destruction of essential natural resources, are potential avenues for the growth of such jurisprudence. International human rights institutions must also support the recognition of the central role of illegal exploitation of natural resources in the perpetration of serious violations during conflicts, and how this could lead to war crimes. For example, the Office of the High Commissioner for Human Rights mapped the crimes in the DRC, proving how control of natural resources played a central role in the conflicts. In that sense, international human rights institutions could play a significant role in supporting the evidence on the impact that destruction, pillage, and looting of natural resources play in some of the most 'unimaginable atrocities'.

4. Natural Resources Defenders: The Physical Integrity Approach

According to civil society figures on average, two environmental and land rights activists are killed every week for opposing natural resources exploitation projects.[86] Since 2012, Global Witness has conducted a campaign documenting the killings of land and environmental defenders worldwide, and their annual reports show a year-on-year rise in the numbers of land and environmental defenders who have been assassinated;[87] they note that 'this tide of violence is driven by an intensifying fight for land and natural resources, as mining, logging, hydro-electric and agricultural companies trample on people and the environment in their pursuit of profit'.[88] This is within the context of violence against those who oppose or protest the exploitation of natural resources and who face increased levels of violence, which includes kidnapping, torture, extrajudicial killings, harassment, and disappearances.

International human rights institutions have started to pay specific attention to the situation of those who risk their life to protect natural resources. On World Environment Day in June 2016, three UN Special Rapporteurs (Human Rights and the Environment; Situation of Human Rights Defenders; the Rights of Indigenous People) issued a joint statement highlighting that critical situation faced by 'environmental defenders' noting that they 'are routinely harassed, threatened, unlawfully detained, and even murdered, merely for opposing powerful business and governmental interests bent on exploiting and destroying the natural environment on which we all depend'.[89] The Inter-American Commission on Human Rights (IACHR) also expressed its concern regarding the large number of murders of land

---

[86] See Front Line Defenders, Annual Report 2016: Stop the Killing of Human Rights Defenders (2016); Article 19, *A Deadly Shade of Green—Threats to Environmental Human Rights Defenders in Latin America* (2016); 'The Politics of Death', a report of natural resources defenders killed across the globe. Available at: http://www.thisisplace.org/shorthand/politics-of-death/.

[87] Global Witness, *Defenders of the Earth* (Global Witness, 2016).   [88] Ibid., 6.

[89] See United Nations Human Rights Office of the High Commissioner, 'A Deadly Undertaking—UN Experts Urge All Governments to Protect Environmental Rights Defenders'. Available at: http://www.ohchr.org/EN/NewsEvents/Pages/DisplayNews.aspx?NewsID=20052.

rights and natural resources defenders.[90] In 2016, the UN Special Rapporteur on the situation of human rights defenders issued a specific report on the situation of 'environmental human rights defenders', raising alarm about the increasing and intensifying violence they face.[91]

This section examines the relevance of IHRL in situations of systematic and targeted attacks against 'natural resource defenders', analysing how the protection of human rights defenders remains very disparate across jurisdictions. It also examines how most of these attacks against these defenders are committed by private actors, such as security guards or private firms hired by corporations, ranchers, or other actors having an interest in natural resources exploitation.

4.1 Murders, arbitrary killings, and enforced disappearances: a right to physical integrity

Natural resources defenders have been facing different forms of violence—from extrajudicial killings and murders to enforced disappearances—which have been examined by various international human rights mechanisms. As noted, the UN Special Rapporteur on the situation of human rights defenders has specifically highlighted that environmental human rights defenders face murders, arbitrary killings, and disappearances in many countries across the globe.[92] The UN Special Rapporteur on extrajudicial, summary, or arbitrary executions has also highlighted the connection between natural resources defenders and arbitrary executions, e.g. in the report following an official visit to Honduras, which noted that 'a total of 111 environmental activists, particularly in indigenous communities, were murdered between 2002 and 2014, making Honduras the most dangerous country in the world for land and environmental defenders in that period'.[93] Likewise, the UN Working Group on Enforced or Involuntary Disappearances also reported on the particular situation faced by peoples who oppose large-scale developmental projects, noting that 'in regions where land-grabbing is a growing practice, many human rights defenders and protestors against such practices may also become victims of enforced disappearance'.[94] Additionally, the Working Group declared that 'in such cases, enforced disappearance is used as a repressive measure and a tool to deter the legitimate exercise, defence, or promotion of the enjoyment of economic, social and cultural rights'.[95] These illustrations from the different UN specialized human rights bodies

---

[90] Inter-American Commission on Human Rights, 'IACHR Condemns Murders of Human Rights Defenders in the Region', Press Release No. 011/17, 7 February 2017.

[91] UN Doc. A/71/281 (2016) (n 4).

[92] In this context, 'environmental human rights defenders' refers to 'individuals and groups who, in their personal or professional capacity and in a peaceful manner, strive to protect and promote human rights relating to the environment, including water, air, land, flora and fauna'. UN Doc. A/71/281 (2016) (n 4), para. 7.

[93] Report of the Special Rapporteur on Extrajudicial, Summary or Arbitrary Executions on his Mission to Honduras, UN Doc. A/HRC/35/23/Add.1 (2017), para. 53.

[94] Report of the Working Group on Enforced or Involuntary Disappearances, Study on Enforced or Involuntary Disappearances and Economic, Social and Cultural Rights, UN Doc. A/HRC/30/38/Add.5 (2015), para. 35.

[95] Ibid., para. 33.

show how widespread and specific the violence against natural resources defenders has become.

Attacks against natural resources defenders are not limited to individual killings only, but also concern arbitrary killings during public protests, where excessive use of force, especially during demonstrations, and assaults are common in these contexts. Probably one of the most violent reports of excess aggression concerns the situation in the Peruvian Amazon. The indigenous population resisted the drilling for oil and minerals on ancestral lands,[96] and the bloodshed reached its peak when, following the government's decision to pass regulations allowing companies access to the Amazon, local communities conducted more than a year of declared opposition and advocacy to change this policy, including 65 straight days of civil disobedience.[97] The reaction of the authorities resulted in the June 2009 crisis, as police and military forces violently repressed the protests, resulting in the deaths of more than 30 people.[98] Other cases of violent repression, including the fatal shooting of protesters, have been common in recent years across Latin America.[99] However, this is not limited to Latin America; violent repression of public protests against projects exploiting natural resources is a global phenomenon. The 2015 report of the Special Rapporteur on the rights to freedom of peaceful assembly specifically focused on the repression of protests as well as violence committed against those involved in anti-developmental projects. It highlighted that, in many cases, the most egregious violations of the rights to freedom of peaceful assembly and of association take place in the context of natural resource exploitation.[100] The Special Rapporteur noted that 'those who oppose natural resource exploitation activities are labelled as "anti-development" or "enemies of the State". Attacks are also used as an intimidation tactic to force communities to accept exploitation projects'.[101] While intimidation tactics do not always lead to violence, the Special Rapporteur noted that 'perceived leaders of movements or protests are often subjected to particularly egregious violations of their rights, such as disappearances and arbitrary killings in an effort by States and corporations to intimidate and thus disrupt organized efforts to resist exploitation activities'.[102] Attacks against natural resources defenders are part of the larger criminalization of people who protest and resist natural resources exploitation. Frost, the UN Special Rapporteur on the situation of human rights defenders, notes that

---

[96] See Martí Orta-Martínez and Matt Finer, 'Oil Frontiers and Indigenous Resistance in the Peruvian Amazon', 70(2) *Ecological Economics*, 2010, 207–18; George Stetson, 'Oil Politics and Indigenous Resistance in the Peruvian Amazon: The Rhetoric of Modernity against the Reality of Coloniality', 21(1) *The Journal of Environment & Development*, 76–97.

[97] Interested readers are referred to 'When Two Worlds Collide', a 2016 documentary by Heidi Brandenburg and Mathew Orzel.

[98] See Defensoría del Pueblo Dio a Conocer Relación de Acciones Humanitarias Realizadas ante los Lamentables Sucesos Ocurridos en Bagua, Nota de Prensa No. 120/09/OCII/DP. Available at: http://www.defensoria.gob.pe/modules/Downloads/prensa/notas/2009/NP-120-09.pdf.

[99] See Article 19 (n 86).

[100] See Report of the Special Rapporteur on the Rights to Freedom of Peaceful Assembly and of Association, Maina Kiai, UN Doc. A/HRC/29/25 (28 April 2015).

[101] Ibid., para. 42.   [102] Ibid., para. 46.

'violations are intertwined with the overall climate of criminalization of their work, especially in the context of large-scale development projects'.[103]

Apart from the specialized UN human rights mechanisms, human rights jurisprudence is also on the upswing, the most developed of which (regarding the protection of natural resources defenders) comes from the Inter-American human rights system, which has arguably the largest numbers of cases. *Kawas Fernández* was the first case that put into context the violence faced by environmental and natural resources defenders. Blanca Jeannette Kawas Fernández was murdered in 1995 after having publicly opposed the exploitation of forestlands and illegal logging in a national park on the northern Caribbean coast of Honduras.[104] Despite the government's denial, the IACtHR concluded that her murder was premeditated and that government officials were also involved in its concealment. Additionally, it found that that at least one agent of the State had been involved in the events that ended her life and that such acts were motivated by her work in reporting and opposing the exploitation of natural resources. Consequently, the IACtHR ruled that 'based on the [alleged] participation of State agents in ordering, planning and executing her murder and on the lack of an effective investigation into her death', the government had violated Articles 4 (right to life), 8 (right to fair trial), and 25 (right to judicial protection) of the American Convention. It also found that the authorities had not undertaken an effective investigation of the assassination in violation of the right to life and its relevant standard for investigation required by the American Convention. This case set an important precedent for the requirement that governments must protect at-risk 'environmental human rights defenders'.[105] For example, in 2010, the Court released another similar judgment in *Case of Cabrera García and Montiel Flores*, about two Mexican environmentalists who were arrested by the military and found guilty of various crimes based on confessions extracted under duress. The IACtHR found that the State was responsible for their arbitrary detention and torture.[106]

The other important precedent established by *Kawas Fernández* relates to the legal reasoning of the IACtHR to ensure better protection of environmental defenders. In its reasoning the IACtHR declared the need for States to develop better legal frameworks to protect the 'life and integrity' of environmentalists. Fernandez's murder was paramount to the Court's decision, which placed her attacks within a larger context of increased harassment and assassination of environmentalists that have taken place since her death. The Court specifically noted that:

the threats and attempts against the integrity and life of human right supporters and impunity in this type of events are particularly serious in a democratic society. In accordance with the general obligation to respect and guarantee human rights enshrined in Article 1(1)

---

[103] UN Doc. A/71/281 (2016) (n 4) para. 30

[104] *Kawas Fernández v Honduras*, Merits, Reparations, and Costs, Judgment. Series C No. 196, (2009).

[105] See Laurie R. Tanner, '*Kawas v. Honduras*—Protecting Environmental Defenders', 3(3) *Journal of Human Rights Practice*, 2011, 309–26.

[106] *Case of Cabrera García and Montiel Flores v México*, Judgment. Series C No. 220 (2010).

of the Convention, the State has a duty to adopt legislative, administrative and judicial measures, or to fulfill those already in place, guaranteeing the free performance of environmental
advocacy activities; the instant protection of environmental activists facing danger or threats
as a result of their work; and the instant, responsible and effective investigation of any acts
endangering the life or integrity of environmentalists on account of their work.[107]

There are two important points regarding the specificity of these cases of violence
against natural resources defenders. First, in relying on the notion of 'integrity', the
IACtHR proposes a relevant legal framework to collectively define the different
types of violence faced by natural resources defenders, including mental violence.
From this perspective, the reliance of the IACtHR on the notion of the environmental defenders' right to 'integrity' offers a more encompassing approach which
could cover any type of violence, including severe harm, and, going beyond physical
integrity of the body, mental integrity.[108] It concerns protection against physical
assaults, harassment, and mental or physiological harms. Hence, in relying on the
notion of a right to personal integrity, which is stipulated in both the American and
African human rights treaties,[109] the Court offers a relevant framework to cover all
the different types of violence faced by natural resources defenders and the overall
integrity of life.

Secondly, they establish the connection between State authorities and private
actors. Fernandez Kawas's murder was not a direct act of a State agent, but the
IACtHR held that the Honduran government had failed to properly investigate her
murder and prosecute her killers. Additionally, the IACtHR highlighted that the
killing done by a State agent was purposefully concealed. The murder of Kawas is
not an isolated incident; in many violent attacks against natural resources defenders,
there is a high correlation between concealment, lack of prosecution by State authorities, and the actions of private actors who want to exploit the natural resources.
From this perspective, *Kawas Fernández* only touches on the role of private actors
when it comes to obligations to respect life and personal integrity under IHRL and
violence committed against natural resources defenders.

4.2 Violence from non-State actors: from impunity to extraterritorial litigation

Peoples and individuals resisting exploitation of natural resources often face harassment, death threats, and intimidation with little or no protection from the authorities (who often are on the side of the corporations or private actors involved),
especially when large-scale extractives projects are at stake. As Raftopoulos notes,
'[p]rotecting the large revenues associated with extraction often requires high levels

---

[107] Ibid., para. 213.

[108] See Nigel S. Rodley, 'Integrity of the Person'. In: Daniel Moeckli, Sangeeta Shah, and Sandesh
Sivakumaran, *International Human Rights Law*, 2nd edition (OUP, 2014), pp. 175–94.

[109] See Article 5 of the American Convention: 'Every person has the right to have his physical, mental,
and moral integrity respected', and Article 4 of the African Charter: 'Every human being shall be entitled
to respect for his life and the integrity of his person'.

of violence and repression in the extractive enclaves as multinational companies and governments seek to guarantee the supply of natural resources though the opening up of remote frontiers and networks of connectivity.'[110] The Inter-American Commission referenced a specific report from 2013[111] on the impact of extractive industries in Latin America, and in its 2015 report highlighted that 'one of the most serious effects of extractive or development projects is the adverse effects on the life of members of indigenous peoples and Afro-descendent communities, as well as those situations that jeopardize the right to life'.[112] The 2015 report establishes a clear connection between the right to life and the right to personal integrity of the person in situations of violence against community leaders who have opposed extractive projects.

The role of private actors, notably international and transnational corporations, has increased in recent years, with States transferring more powers to investors and corporations involved in the exploitation of natural resources. Greater numbers of lands and natural resources are also allocated to private actors, e.g. up to 40 per cent of the territory of Peru has been handed over by the government to private for-profit entities to exploit natural resources, and in Liberia and in Indonesia 35 and 30 per cent, respectively, of the land is in the hands of the private sector for exploitation operations.[113] The UN Special Rapporteur on the rights to freedom of peaceful assembly and of association noted that this situation can lead to complex and blurred relationships, saying that 'the obligations may appear to be somewhat distorted owing to the sometimes complex relationships that exist between Governments and the private sector'.[114] Importantly, in many situations the violence does not stem from public authorities, but rather it is committed by private actors, e.g. landlords, private security personals, paramilitaries, private park rangers. Common to all these attacks is the lack of prosecution, or even inquiry, including into the acts of States' agents as well as those committed by non-State actors. Mostly there is no inquiry and prosecution in situations where crimes are indirectly sanctioned by, or in the interests of, the authorities.

In terms of IHRL, this complicity between public authorities and private corporations falls within the expanding field of business and human rights. Since the 2011 adoption by the UN Human Rights Council of the UN Guiding Principles on Business and Human Rights, there has been an increased focus from international institutions on the role and place of corporations when it comes to human rights

---

[110] Malayna Raftopoulos, 'Contemporary Debates on Social-Environmental Conflicts, Extractivism and Human Rights in Latin America', 21(4) *International Journal of Human Rights*, 2017, 387–404.

[111] *Truth, Justice and Reparation—Report on the Situation of Human Rights in Colombia*, OEA/Ser.L/V/II. Doc. 49/13, 31 December 2013, para. 827.

[112] 'Indigenous Peoples, Afro-Descendent Communities, and Natural Resources: Human Rights Protection in the Context of Extraction and Exploitation' (IACHR, 2015), p. 141.

[113] Andrea Alforte, Joseph Angan, Jack Dentith, Karl Domondon, Lou Munden, Sophia Murday, and Leonardo Pradela, *Communities as Counterparties: Preliminary Review of Concessions and Conflict in Emerging and Frontier Market Concessions* (Rights and Resources Initiative, 2014). Available at: http://www.rightsandresources.org/wp-content/uploads/Communities-as-Counterparties-FINAL_Oct-21.pdf.

[114] (n 100) para. 13.

violations.[115] However, despite significant progress, there is still a lack of a strong and enforceable legal framework, and instead 'soft law' and voluntary mechanisms dominate.[116] Overall, a combination of public authorities' compliance with private interests and a lack of a robust and developed international legal framework leads to a dominant situation of impunity for the violence committed by private actors in many situations of protest against natural resources exploitation. International UN human rights-monitoring bodies have started to address this specific gap, highlighting the obligations of public authorities to take action against the violence of private actors against natural resource defenders. Treaty-monitoring bodies have asked governments to pay specific attention to the situation of human rights activists and defenders. For example, the CESCR urged the government of Cambodia 'to take all necessary measures to combat the culture of violence and impunity prevalent in the State party, and for the protection of human rights defenders, defending the economic, social and cultural rights of their communities against any intimidation, threat and violence, regardless of whether it is perpetrated by the government security forces or non-state actors'.[117]

However, one added complexity to these situations is the high level of internationalization of these private actors, with most investors or corporations involved in the exploitation of natural resources often being multinational entities. This has led to a gap in terms of responsibilities for human rights violations, with the 'host' States unable or willing to act against these powerful transnational actors, and the 'home' States unwilling to act against acts committed outside their jurisdictions. In terms of IHRL, the debate is on whether 'home' States, where the corporations or investors are based, have an obligation to prosecute or regulate the actions of such private actors when acting in other countries.[118] Despite the diplomatic and political debate about extraterritoriality of human rights obligations, international UN human rights treaty-monitoring bodies have increasingly highlighted States' obligations to adopt such extraterritorial approach to the acts of corporations registered in their country. For example, CERD in its observations regarding the United States noted

---

[115] For review and analysis, see Nadia Bernaz, *Business and Human Rights: History, Law and Policy—Bridging the Accountability Gap* (Routledge, 2016).

[116] At the time of writing, an international treaty is in negotiation; see the Human Rights Council resolution adopted in 2014 which established an 'open-ended intergovernmental working group on transnational corporations and other business enterprises with respect to human rights, whose mandate shall be to elaborate an international legally binding instrument to regulate, in international human rights law, the activities of transnational corporations and other business enterprises'. 'Elaboration of an International Legally Binding Instrument on Transnational Corporations and Other Business Enterprises with Respect to Human Rights', UN Doc. A/HRC/RES/26/9 (2014).

[117] Concluding Observations regarding Cambodia, 12 June 2009, UN Doc. E/C.12/KHM/CO/1, para. 31.

[118] See Amnesty International, 'Comments in Response to the UN Special Representative of the Secretary General on Transnational Corporations and other Business Enterprises' Guiding Principles' (Amnesty International, October 2010); Olivier De Schutter, Asbjørn Eide, Ashfaq Khalfan, Marcos Orellana, Margot Salomon, and Ian Seiderman, 'Commentary to the Maastricht Principles on Extraterritorial Obligations of States in the Area of Economic, Social and Cultural Rights,' 34(4) *Human Rights Quarterly*, 2012, 1084–169; Nadia Bernaz, 'Enhancing Corporate Accountability for Human Rights Violations: Is Extraterritoriality the Magic Potion?', 117(3) *Journal of Business Ethics*, 2013, 493–511.

'the reports of adverse effects of economic activities connected with the exploitation of natural resources in countries outside the United States by transnational corporations registered in the state party on the right to land, health, living environment and the way of life of indigenous peoples living in these regions'.[119] Likewise, the CESCR, in its 2016 Concluding Observations on the United Kingdom, expressed concerns 'about the lack of a regulatory framework to ensure that ... companies domiciled under its jurisdiction acting abroad fully respect economic, social and cultural rights'.[120] More specifically, the CESCR recommended that the United Kingdom 'adopt appropriate legislative and administrative measures to ensure legal liability of companies domiciled under the State party's jurisdiction, regarding violations of economic, social and cultural rights in their projects abroad, committed directly by these companies or resulting from the activities of their subsidiaries'.[121] These two illustrations are part of growing jurisprudence emerging from international human rights treaty bodies which is pushing States to adopt an extraterritorial approach towards the actions of corporations registered in their countries.[122] To support such evolution, the CESCR has adopted a specific General Comment on Business Obligations under the ICESCR, which specifically mentions these exterritorial obligations;[123] these developments could have a beneficial impact on the lack of prosecution of private actors' acts of violence against natural resources defenders, since most host States do not have the willingness to act against multinational corporations. However, it is still too early to see any significant change in the dominant impunity of multinational private actors' acts of violence against natural resource defenders, as they often act with the wilful support of the local authorities.

The fight against impunity is not limited to legal development in the sphere of IHRL; there has been an increase in recourse to transnational litigation against multinational corporations for their involvement in and support of the repression and attacks against human rights defenders. The Business and Human Rights Resource Centre, one of the leading civil society organizations working on the issue, noted that many cases of violence committed by transnational corporations directly relate to the exploitation of natural resources.[124] It notes in one of its reports on legal accountability that:

---

[119] Concluding Observations of the Committee on the Elimination of Racial Discrimination, United States of America, UN Doc. CERD/C/USA/CO/6 (2008), para. 30.

[120] Concluding Observations on the Sixth Periodic Report of the United Kingdom of Great Britain and Northern Ireland, UN Doc. E/C.12/GBR/CO/6 (2016), para. 11.

[121] Ibid., para. 12(b).

[122] See, for example, CERD/C/NOR/CO/19-20, para. 17; and CCPR/C/DEU/CO/6, para. 16. For further analysis, see Nadia Bernaz, 'States Obligations with Regard to Activities of Companies Domiciled on their Territories'. In: Carla Buckley, Philip Leach, and Alice Donald (eds), *The Harmonisation of International Human Rights Law* (Brill, 2016), pp. 435–53.

[123] General Comment No. 24 (2017) on State Obligations under the International Covenant on Economic, Social and Cultural Rights in the Context of Business Activities, UN Doc. E/C.12/GC/24, paras 25–37.

[124] For a list of cases see https://www.business-humanrights.org/en/key-findings-from-the-database-of-attacks-on-human-rights-defenders-feb-2017. See, for example, the Anvil Mining lawsuit (DRC).

[i]n 2014, seven Guatemalan men filed a lawsuit against Tahoe Resources in Canada for injuries suffered during protests. Also in Canada, in 2011, three lawsuits were filed against Hudbay Minerals and its subsidiary HMI Nickel for alleged gang rape, assassination and injuries in Guatemala; all three lawsuits are ongoing. A trade union leader sued BP in a UK court in 2014 over alleged complicity of the oil company with his kidnapping and torture by paramilitary groups in Colombia.[125]

These cases are part of an emerging transnational jurisprudence aiming for admission of and compensation from multinational corporations' human rights violations in the home countries of these corporations.[126] This jurisprudence does not necessarily rely on international human rights standards only, but also on criminal and tort remedies available in home countries of the concerned corporations. Between these developments and the increased pressure put by international human rights treaty-monitoring bodies is the emerging body of doctrine and jurisprudence to remedy the dominant impunity of multinational private actors. However, until these receive proper implementation, most natural resources defenders still face serious risk to life and physical integrity when they engaged in protests against large-scale natural resources exploitation projects involving powerful multinational corporations.

5. Conclusion

In examining the connection between life and natural resources, this chapter has taken some detours to examine many different situations, including famine, wars, assassination, and more generally the lack of access to essential sources of livelihoods. It has shown that there is little doubt of the strong connection between life and natural resources, making the right to life an important element within the larger human rights approach to natural resources. An enlarged human rights approach to the right to life has emerged encapsulating the right to access essential sources of livelihood such as food and water. This livelihood approach entails that the authorities have a duty to refrain from inducing conditions that impede peoples from attaining the necessities of life, including accessing natural resources that are essential to ensure life. Its evolution is nonetheless significant as until recently the right to life was still interpreted as mainly protecting citizens against unlawful and arbitrary deprivation of life by States' authorities. The more expansive approach to the meaning and content of the right to life that links it to a right to access essential natural resources to ensure livelihood is nascent. There is scope for a much more developed and consistent jurisprudence linking life and access to

---

[125] Business and Human Rights Resource Centre, *Latin America Briefing Focus on Human Rights Defenders under Threat & Attack* (Business & Human Rights Resource Centre, Briefing Note, January 2017).

[126] For review and analysis, see Judith Schrempf-Stirling and Florian Wettstein, 'Beyond Guilty Verdicts: Human Rights Litigation and its Impact on Corporations' Human Rights Policies', 145(3) *Journal of Business Ethics*, 2015, 1–18.; Anna Grear and Burns H. Weston, 'The Betrayal of Human Rights and the Urgency of Universal Corporate Accountability: Reflections on a Post-Kiobel Lawscape', 15(1) *Human Rights Law Review*, 2015, 21–44.

livelihood. Sadly, it is only the increased loss of access to essential natural resources by many local communities across the globe that will increase the push for further extension of this emerging jurisprudence. While the connection between the right to life and access to essential natural resources has been mainly developed under the banner of indigenous peoples' rights, it may expand to other non-indigenous communities, as the vast majority of peoples suffering from hunger and malnutrition due to restriction of their access to essential sources of livelihood are poor and marginalized, rural communities lacking secure land tenure and access agricultural production.[127]

The other significant correlation between the right to life and natural resources relates to the potential role that IHRL can play in situations of armed conflicts and the general violence that can surround the exploitation of natural resources. Here, IHRL places itself at the junction of IHL and ICL, two fields that have started to recognize the intimate link between exploitation of natural resources and criminal activities. As noted, they are some good indications that the ICC might take more seriously the nexus between illegal exploitation of natural resources and serious atrocities. In this context, IHRL places itself in the expanding international legal approach to accountability to potentially play an important role in supporting evidence on the link between natural resources and loss of life. The development of IHRL supports the emergence of a stronger corpus of international norms to regulate resource conflicts, which could also apply to post-conflicts situations. Indeed, control of natural resources is not only a cause of conflicts, but also equally an essential element of long-term peace and stability in post-conflict situations. Young and Goldman note that 'conflicts associated with natural resources are both more likely to relapse than non-resources related conflicts, and to relapse twice as fast'.[128] Increasingly, post-conflict agreements and peace settlements are addressing the redistribution of natural resources as an important element to ensure long-term peace, e.g. Iraq, South Sudan.[129] From this perspective, the complementary nature of IHL, ICL, and IHRL not only ensures the accountability of public authorities, private actors, and multinational corporations and, when guilty, their prosecution, but also helps to develop a stronger legal framework to ensure the transition to peace and long-term security.

Lastly, IHRL can further protect the right to life in the context of natural resources, by developing a human rights jurisprudence to protect those who put their life at risk by opposing or resisting projects that exploit natural resources. This development will also establish a clearer definition of the obligations of multinational corporations when it comes to violence committed against natural resources defenders. In the global quest for the natural resources left to be exploited, States are

---

[127] See Millennium Project, *Halving Hunger: It Can Be Done* (United Nations Publications, Sales No. 05.III.B.5).

[128] Helen Young and Lisa Goldman (eds), *Livelihoods, Natural Resources, and Post-Conflict Peacebuilding* (Routledge, 2015), p. ix.

[129] See Nicholas Haysom and Sean Kane, *Negotiating Natural Resources for Peace: Ownership, Control and Wealth-Sharing* (Henry Dunant Centre for Humanitarian Dialogue, 2009).

increasingly giving away land and territories to powerful multinational extractive industries, but there is still a legal gap concerning their obligations to respect the fundamental human rights of the local populations, especially in light of the increasing numbers of serious life-threating attacks faced by local communities who resist exploitation of natural resources found on their lands.

5

Cultural Rights and Natural Resources

Cultural Heritage, Traditional Knowledge, and Spirituality

> For the indigenous communities, the relationship with the land is not merely a question of possession and production, but rather a material and spiritual element that they should be able to enjoy fully, including to preserve their cultural legacy and transmit it to the future generations.
>
> *Case of the Mayagna (Sumo) Awas Tingni Community v Nicaragua*, Merits, Reparations and Costs, Judgment, Series C No. 79 (2001), para. 149

1. Introduction

Social and artistic expressions, behaviour patterns, arts, and beliefs that are characteristic of a community or population, and the customary beliefs, social forms, and material traits of a racial, religious, or social group, all fall under the umbrella of 'culture'.[1] The UNESCO Universal Declaration on Cultural Diversity defines culture as a 'set of distinctive spiritual, material, intellectual and emotional features of a society or a social group, [which] encompasses, in addition to art and literature, lifestyles, ways of living together, value systems, traditions and beliefs'.[2] These elements are all relevant to the connection between peoples and natural resources, which not only have a market value, but also important cultural values for many, especially rural communities. Additionally, culture encompasses traditional practices related to use of natural resources, including food production, e.g. rotational farming, pastoralism, artisanal fisheries, hunting.

---

[1] See Rodolfo Stavenhagen, 'Cultural Rights: A Social Science Perspectives'. In: H. Nieć (ed.), *Cultural Rights and Wrongs* (UNESCO, 1988), pp. 1–20.

[2] UNESCO Universal Declaration on Cultural Diversity, Preamble, para. 5. See also Fribourg Declaration on Cultural Rights, Art. 2(a) (definitions); (d) 'the sum total of the material and spiritual activities and products of a given social group which distinguishes it from other similar groups [and] a system of values and symbols as well as a set of practices that a specific cultural group reproduces over time and which provides individuals with the required signposts and meanings for behaviour and social relationships in everyday life'.

Natural Resources and Human Rights: An Appraisal. Jérémie Gilbert. © J. Gilbert 2018. Published 2018 by Oxford University Press.

This chapter focuses on the connections between cultural practices and natural resources and explores the correlation between them. Cultural rights represent an important element of international human rights law (IHRL), and several international and regional human rights treaties promote cultural rights.[3] These rights include the right to take part in cultural life, the right to enjoy one's own culture, the right to enjoy the benefits of scientific progress, the right to education, and the right of authors and inventors to the protection of their moral and material interests.[4] These different approaches to cultural rights all are relevant to natural resources. This chapter is not restricted to discussing international human rights treaties, per se, but also examines some of the relevant aspects of international law on cultural heritage. It includes instruments developed under the auspices of the United Nations Educational, Scientific and Cultural Organization (UNESCO) and the World Intellectual Property Organization (WIPO). Indeed, cultural rights over natural resources includes cultural heritage, biocultural heritage, protection of traditional knowledge, and intellectual property rights (IPR), all of which overlap with the work of these specialized international institutions. However, while the chapter engages with other relevant fields of international law, it focuses on the human rights-based approach to culture and natural resources.

It analyses the connection between cultural rights and natural resources using three different approaches. Firstly, via the human rights discourse on cultural diversity it examines how IHRL supports the rights of minorities and indigenous peoples to perpetuate cultural practices and manage natural resources. It also explores how the developing legal framework on the promotion of cultural diversity could have some potential beneficial impact on the perpetuation of specific cultural practices connected to these uses of natural resources. Secondly, it explores how the legal framework governing cultural heritage protects certain traditional cultural practices and traditional knowledge connected to the use of natural resources. Lastly, it discusses the connection between spirituality, religion, and natural resources to IHRL.

2. The Diversity Approach: Natural Resources as a Way of Life

In the context of a way of life of specific groups or communities, cultural rights refer to the anthropological meaning of culture, which includes any social activity or expression specific to a given population, including any customs or practices connected to natural resources. In terms of IHRL, this definition forms part of the treaties and

---

[3] Article 27 of the Universal Declaration of Human Rights; Article 15 of the International Covenant on Economic, Social and Cultural Rights; Article 17 of the African Charter on Human and Peoples' Rights; Article 13 of the American Declaration of the Rights and Duties of Man. For analysis, see Elsa Stamatopoulou, *Cultural Rights in International Law* (Brill, 2007); Ana Vrdoljak (ed.), *The Cultural Dimension of Human Rights* (OUP, 2013).

[4] See Dominic McGoldrick, 'Culture, Cultures, and Cultural Rights'. In: Mashood Baderin and Robert McCorquodale (eds), *Economic, Social and Cultural Rights in Action* (OUP, 2007), pp. 447–73; Elsa Stamatopoulou, *Cultural Rights in International Law* (Brill, 2007); Francesco Francioni and Martin Scheinin (eds), *Cultural Human Rights* (Martinus Nijhoff, 2008).

jurisprudence supporting the right to enjoy one's own culture. Traditionally, IHRL was more concerned with culture in the sense of intellectual and artistic expressions, rather than in the sense of a way of life.[5] However, this approach has been largely extended and developed to include cultural rights, resulting in a more developed legal doctrine that connects minority rights and cultural rights to the right to a specific way of life. This approach also unites minorities and indigenous peoples with the larger integration of a human rights-based approach to cultural diversity that includes recognizing the diversity of cultural practices over natural resources.

2.1 Minorities' way of life: indigenous peoples and cultural survival

When the international architecture of IHRL was developed after the Second World War, the rights of minorities were meant to be one of its strong and specific components, along with the adoption of a specific treaty to protect minorities;[6] however, this treaty never materialized.[7] This does not mean that there is no protection for minority rights under international law, as several regional treaties and instruments have since been adopted and a strong jurisprudence has emerged to protect minority rights.[8] It is within this legal framework protecting minority rights that a strong connection between cultural rights and natural resources has developed.

This approach appeared under a progressive interpretation of the minority rights provision in the International Covenant on Civil and Political Rights (ICCPR) where Article 27 of the ICCPR declares that:

[i]n those States in which ethnic, religious or linguistic minorities exist, persons belonging to such minorities shall not be denied the right, in community with the other members of their group, to enjoy their own culture, to profess and practise their own religion, or to use their own language.[9]

While nothing in this article mentions natural resources, the right of minorities to enjoy their own culture has been progressively interpreted as embracing specific usage of natural resources, especially for indigenous peoples. The connection

---

[5] See Julie Ringelheim, 'Cultural Rights'. In: Daniel Moeckli, Sangeeta Shah, and Sandesh Sivakumaran (eds), *International Human Rights Law*, 2nd edition (OUP, 2014), pp. 286–302.

[6] See Patrick Thornberry, 'Self-Determination, Minorities, Human Rights: A Review of International Instruments,' 38(4) *International and Comparative Law Quarterly*, 1989, 867–89; Patrick Thornberry, *International Law and the Rights of Minorities* (Clarendon Press, 1991); John Humphrey, 'The United Nations Sub-Commission on the Prevention of Discrimination and the Protection of Minorities', 62 *American Journal of International Law*, 1968, 869, 872

[7] However, see David Keane and Joshua Castellino, 'Is the International Convention on the Elimination of All Forms of Racial Discrimination the De Facto Minority Rights Treaty?'. In: Carla Buckley, Alice Donald, and Philip Leach (eds), *Towards Convergence in International Human Rights Law: Approaches of Regional and International Systems* (Brill, 2017).

[8] See Gaetano Pentassuglia, *Minorities in International Law: An Introductory Study* (Council of Europe Publications, 2002); Li-Ann Thio, *Managing Babel: The International Legal Protection of Minorities in the Twentieth Century* (Martinus Nijhoff, 2005); Kristin Henrard and Robert Dunbar (eds), *Synergies in Minority Protection: European and International Law Perspectives* (CUP, 2008).

[9] International Covenant on Civil and Political Rights opened for signature 16 December 1966, 999 UNTS 171, Art. 27.

between cultural rights and indigenous peoples constitutes one of the strong features of the Human Rights Committee's (HRC) interpretation of Article 27 of the ICCPR. In an often-quoted General Comment on Article 27, the HRC stated that:

[w]ith regard to the exercise of the cultural rights protected under article 27, the Committee observes that culture manifests itself in many forms, including a particular way of life associated with the use of land resources, especially in the case of indigenous peoples. That right may include such traditional activities as fishing or hunting and the right to live in reserves protected by law.[10]

Since then, the connection between cultural rights and cultural practices connected to the use of natural resources has been at the heart of several concluding observations and decisions on individual communications of the HRC.[11] There have been several individual complaints by indigenous peoples throughout the 1990s, and some of these decisions, e.g. *Ominayak v Canada*,[12] *Lansman v Finland*,[13] and *Lovelace v Canada*,[14] have become key elements of the international jurisprudence and doctrines regarding the connection between cultural rights and a traditional way of life.[15] All these recommendations and decisions highlight the fact that traditional cultural activities which form an essential element of indigenous peoples' culture should be protected under the minority protection offered by Article 27 of the ICCPR.

The use of the terms 'traditional activities' and 'traditional way of life' have led to some controversies, notably concerning the definition of what constitutes a 'traditional usage' of natural resources. Some governments have raised the fact that some of the activities undertaken by indigenous peoples are no longer 'traditional' as they use modern technology, e.g. the use of skidoos and helicopters by Sami reindeer herders in Finland. In addressing such objection, the HRC noted 'that the authors may have adapted their methods of reindeer herding over the years and practi[sing] it with the help of modern technology does not prevent them from invoking article 27 of the Covenant'.[16] Likewise, in *Apirana Mahuika et al.*, the HRC reaffirmed 'that article 27 does not only protect traditional means of livelihood of minorities, but allows also for adaptation of those means to the modern way of life and ensuing technology'.[17] *Apirana Mahuika et al.* debated the modern use of fishing nets

[10] Human Rights Committee, General Comment No. 23, Art. 27 (50th Session, 1994), Compilation of General Comments and General Recommendations Adopted by Human Rights Treaty Bodies, UN Doc. HRI/GEN/1/Rev.1 at 38 (1994), para. 7.

[11] See Fergus MacKay, 'Indigenous Peoples and United Nations Human Rights Treaty Bodies', Vol. 5 (Forest Peoples Programme, 2011–2012).

[12] UN Doc. CCPR/C/60/D/549/1993/Rev. 1, Communication No. 549/1993.

[13] UN Doc. CCPR/C/52/D/511/1992, Case No. 511/1992.

[14] A/36/40, Annex 7(G) (1998).

[15] For analysis, see Martin Scheinin, 'The Right to Enjoy a Distinct Culture: Indigenous and Competing Uses of Land'. In: Theodore S. Orlin, Allan Rosas, and Martin Scheinin (eds), *The Jurisprudence of Human Rights Law: A Comparative Interpretive Approach* (Institute for Human Rights, 2000), pp. 163–4.

[16] *Ilmari Länsman et al. v Finland*, Communication No. 511/1992, UN Doc. CCPR/C/52/D/511/1992 (1994), para. 9.3.

[17] *Apirana Mahuika et al. v New Zealand*, Communication No. 547/1993, UN Doc. CCPR/C/70/D/547/1993 (2000), para. 9.4.

rather than traditional Maori fishing techniques, and in adopting this approach, the HRC highlighted that the notion of culture is not static, and while it does protect 'traditional' cultural practices, these practices may have evolved over the centuries. Importantly, by avoiding the danger of adopting a very rigid or 'frozen' approach to the meaning of cultural activities, the HRC has consistently stated that indigenous peoples who adapt their traditional cultural activities over the years with the help of modern technology are not prevented from invoking international covenant protections.[18]

This 'non-frozen' rights approach is also reflected in that adopted by the African Court on Human and Peoples' Rights in its 2017 decision concerning the Ogiek community in Kenya (the *Ogiek* Case). The *Ogiek* Case raised the issue of 'authenticity' of cultural practices, with the court stressing 'that stagnation or the existence of a static way of life is not a defining element of culture or cultural distinctiveness. It is natural that some aspects of indigenous populations' culture such as a certain way of dressing or group symbols could change over time'.[19] These decisions are important as they highlight the fact that IHRL does not adopt a rigid and frozen approach to cultural practices and 'authenticity', as this type of approach would make it irrelevant to most communities who have adapted their traditional cultural use of natural resources to modern living.[20] Wolfe analyses the danger of 'repressive authenticity' in his study of Australian aboriginal people forced to prove their 'authentic' and 'traditional' ways of using natural resources in order to establish native title claims.[21] According to (former) Australian Aboriginal and Torres Strait Islanders Social Justice Commissioner, 'the right to enjoy a culture is not "frozen" at some point in time when culture was supposedly "pure" or "traditional". The enjoyment of culture should not be falsely restricted as a result of anachronistic notions of the "authenticity" of the culture.'[22]

Another debate concerning this legal approach relates to defining whether activities that have an economical aspect could qualify as traditional cultural practices. Some States have argued that economic activities should not been regarded as traditional cultural activities, but rather as economic activities. For example, when the HRC examined *Ivan Kitok* regarding reindeer herding by a Sami community in Sweden, one of the arguments developed by the government was that reindeer herding was more an economic, rather than a purely cultural, activity. Here, the HRC noted that, while 'the regulation of an economic activity is normally a matter for the State alone', if 'that activity is an essential element in the culture of an ethnic community, its application to an individual may fall under article 27 of the Covenant'.[23]

---

[18] *Ilmari Länsman et al.* (n 16).

[19] *African Commission on Human and Peoples' Rights v Republic of Kenya*, Application No. 006/2012 (2017), para. 185 (the *Ogiek* Case).

[20] See John Borrows, 'Frozen Rights in Canada: Constitutional Interpretation and the Trickster', 22(1) *American Indian Law Review*, 1997, 37–64.

[21] Patrick Wolfe, *Settler Colonialism and the Transformation of Anthropology: The Politics and Poetics of an Ethnographic Event* (Cassell, 1999).

[22] Report of the Aboriginal and Torres Strait Islanders Social Justice Commissioner to the Attorney General, Aboriginal and Torres Strait Islander Social Justice Commissioner, Native Title Report 2000.

[23] *Ivan Kitok v Sweden*, Communication No. 197/1985, CCPR/C/33/D/197/1985 (1988), para. 9.2.

The point of the HRC here is that ultimately, if for the concerned communities such an activity is part of their cultural way of life, then States should recognize it as such, even if such cultural activity has an economical element. This decision was later re-affirmed in other cases in which the HRC declared that economic activities might come within the realm of Article 27 if they constitute an essential element of the culture of an indigenous community, e.g. fishing, herding, hunting.[24] However, to the contrary, the HRC has also rejected cultural claims, for example, *J.G.A. Diergaardt (late Captain of the Rehoboth Baster Community) et al.*, concerning cattle herders in Namibia (the Rehoboth community), where it did not find a violation of Article 27. In its decision, it stated that although 'the link of the Rehoboth community to the lands in question dates back some 125 years, it is not the result of a relationship that would have given rise to a distinct culture'.[25] In their concurring opinion, HRC members Evatt and Quiroga further clarified that point, arguing that:

the authors have defined their culture almost solely in terms of the economic activity of grazing cattle. They cannot show that they enjoy a distinct culture which is intimately bound up with or dependent on the use of these particular lands, to which they moved a little over a century ago, or that the diminution of their access to the lands has undermined any such culture. Their claim is, essentially, an economic rather than a cultural claim and does not draw the protection of article 27.[26]

The distinction between cultural and economic activities has also been an issue examined by the Inter-American Court of Human Rights (IACtHR). In *Saramaka People*, the IACtHR analysed the impact of logging and mining activities undertaken on indigenous territory and to what extent these extractive activities affected the traditional use of natural resources essential to the cultural survival of the concerned community. The IACtHR declared that 'the members of the Saramaka people have not traditionally used gold as part of their cultural identity or economic system. Despite possible individual exceptions, members of the Saramaka people do not identify themselves with gold nor have demonstrated a particular relationship with this natural resource.'[27] More generally, it is difficult to demonstrate a cultural attachment to sub-soil resources, notably primary resources exploited by the mining industry.[28]

The IACtHR also declares that 'another crucial factor to be considered is whether the restriction amounts to a denial of their traditions and customs in a way that endangers the very survival of the group and of its members'.[29] The Court noted that 'survival' entails much more than physical survival. It also includes a people's need to

[24] See *Apirana Mahuika et al. v New Zealand*, Communication No. 547/1993, UN Doc. CCPR/C/70/D/547/1993 (2000).

[25] *J.G.A. Diergaardt (late Captain of the Rehoboth Baster Community) et al. v Namibia*, Comm. No. 762/1997, UN Doc CCPR/C/69/D/760/1997 (2000), 7.

[26] Ibid., Concurring Opinion, Evatt and Quiroga.   [27]   Ibid., para. 155.

[28] However, see the Constitutional Court of South Africa, *Alexkor v Richtersveld Community*, 2003 (12) BCLR 1301; in this case the community managed to prove a traditional usage of copper (see para. 61 and ss).

[29] *Case of the Saramaka People v Suriname*, Preliminary Objections, Merits, Reparations and Costs, Judgment. Series C No. 172 (2007), para. 128.

'preserve, protect and guarantee the special relationship that [they] have with their territory', so that 'they may continue living their traditional way of life, and that their distinct cultural identity, social structure, economic system, customs, beliefs and traditions are respected, guaranteed and protected'.[30] This does not mean that any restriction on access to natural resources is prohibited, but rather that these restrictions should not affect the 'cultural survival' of the concerned communities,[31] and this notion of 'cultural survival' has been affirmed in several other rulings of the court.[32] This approach is also consistent with Article 8 of UNDRIP, which provides that States shall effectively prevent and provide redress for 'any action which has the aim or effect of depriving [indigenous peoples] of their integrity as distinct peoples, or of their cultural values or ethnic identities; [and] [a]ny action which has the aim or effect of dispossessing them of their lands, territories or resources'.

Overall, IHRL recognizes that the protection of cultural practices and traditional methods of using natural resources is essential to ensure the cultural survival of indigenous peoples. This link between cultural practices using natural resources and a specific 'minority way of life' falls under the umbrella of indigenous peoples' rights, which also has been expanded to Afro-descendant communities in Latin America.[33] For example, the IACtHR recognized this link in *Moiwana Village* and *Saramaka People*.[34] It is still undecided as to whether this approach might extend to other minorities under the broader framework of cultural diversity.

2.2 Cultural diversity, natural resources, and identity

Traditional and cultural use of natural resources can constitute an important element of a particular group's or community's culture. Traditional ways of using natural resources constitute an important factor in maintaining nature's biodiversity as well as humanity's cultural diversity. Recently, international law has increasingly supported and promoted cultural diversity.[35] The preamble of the 2001 UNESCO Universal Declaration on Cultural Diversity declares that 'culture should be regarded as the set of distinctive spiritual, material, intellectual and emotional features of society or a social group [that] ... encompasses, in addition to art and literature, lifestyles, ways

---

[30] Ibid., paras 125–7.
[31] Ibid., para. 128: 'the State may restrict the Saramakas' right to use and enjoy lands and resources only when such restriction complies with the aforementioned requirements and, additionally, when it does not deny their survival as a tribal people'.
[32] See, for example, *Case of the Kichwa Indigenous People of Sarayaku v Ecuador*, Series C No. 245 (2012), 146; and see *Rio Negro Massacres v Guatemala*, Series C No. 250 (2012), 177.
[33] See Ariel E. Dulitzky, 'When Afro-Descendants Became "Tribal Peoples": The Inter-American Human Rights System and Rural Black Communities', 15 *UCLA Journal of International Law and Foreign Affairs*, 2010, 45; IACHR, Indigenous Peoples, Afro-Descendent Communities, and Natural Resources: Human Rights Protection in the Context of Extraction, Exploitation, and Development Activities, OEA/Ser.L/V/II., Doc. 47/15 (2015).
[34] *Moiwana Village v Suriname*, Series C No. 124 (2005); *Saramaka People v Suriname*, Series C No. 172 (2007).
[35] See Lilian Richieri Hanania (ed.), *Cultural Diversity in International Law: The Effectiveness of the UNESCO Convention on the Protection and Promotion of the Diversity of Cultural Expressions* (Routledge, 2014).

of living together, value systems, traditions and beliefs'.[36] The 2005 Convention on the Protection and Promotion of the Diversity of Cultural Expressions affirms that cultural diversity can be protected only if human rights are guaranteed, including the right to cultural expression (Art. 2.1).[37] Prior to that, the 2003 Convention on the Safeguarding of Intangible Cultural Heritage included specific references to community participation, cultural practices, and knowledge, including oral traditions and expressions.[38] Several UNESCO instruments have adopted a similar approach highlighting that cultural practices, traditions, and traditional knowledge should be protected and promoted to support cultural diversity.[39]

In terms of IHRL, references to cultural diversity's connection to natural resources have appeared in the work of some of the international human rights treaty bodies.[40] The whole approach of the HRC regarding cultural rights of minorities and their traditional practices related to the use of natural resources is based on the rationale of protecting specific minority ways of life.[41] The HRC declares that the purpose of such protection is 'enriching the fabric of society as a whole'.[42] The echo of this notion appears in the decision of the African Commission on Human and Peoples' Rights (ACHPR) in the *Endorois* Case against Kenya, where the Commission states that 'Article 17 of the Charter is of a dual dimension in both its individual and collective nature, protecting, on the one hand, individuals' participation in the cultural life of their community and, on the other hand, *obliging the state to promote and protect traditional values recognised by a community*'.[43] It added that Article 17 requires governments to take measures 'aimed at the conservation, development and diffusion of culture,' such as promoting 'cultural identity as a factor of mutual appreciation among individuals, groups, nations and regions; … [and] promoting awareness and enjoyment of cultural heritage of national ethnic groups and minorities and of indigenous sectors of the population'.[44]

Outside the field of indigenous peoples' rights, the CESCR has highlighted the importance of natural resources in its General Comment on cultural rights. The CESCR acknowledged that access to cultural life covers the right of everyone (alone, in association with others, or as a community) to follow a way of life associated with

---

[36] Universal Declaration on Cultural Diversity, adopted 2 November 2001, UNESCO Gen. Conf., 31st Session, UNESCO Doc. CLT.2002/WS/9 (2002), Preamble.

[37] Convention on the Protection and Promotion of the Diversity of Cultural Expressions, adopted 20 October 2005, 33d Session, Art. 2(1), UNESCO Doc. CLT/CEI/DCE/2007/PI/32 (2005).

[38] Convention for the Safeguarding of the Intangible Cultural Heritage 2003, Art. 2.

[39] For review and analysis, see Silvia Borelli and Federico Lenzerini (eds), *Cultural Heritage, Cultural Rights, Cultural Diversity: New Developments in International Law* (Martinus Nijhoff, 2012).

[40] See Yvonne Donders, 'Do Cultural Diversity and Human Rights Make a Good Match?' 61(199) *International Social Science Journal*, 2010, 15.

[41] General Comment No. 23, The Rights of Minorities (Art. 27), UN Doc. CCPR/C/21/Rev.1/Add.5.

[42] Ibid., para. 9.

[43] *African Commission on Human and Peoples' Rights: Centre for Minority Rights Development (Kenya) and Minority Rights Group International on behalf of Endorois Welfare Council v Kenya* (February 2010), para. 241.

[44] Ibid., para. 246.

the use of cultural goods and resources, e.g. land, water, and biodiversity.[45] It is noteworthy that the CESCR refers to 'everyone' and not only indigenous peoples or minorities. It also stated that the right includes the 'availability of nature's gifts, such as seas, lakes, rivers, mountains, forests, and nature reserves, including the flora and fauna found there, which give nations their character and biodiversity'.[46] Again, the rights-holders are 'everyone' and not any particular group. In its approach, the CESCR confirms that these cultural connections to using natural resources help protect humanity's cultural diversity.

One specific approach concerns the realization of the right to food; the CESCR noted that this right includes the protection of specific cultural forms of food production. In its General Comment on the right to food, the CESCR stressed that the core content of the right to adequate food implies 'the availability of food in a quantity and quality sufficient to satisfy the dietary needs of individuals, free from adverse substances, and *acceptable within a given culture*'.[47] Adequate food means that it is produced according to local cultural practices. The CESCR also noted that this includes cultural or consumer acceptability which 'implies the need also to take into account, as far as possible, perceived non-nutrient-based values attached to food and food consumption and informed consumer concerns regarding the nature of accessible food supplies'.[48] Similarly, in its General Comment on the right to water, the CESCR paid specific attention to the cultural values and traditions attached to water usage. It noted that water is essential to enjoying certain cultural practices and that 'water should be treated as a social and cultural good'.[49] It particularly noted that States should not arbitrarily interfere 'with customary or traditional arrangements for water allocation'.[50] Overall, whether related to access to water or to food production, the approach of the CESCR is based on supporting the diversity of cultural use of natural resources.

The importance of cultural diversity, and its expression via different uses of natural resources, is recognized in other international instruments. For example, the FAO guidelines on small-scale fisheries declares that:

States, in accordance with their legislation, should ensure that small-scale fishers, fish workers and their communities have secure, equitable, and *socially and culturally appropriate tenure rights to fishery resources* (marine and inland) and small-scale fishing areas and adjacent land, with a special attention paid to women with respect to tenure rights.[51]

At the regional level, the European Union Land Policy Guidelines state that:

---

[45] General Comment No. 21: Right of Everyone to Take Part in Cultural Life (Art. 15, para. 1(a), of the International Covenant on Economic, Social and Cultural Rights), UN Doc. E/C.12/GC/21, para. 15b.
[46] Ibid., para. 16(a).
[47] CESCR, General Comment No. 12 (1999), E/C.12/1999/5, para. 8 (emphasis added).
[48] Ibid., para. 11.
[49] CESCR, General Comment No. 15 (2003), E/C.12/2002/11, paras 6, 11.
[50] Ibid., para. 21.
[51] FAO, *Voluntary Guidelines for Securing Sustainable Small-Scale Fisheries in the Context of Food Security and Poverty Eradication* (Small-Scale Fisheries Guidelines), 2014, Guideline 5.3 (emphasis added).

[l]and constitutes an asset and a source of wealth for families and individuals as well as for communities, *with strong links to cultural and spiritual values* .... The interrelated social, institutional, and political factors involved in land make it an asset different from all others. Land is never just a commodity. *It combines being a factor of production, with its role as family or community property, a capital asset and a source of identity.*[52]

However, it is necessary to note that cultural practices connected to the use of natural resources are not necessarily beneficial, and could lead to violations of human rights, e.g. the prohibition of lower caste Dalits in India from using water wells used by higher castes. In many rural localities across India, access to water is still restricted for Dalits as their physical proximity or touch is meant to 'defile' the natural resource, thus becoming unfit for consumption by upper castes.[53] In 2016, the Special Rapporteur on minorities undertook a specific report on the issue of caste and descendent-based discrimination, specifically noting the restriction on access to water. She noted that:

[i]n Bangladesh and India, Dalits are often systematically excluded from access to water and sanitation. Reports indicate that Dalits may be prohibited from fetching water; have to wait in different queues when accessing wells; and, in the event of water shortage, must give non-Dalits priority. Dalits may be subjected to large-scale violence and physical attacks by members of the dominant caste when attempting to access facilities in areas inhabited by them. Dalit women are particularly vulnerable to physical violence from members of the dominant castes while collecting water from public wells and taps.[54]

More generally, the Special Rapporteur on the human right to safe drinking water and sanitation highlighted the potential stigma associated with lower castes accessing water, as these lower-caste people are often restricted in their access to shared or common water and sanitation facilities.[55] The CESCR General Comment on water declares that '[w]ater and water facilities and services must be accessible to all, including the most vulnerable or marginalized sections of the population, in law and in fact, without discrimination on any of the prohibited grounds'.[56]

Negative cultural practices connected to using natural resources may also result in discrimination against women and restricted women's access and use of some natural resources.[57] These violations have been addressed by international human

---

[52] EU Task Force on Land Tenure, 'EU Land Policy Guidelines: Guidelines for Support to Land Policy Design and Land Policy Reform Processes in Developing Countries', November 2004, at 2 (emphasis added).

[53] See Rakesh Tiwary and Sanjiv J. Phansalkar, 'Dalits' Access to Water: Patterns of Deprivation and Discrimination', 3(1) *International Journal of Rural Management*, 2007, 43–67; and Rakesh Tiwary, 'Explanations in Resource Inequality: Exploring Scheduled Caste Position in Water Access Structure', 2(1) *International Journal of Rural Management*, 2006, 85–106.

[54] Report of the Special Rapporteur on Minority Issues, UN Doc. A/HRC/31/56 (2016), para. 82 (references omitted).

[55] See UN Doc. A/HRC/21/42, para. 12.   [56] Para. 12(c)(iii).

[57] See Bernadette Resurreccion and Rebecca Elmhirst (eds), *Gender and Natural Resource Management: Livelihoods, Mobility and Interventions* (Earthscan, 2008); Ruth S. Meinzen-Dick, Lynn R. Brown, Hilary Sims Feldstein, and Agnes R. Quisumbing, 'Gender, Property Rights, and Natural Resources', 25(8) *World Development*, 1997, 1303–15; Ann Whitehead and Dzodzi Tsikata, 'Policy Discourses on Women's Land Rights in Sub-Saharan Africa: The Implications of the Return to the Customary', 3(1) *Journal of Agrarian Change*, 2003, 67–112.

rights treaty bodies. In its General Recommendation No. 34, CEDAW recalls States' obligations to take measures to 'achieve substantive equality of rural women in relation to land and natural resources', including communal lands, ensuring that customary systems do not discriminate against them. Legislation should also guarantee 'women's rights to land, water and other natural resources on an equal basis with men, irrespective of their civil and marital status'.[58] In General Recommendation No. 21, CEDAW further recommends that States respect women's equal rights in the context of agrarian reform or redistribution of land.[59] Other potential clashes between certain communities' cultural way of life and their use of natural resources could include environmental damages, e.g. traditional indigenous whale-hunting communities.[60] All these potential clashes are not unusual in IHRL. The right of everyone to take part in cultural life is closely linked to the enjoyment of other rights recognized in international human rights instruments. For example, Article 4 of ICESCR gives States the possibility to limit the enjoyment of the rights in the Covenant. This limitation is on the condition that it is determined by law, that it is compatible with the nature of these rights, and that it is solely for the purpose of promoting the general welfare in a democratic society. The CESCR states that 'applying limitations to the right of everyone to take part in cultural life may be necessary in certain circumstances, in particular in the case of negative practices, including those attributed to customs and traditions, that infringe upon other human rights'.[61] The CESCR added that 'a violation also occurs when a State party fails to take steps to combat practices harmful to the well-being of a person or group of persons … including [harmful practices] attributed to customs and traditions'.[62] In general, IHRL strives to offer a flexible balance between the protection of communities' cultural practices and respect for the fundamental rights of individual members of these communities. Allowing for any potential clashes and finding resolutions on a case-by-case basis provides enough flexibility for long-term social and cultural changes, rather than top-down approaches that could lead to further discord.[63] Ultimately, allowing such flexibility is part of the recognition of cultural diversity.

---

[58] CEDAW, General Recommendation No. 34 on the Rights of Rural Women, CEDAW/C/GC/34, para. 58–59.

[59] CEDAW, General Recommendation No. 21 on Equality in Marriage and Family Relations, para. 27 (contained in A/49/38, Chapter I, A).

[60] See Nancy C. Doubleday, 'Aboriginal Subsistence Whaling: The Right of Inuit to Hunt Whales and Implications for International Environmental Law', 17 *Denver Journal of International Law & Policy*, 1988, 373; Chris Wold, 'Integrating Indigenous Rights into Multilateral Environmental Agreements: The International Whaling Commission and Aboriginal Subsistence Whaling', 40 *Boston College of International & Comparative Law Review*, 2017, 63.

[61] General Comment No. 21, Right of Everyone to Take Part in Cultural Life, UN Doc. E/C.12/GC/21 (2009), para. 19.

[62] Ibid., para. 64.

[63] For further analysis, see Johanna Gibson's in-depth analysis: *Community Resources: Intellectual Property, International Trade and Protection of Traditional Knowledge* (Routledge, 2016).

3. The Cultural Heritage Approach: Traditional Knowledge and Natural Resources

There is no single and authoritative definition of what constitutes cultural heritage, but the international legal framework governing cultural heritage has evolved considerably in recent decades.[64] Although distinctions are often made between tangible, intangible, and natural heritage, these three interconnected categories are all relevant to examining connections between cultural heritage, natural resources, and IHRL. For example, intangible cultural heritage includes traditional knowledge connected to ancestral methods of food production, such as *swidden* agricultural methods,[65] or cultural knowledge about gathering natural resources. It also includes biocultural heritage, e.g. cultural use of seeds and plants. The overall international legal framework governing cultural heritage law is extremely complex and fragmented as it is composed of instruments and norms across different legal fields, including cultural heritage law, intellectual property law, and traditional knowledge and folklore heritage norms. All these different elements of what constitutes cultural heritage law are relevant to natural resources.[66] Although IHRL is a latecomer to the field, cultural heritage is increasingly becoming an important element of IHRL.[67] In terms of cultural heritage and natural resources, IHRL has engaged in two main ways with the other fields of international cultural heritage. First, it supports a better inclusion and recognition of indigenous peoples and local communities' rights over their own cultural heritage sites, notably when these natural areas are classified as 'humanity's cultural heritage'. Secondly, it does so via the emergence of a human rights-based approach to the protection of traditional knowledge and practices connected to natural resources.

3.1 'World Heritage Sites', natural resources, and human rights

The main global treaty on 'world heritage' is the 1972 Convention Concerning the Protection of the World Cultural and Natural Heritage.[68] This convention addresses both cultural heritage (such as sacred sites, monuments, or buildings) and natural

---

[64] See Janet Blake, 'On Defining the Cultural Heritage', 49(1) *International & Comparative Law Quarterly*, 2000, 61–85; and Report of the Independent Expert in the Field of Cultural Rights, Farida Shaheed, UN Doc. A/HRC/17/38 (2011).

[65] *Swidden* agriculture, also known as shifting cultivation, refers to a technique of rotational farming in which land is cleared for cultivation (normally by fire) and then left to regenerate after a few years.

[66] See Helaine Silverman and D. Fairchild Ruggles (eds), *Cultural Heritage and Human Rights* (Springer, 2007); Michele Langfield, William Logan, and Mairead Nic Craith (eds), *Cultural Diversity, Heritage and Human Rights: Intersections in Theory and Practice* (Routledge, 2009).

[67] As highlighted in the report of the Special Rapporteur in the Field of Cultural Rights (A/HRC/ 17/38), the right of access to and enjoyment of cultural heritage forms part of IHRL. See Report of the Independent Expert in the Field of Cultural Rights, Farida Shaheed, UN Doc. A/HRC/17/38 (2011). See also Borelli and Lenzerini (n 39).

[68] The Convention Concerning the Protection of the World Cultural and Natural Heritage, 16 November 1972, 11 *International Legal Materials*, 1972, 1358.

heritage (such as biodiversity hotspots or outstanding geological formations).[69] Its goal is to ensure the identification, protection, conservation, presentation, and transmission of cultural and natural heritage of 'outstanding universal value' future generations. However, this approach is still largely based on the difference between 'cultural' and 'natural' heritage, where the latter is defined as (more or less) 'pristine' natural sites that leave little space for interaction between humans and nature.[70] For many indigenous peoples and local communities, this dichotomy does not correspond to their reality, where centuries of interaction between nature and cultural practices have shaped their cultural heritage.[71] The UN Expert Mechanism on the Rights of Indigenous Peoples (EMRIP) notes that, for indigenous peoples, cultural and natural values are inseparably interwoven and should be managed and protected in a holistic manner.[72] The division between 'natural' and 'cultural' heritage does not integrate such a holistic approach to cultural heritage. UNESCO and related cultural heritage agencies have tried to build a bridge between 'culture' and 'nature' to address this dichotomy; it is possible for sites to be listed as 'mixed sites' if they fulfil both natural and cultural criteria for inscription on the World Heritage List. Moreover, in 1992, the category of 'cultural landscape' was added to include places where manifestations of the interaction between people and their natural environment are considered of outstanding universal value.[73] However, despite these efforts, the gap still exists between what is seen as 'cultural' and 'natural' heritage when it comes to the classification and nomination of heritage sites. Disko's in-depth analysis on the issue shows that the approach to declaring World Heritage Sites is still dominated by a distinction between cultural and natural criteria.[74] This results in a divorce between indigenous peoples' and local communities' holistic perception of cultural and natural elements, with the international legal approach favouring 'culture' and 'nature' as two distinct entities.

The other significant issue in terms of human rights relates to the nomination process of sites of 'outstanding universal value'. There is often a serious lack of

---

[69] See Human Rights Council, Promotion and Protection of the Rights of Indigenous Peoples with Respect to their Cultural Heritage, Study by the Expert Mechanism on the Rights of Indigenous Peoples, 19 August 2015, A/HRC/30/53.

[70] See David Lowenthal, 'Natural and Cultural Heritage', 11(1) *International Journal of Heritage Studies*, 2005, 81–92.

[71] See Stefan Disko, 'World Heritage Sites in Indigenous Peoples' Territories: Ways of Ensuring Respect for Indigenous Cultures, Values and Human Rights'. In: Dieter Offenhäußer, Walther Ch. Zimmerli, and Marie-Thérèse Albert (eds), *World Heritage and Cultural Diversity* (German Commission for UNESCO, 2010), p. 167.

[72] Study by the Expert Mechanism on the Rights of Indigenous Peoples, Promotion and Protection of the Rights of Indigenous Peoples with Respect to their Cultural Heritage, UN Doc. A/HRC/EMRIP/2015/2 (2015).

[73] See Kathryn Whitby-Last, 'Article 1: Cultural Landscapes'. In: Francesco Francioni and Federico Lenzerini (eds), *The 1972 World Heritage Convention: A Commentary* (OUP, 2008), pp. 51–62; Ken Taylor, Archer St. Clair, and Nora J. Mitchell (eds), *Conserving Cultural Landscapes: Challenges and New Direction* (Routledge, 2015).

[74] See Stefan Disko, 'Indigenous Cultural Heritage in the Implementation of UNESCO's World Heritage Convention: Opportunities, Obstacles and Challenges'. In: Alexandra Xanthaki, Sanna Valkonen, Leena Heinämäki, and Piia Nuorgam (eds), *Indigenous Peoples' Cultural Heritage: Rights, Debates, Challenges* (Brill, 2017), pp. 39–77.

regulation to ensure the meaningful participation from the most concerned communities living on sites nominated to become World Heritage Sites.[75] The process is usually dominated by governments, heritage experts, and bureaucrats, with a lack of integration of other less 'expert' opinions of heritage sites, notably those of indigenous peoples and local communities. The nomination of a World Heritage Site as a place of 'outstanding universal value' takes place via a process that often leaves no room for the concerned local communities. Sites are nominated by States, although the World Heritage Committee has the final say on whether a site is inscribed on the World Heritage List. As Lixinski suggests, very little place is made for communities' involvement in protecting heritage, and in determining what their heritage actually is, as under the dominant legal system, peoples and local communities 'are assumed to be fairly represented by States in the Convention's processes'.[76]

This is representative of the overarching legal process for nomination, management, and control of World Heritage Sites.[77] As Disko suggests, while the World Heritage Committee 'has over the years increasingly recognized the importance of involving local communities in the protection of World Heritage Sites, and included several references to local communities (and more recently also to indigenous peoples) in the Operational Guidelines, their involvement continues to be largely seen as a means to an end, rather than an end in itself'.[78] Aside from the problematic issue of lack of participation in itself, the disregard for local communities negatively effects their rights to access to their own cultural heritage. In many situations, classification as a World Heritage Site has meant a loss of control over these natural resources and restrictions on traditional uses of them.[79] It is this lack of participation, loss of access rights, and disregard for indigenous peoples' rights over their land and natural resources that has led IHRL to engage more directly with the process governing World Heritage Sites.

Traditionally, IHRL has not engaged with the specific process established by UNESCO, but recent human rights violations have changed this dynamic.[80] For example, listing Kenya's Great Rift Valley Lake System on the World Heritage List in 2011 led to clashes between cultural heritage law and human rights. The listing of Lake

---

[75] See Nicolas Adell, Regina F. Bendix, Chiara Bortolotto, and Markus Tauschek (eds), *Between Imagined Communities and Communities of Practice: Participation, Territory and the Making of Heritage* (Universitätsverlag Göttingen, 2015).

[76] Lucas Lixinski, 'Heritage for Whom? Individuals' and Communities' Roles in International Cultural Heritage Law'. In: Federico Lenzerini and Ana Filipa Vrdoljak (eds), *International Law for Common Goods: Normative Perspectives on Human Rights, Culture and Nature* (Hart Publishing, 2014), pp. 193, 196.

[77] With few exceptions, when States' authorities willingly decide to include indigenous or local communities in the process. For illustrations and analysis, see Stener Ekern, William Logan, Birgitte Sauge, and Amund Sinding-Larsen (eds), *World Heritage Management and Human Rights* (Routledge, 2016).

[78] Stefan Disko (n 74), pp. 74–5.

[79] See Stefan Disko and Helen Tugendhat (eds), *World Heritage Sites and Indigenous Peoples Rights* (International Work Group for Indigenous Affairs, 2014).

[80] See Rosemary J. Coombe and Joseph F. Turcotte, 'Indigenous Cultural Heritage in Development and Trade: Perspectives from the Dynamics of Intangible Cultural Heritage Law and Policy'. In: Christoph Graber, Karolina Kuprecht, and Jessica Lai (eds), *International Trade in Indigenous Cultural Heritage: Legal and Policy Issues* (Edward Elgar, 2012), pp. 272–305.

Bogoria National Reserve as part of this process occurred without the involvement of the indigenous Endorois community upon whose ancestral land the reserve is located. Lake Bogoria has been at the centre of an ongoing dispute between the Endorois community and the public authorities for decades, leading to a 2010 decision by the ACHPR supporting indigenous peoples' rights.[81] Consequently, in 2011, the ACHPR took the unusual decision of adopting a specific resolution condemning the inscription of Lake Bogoria National Reserve in Kenya on the World Heritage List,[82] noting its concern that the classification of the reserve had occurred in violation of the human rights of the Endorois community. Outside the specific case of Lake Bogoria, the ACHPR also chose to highlight a general lack of integration of, and respect for, the human rights of indigenous peoples concerning the inscription of ancestral territories on the World Heritage list. The resolution notes 'with concern that there are numerous World Heritage Sites in Africa that have been inscribed without the free, prior and informed consent of the indigenous peoples in whose territories they are located and whose management frameworks are not consistent with the principles of the UN Declaration on the Rights of Indigenous Peoples.' The fact that the ACHPR chose to highlight the issue through the adoption of such a resolution is indicative of a common lack of respect for the rights of indigenous peoples in the implementation of the World Heritage Convention. The resolution is also an indication of the general lack of integration of and understanding on the rights of indigenous peoples in the context of World Heritage.

Because of this, the UN specialized human rights institutions working to support the rights of indigenous peoples have called for reforms in the way the World Heritage Convention and its related processes ignore the rights of indigenous peoples.[83] In its General Comment on Cultural Rights, the CESCR highlighted that States should 'allow and encourage the participation of persons belonging to minority groups, indigenous peoples or to other communities in the design and implementation of laws and policies that affect them. In particular, States parties should obtain their free and informed prior consent when the preservation of their cultural resources, especially those associated with their way of life and cultural expression, are at risk.'[84] More generally, international human rights monitoring bodies have called for better inclusion and respect of indigenous peoples' rights in the process of designing and managing World Heritage Sites.[85] From this perspective, IHRL has clearly started to engage more systematically with the process governing World Heritage Sites. Lixinski notes that this gives a more 'human' dimension to cultural heritage law,

---

[81] See Korir Sing'Oei Abraham, 'Ignoring Indigenous Peoples' Rights: The Case of Lake Bogoria's Designation as a UNESCO World Heritage Site'. In: Disko and Tugendhat (n 79), pp. 163, 171.

[82] Resolution on the Protection of Indigenous Peoples' Rights in the Context of the World Heritage Convention and the Designation of Lake Bogoria as a World Heritage Site, adopted at the ACHPR's 50th Ordinary Session held from 24th October to 5th November 2011.

[83] For references, see Study by the Expert Mechanism on the Rights of Indigenous Peoples, Promotion and Protection of the Rights of Indigenous Peoples with Respect to their Cultural Heritage, UN Doc. A/HRC/EMRIP/2015/2 (2015).

[84] (n 61) para. 55.   [85] For analysis and references, see Disko and Tugendhat (n 79).

but that it should also be taken with a 'pinch of salt', as ultimately the process is still very much dominated by States, international organizations, and heritage experts.[86]

3.2 Intangible heritage, traditional knowledge, and human rights

There is a direct correlation between intangible heritage and natural resources. According to the 2003 UNESCO Convention for the Safeguarding of the Intangible Cultural Heritage, intangible cultural heritage refers to 'practices, representations, expressions, knowledge, skills, . . . that communities, groups and, in some cases, individuals recognize as part of their cultural heritage'.[87] This includes 'knowledge and practices concerning nature and the universe', including traditional knowledge which emerged from the interaction between communities and groups with their natural environment.[88] The term 'traditional knowledge' refers to a living body of knowledge that is developed, sustained, and passed on through generations within a community, often forming part of its cultural and spiritual identity.[89] Traditional knowledge also includes cultural practices on the use of natural resources, for example, agricultural knowledge or knowledge associated with genetic resources. The international legal protection of traditional knowledge is emerging from several legal fields, including cultural heritage,[90] protection of biodiversity,[91] desertification,[92] food and agriculture,[93] health,[94] and sustainable development.[95] Once again, IHRL is a latecomer, and has arguably been influenced by the developments taking place under other legal frameworks.[96]

---

[86] Lucas Lixinski, 'Heritage for Whom? Individuals' and Communities' Roles in International Cultural Heritage Law'. In: Federico Lenzerini and Ana Filipa Vrdoljak (eds), *International Law for Common Goods: Normative Perspectives on Human Rights, Culture and Nature* (Hart Publishing, 2014), p. 213.

[87] UNESCO Convention for the Safeguarding of the Intangible Cultural Heritage (2003), Art. 2.

[88] Ibid.

[89] As noted by WIPO, traditional knowledge refers to 'the know-how, skills and practices that are developed, sustained and passed on from generation to generation within a community, often forming part of its cultural or spiritual identity'. See Intergovernmental Committee on Intellectual Property and Genetic Resources, Traditional Knowledge and Folklore, 'List and Brief Technical Explanation of Various Forms in which Traditional Knowledge May be Found', 17th Session, WIPO/GRTKF/IC/17/INF/9 (November 2010), para. 3.

[90] See UNESCO Convention on the Protection and Promotion of the Diversity of Cultural Expressions (2007), 2440 UNTS 311, Preamble at 8.

[91] Convention on Biological Diversity (1992) 1760 UNTS 79 ['CBD'] Arts 8(j) and 10(c).

[92] UN Convention to Combat Desertification in Countries Experiencing Serious Drought and/or Desertification, Particularly in Africa (1994) 1954 UNTS 3 ['UNCCD'], Art. 18.2(b).

[93] International Treaty on Plant Genetic Resources for Food and Agriculture (2001) 2400 UNTS 303 ['ITPGR'], Art. 9.2(a).

[94] World Health Organization Declaration of Alma-Ata, International Conference on Primary Health Care, Alma-Ata, (1978), Art. VII.7.

[95] See Rio Declaration on Environment and Development (1993) A/Res/48/190, Principle 22; and Agenda 21, in Report of the United Nations Conference on Environment and Development (1992) A/CONF.151/26/Rev.1, Vol. 1, 9, at 26.3(a)(iii).

[96] See Anja Meyer, 'International Environmental Law and Human Rights: Towards the Explicit Recognition of Traditional Knowledge', 10(1) *Review of European Community and International Environmental Law*, 2001, 37–46.

Probably one of the most significant international legal frameworks concerning traditional knowledge and natural resources emerges from the Convention on Biological Diversity (CBD), which specifically acknowledges traditional knowledge and practices of indigenous peoples and local communities.[97] Its emphasis is on the obligations to 'protect and encourage customary use of biological resources in accordance with traditional cultural practices that are compatible with conservation or sustainable use requirements'.[98] In this context, traditional knowledge is protected insofar as it is relevant to the conservation of biological diversity.[99] It is important to note that the impact of the CBD on traditional knowledge goes beyond the objectives of conservation and biological diversity. A significant element of the process put in place relates to the direct participation, control, and management of traditional knowledge by the most concerned communities. The 2010 Nagoya Protocol, which was adopted to complement the CBD, includes several provisions supporting the rights of indigenous peoples and local communities over their traditional knowledge.[100] Drawing on the UNDRIP and IHRL, the protocol calls for the respect of the prior and informed consent of indigenous and local communities before any outside use of traditional knowledge associated with genetic resources.[101] It includes a number of defences against outsiders accessing indigenous and local communities' traditional knowledge and the obligation for 'not restricting the customary use of genetic resources and associated traditional knowledge within and among indigenous communities.'[102]

Conversely, IHRL has increasingly been integrating recognition of traditional knowledge as an important element of indigenous peoples' rights.[103] Article 31 of UNDRIP proclaims that:

Indigenous peoples have the right to maintain, control, protect and develop their cultural heritage, traditional knowledge and traditional cultural expressions, as well as the manifestations of their sciences, technologies and cultures, including human and genetic resources,

---

[97] Under Article 8(j) of the Convention on Biological Diversity, States shall 'respect, preserve and maintain knowledge, innovations and practices of indigenous and local communities embodying traditional lifestyles relevant for the conservation and sustainable use of biological diversity and promote their wider application with the approval and involvement of the holders of such knowledge, innovations and practices and encourage the equitable sharing of the benefits arising from the utilization of such knowledge, innovations and practices'.

[98] Article 10(c) CBD.

[99] This is examined in more detail in Chapter 6, which focuses on the connection between environmental protection and IHRL.

[100] Nagoya Protocol on Access to Genetic Resources and the Fair and Equitable Sharing of Benefits Arising from Their Utilization to the Convention on Biological Diversity 2010 (Nagoya Protocol), Arts 5(2), 12(1), and 12(2).

[101] See Kabir Bavikatte and Daniel F. Robinson, 'Towards a People's History of the Law: Biocultural Jurisprudence and the Nagoya Protocol on Access and Benefit Sharing', 7 *Law, Environment and Development Journal*, 2011, 35.

[102] Ibid., Art. 12.4.

[103] See Rosemary J. Coombe, 'The Recognition of Indigenous Peoples' and Community Traditional Knowledge in International Law', 14 *St Thomas Law Review*, 2001, 275–85; Silke von Lewinski, *Indigenous Heritage and Intellectual Property: Genetic Resources, Traditional Knowledge and Folklore* (Kluwer Law International, 2008).

seeds, medicines, knowledge of the properties of fauna and flora, oral traditions, literatures, designs, sports and traditional games and visual and performing arts.[104]

Article 31 has been instrumental in supporting the rise of a more developed human rights-based approach to the recognition of indigenous peoples' traditional knowledge over their natural resources.[105] Significantly, this language has been directly integrated in the General Comment adopted by the CESCR on the right of everyone to take part in cultural life, which states that:

Indigenous peoples have the right to act collectively to ensure respect for their right to maintain, control, protect and develop their cultural heritage, traditional knowledge and traditional cultural expressions, as well as the manifestations of their sciences, technologies and cultures, including human and genetic resources, seeds, medicines, knowledge of the properties of fauna and flora, oral traditions, literature, designs, sports and traditional games, and visual and performing arts.[106]

The reference to genetic resources, seeds, knowledge of the properties of fauna and flora is particularly noteworthy. This approach is not only limited to norms and declarations, but is also integrated in the case law and jurisprudence.[107] In several of its cases on indigenous peoples' rights, the IACtHR has highlighted how traditional knowledge over natural resources forms an essential element of indigenous peoples' right to cultural identity. For example, in *Yakye Axa Indigenous Community*, the IACtHR acknowledged the importance of traditional knowledge over natural resources, noting that '[b]ased on their environment, their integration with nature and their history, the members of indigenous communities transmit this non-material cultural heritage from one generation to the next, and it is constantly recreated by the members of the indigenous groups and communities'.[108]

In *Sarayaku*, the IACtHR considered that the failure to consult indigenous peoples before undertaking development on their lands 'affected their cultural identity, since there is no doubt that the intervention in and destruction of their cultural heritage entailed a significant lack of respect for their social and cultural identity, their customs, traditions, worldview and way of life, which naturally caused great concern, sadness and suffering among them'.[109] A similar approach was adopted in the decisions of the African Commission and the ACHPR highlighting the connection between traditional knowledge and natural resources.[110] Overall, there is now

---

[104] United Nations Declaration on the Rights of Indigenous Peoples, General Assembly, UN Doc. A/RES/61/295, Adopted on 13 September 2007, Art. 31.

[105] For analysis on the drafting of this article and the evolution of indigenous biodiversity rights, see Alexandra Xanthaki, *Indigenous Rights and United Nations Standards: Self-Determination, Culture and Land* (CUP, 2007), pp. 224–6,

[106] (n 61) para. 37.

[107] See also specific article on traditional knowledge in the American Declaration on the Rights of Indigenous Peoples (Art. 28).

[108] *Case of the Yakye Axa Indigenous Community*, Merits, Reparations and Costs. Series C No. 125 (2005), para. 154.

[109] *Case of the Kichwa Indigenous People of Sarayaku* (n 32) para 220.

[110] See *African Commission on Human and Peoples' Rights: Centre for Minority Rights Development (Kenya) and Minority Rights Group International on behalf of Endorois Welfare Council v Kenya* (February 2010); *ACHPR v Kenya*, Judgment, Application No. 006/2012 (2017) (the '*Ogiek* Judgment').

a substantial body of IHRL supporting the protection of indigenous peoples' trad-itional knowledge over their natural resources.[111]

The other relevant field of international law is the specialized legal framework governing food production, food security, and agriculture developed under the lead-ership of the Food and Agricultural Organization (FAO). Of particular relevance is the Treaty on Plant Genetic Resources for Food and Agriculture (ITPGRFA), which calls for the protection of farmers' traditional knowledge relevant to plant genetic resources for food and agriculture.[112] While the treaty is principally concerned with ensuring food security through the conservation, exchange, and sustainable use of genetic resources, it puts forward the importance of the rights of small-scale farmers. It highlights 'the enormous contribution that the local and indigenous communi-ties and farmers of all regions of the world, particularly those in the centres of origin and crop diversity, have made and will continue to make for the conservation and development of plant genetic resources which constitute the basis for food and agri-culture production throughout the world'.[113] It calls on governments to protect the traditional knowledge relevant to plant genetic resources for food and agriculture. This treaty was one of the first international legal instruments to formally put for-ward the rights of farmers to their traditional knowledge, but since then, IHRL has slowly started to address the issue as well. International human rights institutions are increasingly mentioning the rights of small-scale farmers and peoples working in rural environments over their traditional knowledge. For example, in 2017 the HRC adopted a resolution highlighting the importance of traditional sustainable agricultural practices, e.g. traditional seed supply systems, for many smallholder and subsistence farmers.[114] The current negotiations for the eventual adoption of the UN Declaration on the Rights of Peasants and other people working in rural areas include many direct references to traditional knowledge over natural resources.[115] The draft text puts forward the right to seeds and traditional agricultural knowledge and practice, as well as the right to the protection of local agricultural values.[116] This is part of a larger movement of peasants and rural peasants' organizations in-creasingly pushing IHRL to recognize their rights over their traditional agricultural knowledge, including a specific right over their traditional seeds.[117]

Finally, the field of IPR is slowly beginning to focus on traditional knowledge, specifically on protecting traditional knowledge holders against third-party abuse.

---

[111] See Sarah A. Laird (ed.), *Biodiversity and Traditional Knowledge: Equitable Partnerships in Practice* (Routledge, 2010); Laura Westra (ed.), *Environmental Justice and the Rights of Indigenous Peoples: International and Domestic Legal Perspectives* (Earthscan, 2012).

[112] Treaty on Plant Genetic Resources for Food and Agriculture (2001), Art. 9.   [113] Ibid.

[114] Human Rights Council, UN Doc. A/HRC/34/L.21 (2017).

[115] See Open-Ended Intergovernmental Working Group on a United Nations Declaration on the Rights of Peasants and other People Working in Rural Areas. Available at: http://www.ohchr.org/EN/HRBodies/HRC/RuralAreas/Pages/WGRuralAreasIndex.aspx.

[116] Draft Declaration on the Rights of Peasants and other People Working in Rural Areas, presented by the Chair-Rapporteur of the Working Group, UN Doc. A/HRC/WG.15/4/2 (2017); see Arts 5 and 9.

[117] See Priscilla Claeys, 'Food Sovereignty and the Recognition of New Rights for Peasants at the UN: A Critical Overview of La Via Campesina's Rights Claims over the Last 20 Years', 12(2) *Globalizations*, 2015, 452–65.

However, the international legal framework governing IPR tends to focus quite heavily on elite forms of knowledge to capture the complexity of local communities' traditional knowledge. As traditional knowledge over natural resources has ancient roots and is often oral, it is usually not well protected by conventional intellectual property systems. Gibson notes that 'the symbiotic relationship between community and its resources, inextricable from knowledge and expression emanating from that community, is not readily compatible with intellectual property models which induce an objectification of knowledge in ways inconsistent with traditional knowledge development and dissemination'.[118] However, innovations based on traditional knowledge may benefit from patent, trademark, and geographical indication protection, or be protected as a trade secret or confidential information. In 2000, the WIPO established an Intergovernmental Committee on Intellectual Property and Genetic Resources, Traditional Knowledge and Folklore (IGC), to serve as a forum to discuss the intellectual property issues that arise in the context of access to genetic resources (GR).[119] The issue of protecting traditional knowledge over natural resources forms an important element of the negotiations to develop international instruments for the protection of traditional knowledge, traditional cultural expressions, and genetic resources.[120] Furthermore, these discussions on IPR are also touching on another field of the law regarding bio-piracy and trade patents on use of plants and seeds. However, the dominant regime remains extremely top-down and heavily focused on market-orientated patents. Dodson notes that 'Western constructs of intellectual property focus on individual knowledge and creativity, rather than communal trans-generational knowledge'.[121] Nevertheless, it is clearly an area where IHRL can have a beneficial impact to expand the protection of IPR to local communities' traditional knowledge over natural resources. In terms of IHRL, there is an increasing significant focus on these issues.[122] Probably one of the most significant encounters between the two fields concerns the rights of indigenous peoples, and there has been some impact of the UNDRIP in the current negotiations to improve the system of patents.[123] There is nonetheless still a long way for IHRL to fully develop in order to protect traditional small-scale farmers and local communities'

---

[118] Johanna Gibson, *Community Resources: Intellectual Property, International Trade and Protection of Traditional Knowledge* (Routledge, 2016), Ch. 9.

[119] For analysis, see Daphne Zografos Johnsson and Hai-Yuean Tualima, 'Cultural Heritage, Traditional Knowledge and Intellectual Property Rights'. In: Alexandra Xanthaki, Sanna Valkonen, Leena Heinämäki, and Piia Kristiina Nuorgam (eds), *Indigenous Peoples' Cultural Heritage Rights, Debates, Challenges* (Brill, 2017), pp. 218–28.

[120] At the time of writing the negotiations are still ongoing. For updates see WIPO's website at: http://www.wipo.int/tk/en/igc/.

[121] UN Permanent Forum on Indigenous Issues, Report of the Secretariat on Indigenous Traditional Knowledge, prepared by Special Rapporteur M. Dodson, UN Doc. E/C.19/2007/10 (2007), para. 20.

[122] See Laurence R. Helfer and Graeme W. Austin, *Human Rights and Intellectual Property: Mapping the Global Interface* (CUP, 2011).

[123] See Mauro Barelli, 'The United Nations Declaration on the Rights of Indigenous Peoples: A Human Rights Framework for Intellectual Property Rights'. In: Matthew Rimmer (ed.), *Indigenous Intellectual Property: A Handbook of Contemporary Research* (Edward Elgar Publishing, 2015).

IPR over their seeds and plants as the rights and views of the large agribusiness corporations are still largely dominant.[124]

4. The Spiritual Approach: Sacred Sites, Sacred Practices, and Natural Resources

For many local, rural, and indigenous communities, natural resources constitute an important part of their belief systems and cosmology. Berkes discusses how sacred, spiritual, and cosmological knowledge and connection with natural resources constitute an important element of traditional ecological knowledge.[125] Ecological knowledge also includes sacred knowledge of plants, prayers, chants, and performances connected to certain natural resources, as well as of sacred species of plants, animals, microorganisms, and minerals.[126] This cultural knowledge can also include spiritual aspects of healing practices connected with use of certain plants. IHRL is increasingly recognizing these sacred, spiritual, and cosmological connections to natural resources. The closest reference to 'spirituality' in human rights treaties comes under the right to freedom of thought, conscience, religion, or belief. Even if the right to freedom of religion has been controversial and often underdeveloped,[127] it potentially offers an avenue to recognize spiritual ties to natural resources. One of the first breakthroughs connecting freedom of religion, or belief, and natural resources came via indigenous peoples who have convinced legal institutions to recognize the importance of 'sacred natural sites' as part of their right to freedom of religion. The second significant advance concerns the recognition of specific sacred practices as forms of spiritual expression that are protected under cultural and property rights.

4.1 Freedom of religion, sacred natural sites, and spirituality

The notion of 'sacred sites' refers to areas that symbolize or pertain to religious and spiritual beliefs, practices, or customs. Sacred natural sites includes 'areas of land or water having special spiritual significance to peoples and communities'.[128] For many communities across the globe sacred natural sites include mountains, rivers, forests, and other natural resources that are at the genesis of their spirituality.[129]

---

[124] See Olivier De Schutter and Gaëtan Vanloqueren, 'The New Green Revolution: How Twenty-First-Century Science Can Feed the World', 2(4) *Solutions*, 2011, 33–44.

[125] See Fikret Berkes, *Sacred Ecology*, 4th edition (Routledge, 2017), Chs 1 and 2.

[126] See Daniel J. Gervais, 'Spiritual but not Intellectual: The Protection of Sacred Intangible Traditional Knowledge', 11 *Cardozo Journal of International and Comparative Law*, 2003, 467, 469–90.

[127] See Malcolm David Evans, Peter Petkoff, and Julian Rivers (eds), *The Changing Nature of Religious Rights Under International Law* (OUP, 2015), pp. 1–9.

[128] Robert Wild, Christopher McLeod, and Peter Valentine, *Sacred Natural Sites: Guidelines for Protected Area Managers* (No. 16. IUCN, 2008); World Conservation Congress Resolution 4.038 (2008, Barcelona); and World Conservation Congress Recommendation 5.147 (2012, Jeju).

[129] See Bas Verschuuren, Robert Wild, Jeffrey McNeely, and Gonzalo Oviedo (eds), *Sacred Natural Sites: Conserving Nature and Culture* (Routledge, 2010).

Many indigenous peoples' representatives have highlighted that the spiritual life of indigenous peoples is 'different from that of monotheistic faiths in that they are "geosophical" or earth-centred, rather than "theosophical" or god-centred'.[130] Graber notes that, for many indigenous peoples, these traditional forms of cultural expressions 'fulfil indicative and liturgical functions and are closely related to landscape, ancestors and custom',[131]

These connections between natural sites and religion are not included as such in international human rights treaties. However, in its General Comment on the Right to Freedom of Thought, Conscience and Religion, the HRC advocates for a wide understanding of religion, including the right to hold 'theistic, non-theistic and atheistic beliefs, as well as the right not to profess any religion or belief.'[132] The HRC also highlights that the terms 'belief' and 'religion' are to be broadly construed and should not be limited to traditional religions or to religions and beliefs with institutional characteristics.[133] Regarding religious practices, the HRC noted that '[t]he freedom to manifest religion or belief in worship, observance, practice and teaching encompasses a broad range of acts'. Hence, while there is no direct mention of 'sacred sites' or 'sacred practices' connected to natural resources, the approach is opened to all forms of spirituality. Bielefeldt suggests that freedom of religion or belief 'recognizes all human beings in their deep convictions and conviction-based practices, instead of privileging the *homo religiosus* in any narrow sense . . .'.[134]

The connection between freedom of religion, or belief, and natural sites has emerged under the rights of indigenous peoples. This has taken place at two levels: normative and jurisprudential. In terms of the normative development, Article 25 of the UNDRIP declares that:

Indigenous peoples have the right to maintain and strengthen their distinctive spiritual relationship with their traditionally owned or otherwise occupied and used lands, territories, waters and coastal seas and other resources and to uphold their responsibilities to future generations in this regard.[135]

Likewise, the ILO Convention No. 169 affirms that, in applying the Convention, 'governments shall respect the special importance for the cultures and spiritual values of the peoples concerned of their relationship with the lands or territories, or both as applicable, which they occupy or otherwise use, and in particular the

---

[130] See Katja Mikhailovich and Alexandra Pavli, *Freedom of Religion, Belief, and Indigenous Spirituality, Practice and Cultural Rights* (Australian Institute of Aboriginal and Torres Strait Islanders Studies, 2011).

[131] Christoph Beat Graber, 'Using Human Rights to Tackle Fragmentation in the Field of Traditional Cultural Expressions: An Institutional Approach'. In: Christoph Beat Graber and Mira Burri-Nenova (eds), *Intellectual Property and Traditional Cultural Expressions in a Digital Environment* (Edward Elgar, 2008), p. 111.

[132] Human Rights Committee, General Comment No. 22: The Right to Freedom of Thought, Conscience and Religion (Art. 18), UN Doc. CCPR/C/21/Rev.1/Add.4, para. 2.

[133] Ibid.

[134] Heiner Bielefeldt, 'Privileging the Homos Religiosus? Towards a Clear Conceptualization of Freedom of Religion or Belief'. In: Malcolm David Evans, Peter Petkoff, and Julian Rivers (eds), *The Changing Nature of Religious Rights Under International Law* (OUP, 2015), p. 22.

[135] United Nations Declaration on the Rights of Indigenous Peoples, General Assembly, UN Doc. A/RES/61/295, Adopted on 13 September 2007, Art. 25.

collective aspects of this relationship'.[136] This approach has also been integrated in the interpretation of the mainstream human rights treaties. In its General Comment No. 21, the CESCR especially emphasized that State parties must 'respect the rights of indigenous peoples to their culture and heritage and to maintain and strengthen their spiritual relationship with their ancestral lands and other natural resources traditionally owned, occupied or used by them, and indispensable to their cultural life'.[137] The HRC has also made references to the connection between indigenous peoples' rights and spirituality over natural sites. For example, in its Concluding Observations on Australia in 2000, the HRC expressed 'its concern that securing continuation and sustainability of traditional forms of economy of indigenous minorities (hunting, fishing and gathering), and protection of sites of religious or cultural significance for such minorities, which must be protected under Article 27, are not always a major factor in determining land use'.[138]

At the regional level, the connection between freedom of religion, natural resources, and sacred sites has been examined in detail by the African human rights system. In its Article 8, the ACHPR guarantees the right to practise religion. This article was invoked when the Endorois community of Kenya lost access to their ancestral territory—an area including Lake Bogoria, which was used for tourism and wildlife protection. In their claim, the Endorois declared that access to Lake Bogoria was of fundamental religious significance since religious ceremonies are regularly held there, including an annual religious ritual that occurs when the lake undergoes seasonal changes.[139] For the African Commission, the issue was to determine whether the Endorois' spiritual beliefs about the lake constituted religion under the African Charter and international law. After having examined all the arguments put forward by the community relating to their spiritual connection to the lake, the Commission endorsed their claim, recognizing that 'the Endorois spiritual beliefs and ceremonial practices constitute a religion under the African Charter'.[140] In its 2010 decision, the African Commission concluded that the government had violated Article 8 in interfering with the Endorois' right to religious freedom and removed them from the sacred grounds essential to the practice of their religion. In terms of the legal argumentation, this claim put forward a direct violation of the right to practice religion in connection to access to a natural site, hence opening a new legal avenue between the human rights to freedom of religion and natural resources.

In 2017, a similar issue was brought to the ACHPR in the *Ogiek* Case, in which the traditionally hunter-gatherer community had put forward the argument that

---

[136] ILO Convention 169, Art. 13.   [137] (n 61) para. 49(d).

[138] Concluding Observations of the Human Rights Committee: Australia. 28/07/2000. CCPR/CO/69/AUS. (Concluding Observations/Comments), paras 9–12. For analysis, see Leena Heinämäki and Thora Martina Herrmann, 'The Recognition of Sacred Natural Sites of Arctic Indigenous Peoples as a Part of Their Right to Cultural Integrity', 4(2) *Arctic Review on Law and Politics*, 2013, 207–33.

[139] *African Commission on Human and Peoples' Rights: Centre for Minority Rights Development (Kenya) and Minority Rights Group International on behalf of Endorois Welfare Council v Kenya* (February 2010), para. 77.

[140] Ibid., para. 168.

their forced eviction from their ancestral forests constituted a violation of the right to practise their religion. The Ogiek people highlighted that they could not access significant sacred places in the Mau Forest, such as caves, hills, and specific trees which were of importance to their spiritual beliefs. Adopting a similar line of reasoning connecting Article 8 on Freedom to Practice Religion and Natural Sites, the ACHPR noted that 'in the context of traditional societies, where formal religious institutions often do not exist, the practice and profession of religion are usually inextricably linked with land and the environment. In indigenous societies in particular, the freedom to worship and to engage in religious ceremonies depends on access to land and the natural environment.'[141] This jurisprudence emerging from the African system of human rights establishes a direct connection between the right to practise a religion and access to traditional sacred sites allowing the exercise of traditional practices connected to natural resources. Adding to this approach, the African Commission adopted a specific resolution on the issue of sacred natural sites in 2017 in its 'Resolution on the Protection of Sacred Natural Sites and Territories'. Here, the African Commission made direct connection between human rights and States' obligations to protect and respect natural sacred sites and called on 'States Parties to recognise sacred natural sites and territories, and their customary governance systems, as contributing to the protection of human and peoples' rights'.[142] Overall, the African human rights system has clearly engaged in the recognition of sacred natural sites and practices connected to the natural resources as a form of spirituality covered by the right to freedom of religion. However, until now, other regional systems have not yet embraced such an approach and have instead focused on other human rights, e.g. property and cultural rights.[143]

4.2 Sacred practices and indigenous peoples' 'cosmovision'

This section focuses on the protection of spiritual connections under cultural and property rights, rather than freedom of religion. The Inter-American system of human rights, both Commission and Court, have recognized the right of indigenous peoples to their spiritual connection to natural sites and natural resources, but mainly under their rights to property and culture. In *Case of the Mayagna (Sumo) Awas Tingni Community*, the IACtHR declared that:

the close relationship that the communities have with the land must be recognised and understood as a foundation for their cultures, spiritual life, cultural integrity and economic survival. For indigenous communities, the relationship with the land is not merely one of possession and production, but also a material and spiritual element that they should fully

---

[141] *African Commission on Human and Peoples' Rights v Republic of Kenya*, Judgment. Application No. 006/2012 (2017), para. 164.

[142] Resolution on the Protection of Sacred Natural Sites and Territories, ACHPR/Res. 372 (LX) 2017.

[143] For analysis of the shortcomings of European and American systems, see Dwight Newman, Elisa Ruozzi, and Stefan Kirchner, 'Legal Protection of Sacred Natural Sites Within Human Rights Jurisprudence: Sápmi and Beyond'. In: Leena Heinämäki and Thora Martina Herrmann (eds), *Experiencing and Protecting Sacred Natural Sites of Sámi and other Indigenous Peoples* (Springer, 2017), pp. 11–26.

enjoy, as well as a means through which to preserve their cultural heritage and pass it on to future generations.[144]

This approach has been reaffirmed in many of the cases examined by the IACtHR, and highlights the importance of spiritual ties to a territory as an important element of the right to property.[145] This approach has been grounded into Article 21 of the American Convention protecting property rights rather than freedom of religion. This is part of a larger jurisprudence on the collective and cultural rights of indigenous peoples over their land and territories, rather than a sole focus on the right to freedom religion. For example, in *Case of Yakye Axa Indigenous Community*, the IACtHR declared that 'the culture of the members of the indigenous communities directly relates to a specific way of being, seeing, and acting in the world, developed on the basis of their close relationship with their traditional territories and the resources therein, not only because they are their main means of subsistence, but also because they are part of their worldview, their religiosity, and therefore, of their cultural identity'.[146] In *Case of the Kichwa Indigenous People of Sarayaku*, the IACtHR also acknowledged the importance that sites of symbolic value have for the cultural identity of the community. It noted that 'for the Sarayaku, the destruction of sacred trees, such as the Lispungu tree, by the company entailed a violation of their worldview and cultural beliefs'.[147] In many of its decisions, the IACtHR referred to the concept of 'cosmovision' as a way of capturing the connection between natural sites, natural resources, and indigenous peoples' spirituality, declaring that such 'cosmovision' should be protected as part of indigenous peoples' property rights over their land and natural resources.[148] For example, in *Rio Negro Massacres*, the Court emphasized that connection to natural sites and natural resources is an 'integral part of their cosmovision, religious beliefs and, consequently, their cultural identity or integrity, which is a fundamental and collective right of the indigenous communities that must be respected'.[149]

This link between sacred sites, sacred practices, and natural sites is also recognized under the right to access ancestral burial grounds. The HRC has examined this link in its individual opinion in *Francis Hopu and Tepoaitu Bessert*, regarding two Polynesians' rights over traditionally important spiritual land where the authorities had authorized building of a hotel.[150] The contested land contained a traditional burial ground and a fishing lagoon, and the HRC concluded that the construction

---

[144] *Case of the Mayagna (Sumo) Awas Tingni Community v. Nicaragua*, Reparations and Costs, Judgment. Series C No. 79 (2001), para. 149.

[145] See Newman, Ruozzi, and Kirchner (n 143), 11–26.

[146] *Case of Yakye Axa Indigenous Community v Paraguay* (n 108) para. 135.

[147] *Case of the Kichwa Indigenous People of Sarayaku*, (n 32) para. 218.

[148] 'The term cosmovision has to do with basic forms of seeing, feeling and perceiving the world. It is made manifest by the forms in which a people acts and expresses itself.' See Jorge Ishizawa, 'Affirmation of Cultural Diversity: Learning with Communities in the Central Andes', 2 *Development Dialogue*, 2009, 105–39, 118. Note that the IACtHR also uses the term 'world vision' (see *Kaliña and Lokono Peoples v Suriname*, Merits, Reparations and Costs. Series C No. 309 (2015), para. 164).

[149] *Rio Negro Massacres* (n 32) at 160.

[150] *Francis Hopu and Tepoaitu Bessert v France*, Communication No. 549/1993, UN Doc. CCPR/C/60/D/549/1993/Rev.1. (1997).

of a hotel on the traditional Polynesian burial grounds interfered with the right to privacy and family life, which was neither reasonable nor justified. The HRC highlighted that relationship to their ancestors was an essential element of their identity and played an important role in their family life.[151] A similar approach can also be found in the approach of the Inter-American Commission associating family life with access to ancestral burial grounds. In *Maya Indigenous Communities of the Toledo District*, the IACHR highlighted that 'the concept of family and religion within the context of indigenous communities, including the Maya people, is intimately connected with their traditional land, where ancestral burial grounds, places of religious significance and kinship patterns are linked with the occupation and use of their physical territories'.[152] The connection between property rights, burial ceremonies, and burial grounds was also at the heart of the decision from the IACtHR in *Case of the Moiwana Community*.[153] The IACtHR declared that the lack of access to their traditional territories did not allow 'the community to appease the angry spirits of their deceased family members and purify their traditional land'.[154]

Despite these evolutions in the international jurisprudence, many indigenous peoples still face challenging legal frameworks at the national level. There have been many cases where indigenous peoples' spiritual connection to land and natural resources have been ignored or rejected as not constituting 'proper' religious practices. An infamous example includes the US Supreme Court in *Lyng v Northwest Indian Cemetery Protective Association*, which refused to recognize the specific religious relationship between the indigenous community and their land and natural resources.[155] In this case a road was being built on public land that had specific religious significance for the plaintiffs who argued that the road would destroy the tranquillity necessary for the religion that had been practised on the land for generations.[156] As pointed out by Kingsbury, in this case the judge did not take into consideration such historical and cultural issues and decided that the Indian had the same religious right as any other citizen that would not extend to controlling the use of public lands.[157]

Other challenging issues for indigenous peoples concern the complexity of having to divulge sacred spiritual connections to the outside world, despite

[151] However, see dissenting individual opinion by Committee members David Kretzmer and Thomas Buergenthal, co-signed by Nisuke Ando and Lord Colville, which highlights that this was the case due to France's reservations regarding Article 27.

[152] Inter-American Court of Human Rights, Report No. 40/04, Case 12.053, *Maya Indigenous Communities of the Toledo District*, 12 October 2004, para 155.

[153] *Case of the Moiwana Community v Suriname*, Preliminary Objections, Merits, Reparations and Costs, Judgment (2005).

[154] Ibid., para. 118.

[155] *Lyng v Northwest Indian Cemetery Protective Association*, 485 US 439 (1988).

[156] For analysis, see René Kuppe, 'Religious Freedom Law and the Protection of Sacred Sites'. In: Thomas G. Kirsch and Bertram Turner (eds), *Permutations of Order: Religion and Law as Contested Sovereignties* (Ashgate, 2009), pp. 49–66.

[157] Benedict Kingsbury, 'Reconciling Five Competing Conceptual Structures of Indigenous Peoples' Claims in International and Comparative Law'. In: Philp Alston (ed.) *Peoples' Rights* (OUP, 2001), p. 74. See Kristen Carpenter, 'A Property Rights Approach to Sacred Sites Cases: Asserting a Place for Indians as Nonowners,' 52 *UCLA Law Review*, 2005, 1061.

traditional prohibition of such divulgation. An example of such a situation concerns the Kumargank, or Hindmarsh Island, dispute in South Australia.[158] In this case, an Aboriginal community was forced to reveal a secret practice to challenge the building of a bridge over their traditional territory.[159] This case is often referred to as the 'Ngarrindjeri women's secret business,' as the concerned practices connected to this specific land were sacred to Aboriginal women, and such business was not to be divulged outside women's circles.[160] However, to get protection of their cultural attachment to their land, the community had to reveal 'the secret women's business' in front of a public commission.[161] In the end, the project went ahead and the bridge was built, as the Aboriginal women's business was regarded as being 'fabricated'.[162]

Another significant issue concerns the exploitation of some of the traditional spiritual practices for trade or tourism. Many communities have seen their spiritual and sacred connection with natural resources used for commercial purposes, in tourism, by cultural industries, in the mass media, or as part of showcasing national culture, without proper authorization or shared benefits. This link between spiritual connection to land and natural resources and artistic and spiritual expression of this connection has been extensively documented in the context of Aboriginal art in Australia.[163] As Graber notes, in such a context, human rights could play a substantial role in pushing for a better recognition of the spiritual, cultural, and sacred values of indigenous peoples' connection to natural resources, notably to challenge the fragmentation of international law on the issue of copyrights.[164] However, there is still a lot of progress to be made as IHRL is still only starting to engage in these issues.

---

[158] See James F. Weiner, 'Religion, Belief and Action: The Case of Ngarrindjeri "Women's Business" on Hindmarsh Island, South Australia, 1994–1996', 13(1) *The Australian Journal of Anthropology*, 2002, 51–71.

[159] See *Wilson v Minister for Aboriginal and Torres Strait Islander Affairs* (1996), 189 *Commercial Law Review* 1—High Court of Australia.

[160] See Diane Bell, *Ngarrindjeri Wurruwarrin: A World That Is, Was, and Will Be* (Spinifex Press, 1998).

[161] See the cases from the Supreme Court of South Australia: *Aboriginal Legal Rights Movement v South Australia* (26 July 1995); *Aboriginal Legal Rights v South Australia* [No. 1] (1995) 64 S.A.S.R. 551; *Aboriginal Legal Rights v South Australia* [No 2] (1995) 64 S.A.S.R. 558; *Aboriginal Legal Rights v South Australia* [No 3] (1995) 64 S.A.S.R. 566.

[162] See Mark Harris, 'The Narrative of Law in the Hindmarsh Island Royal Commission', 14(2) *Law in Context*, 1996, 115. See also *Kartinyeri v The Commonwealth* (1998) H.C.A. 22; and Mark Harris, '"... another box of tjuringas under the bed": The Appropriation of Aboriginal Cultural Property to Benefit Non-Indigenous Interests'. In: Joshua Castellino and Niamh Walsh (eds), *International Law and Indigenous Peoples* (Martinus Nijhoff, 2005), p. 133.

[163] See Ronald M. Berndt and Catherine H. Berndt, *Aboriginal Australian Art* (Methuen, 1982); Ronald M. Berndt and Catherine H. Berndt, *The World of the First Australians—Aboriginal Traditional Life: Past and Present* (Aboriginal Studies Press, 1996), pp. 367–446; Howard Morphy, *Aboriginal Art* (Phaidon, 1998); Michael L. Blakeney, 'Protecting the Spiritual Beliefs of Indigenous peoples: Australian Case Studies' 22 *Pacific Rim Law and Policy Journal*, 2013, 391.

[164] Christoph Beat Graber, 'Using Human Rights to Tackle Fragmentation in the Field of Traditional Cultural Expressions: An Institutional Approach'. In: Christoph Beat Graber and Mira Burri Nenova (eds), *Intellectual Property and Traditional Cultural Expressions in a Digital Environment* (Edward Elgar, 2008), p. 98.

5. Conclusion

This chapter has discussed the connection between cultural rights and natural resources that is taking place under three main different but complementary approaches. The first relates to the protection of cultural diversity and notably the rights of minorities. Under this approach, the most developed jurisprudence concerns the rights of indigenous peoples to practise their traditional way of life, including traditional use of natural resources. Despite being embedded within a minority rights framework, this approach applies to indigenous peoples to ensure their 'cultural survival'. There are traces of expansion of this recognition under the larger heading of cultural diversity, e.g. the CESCR highlighting that the right to food and water is based on the recognition of cultural practices regarding the use of the concerned natural resources. The second important legal lens used to examine cultural rights and natural resources comes under the banner of cultural heritage law, a field largely dominated by the UNESCO and other specialized agencies mandated to focus on cultural heritage. The role of IHRL as latecomer to this field has mainly been to challenge the very top-down and expert approach to cultural heritage, which has tended to divide 'cultural' and 'natural' heritage. This particularly concerns the nomination of natural sites as World Heritage Sites, a process often resulting in the encroachment upon indigenous and local communities' human rights.

On a more encouraging note, IHRL plays an increasingly significant role in supporting the development of a strong international legal framework to protect and promote indigenous and local communities' traditional knowledge over natural resources. Here, the interaction between the different fields of international law has resulted in a positive working relationship between cultural heritage, intellectual property, biodiversity, and IHRL. However, the process for patents and protection of IPR over natural resources, notably seeds and plants, is still largely dominated by market and economic capacity, rather than local and small-scale traditional knowledge holders. From this perspective, the engagement of IHRL in this field is both important and urgent. Hopefully, a stronger recognition of the importance of traditional knowledge over natural resources by indigenous, local, and small-scale rural communities will allow IHRL to play a more significant role in the development of the international legal framework on these issues.

Lastly, in focusing on spiritual and religious relationships with natural resources, this chapter examined the potential connection between freedom of religion and natural resources, although this connection is still tenuous and has mainly developed under the auspices of the African human rights system for indigenous peoples. Other regional human rights institutions still rely on other rights-based approaches, e.g. property rights and the right to family life, again in the context of indigenous and tribal peoples' rights only. These rights over natural resources for other groups and communities are not yet well developed or addressed by IHRL.

Overall, via cultural diversity, cultural heritage, and spirituality, IHRL recognizes natural resources as an important element of cultural rights. Traditional knowledge, traditional cultural activities, and the way natural resources are used all form essential parts of the cultural rights of many local communities . However, the fragmented legal specialized regimes on cultural heritage, cultural diversity, traditional knowledge, IPR, and religious rights could, via a more holistic approach, be integrated into international legal norms to govern cultural rights and cultural heritage. From this perspective, the divided international legal framework between specialized fields that governs cultural rights and cultural heritage could benefit from a more integrated human rights-based approach to cultural rights over natural resources. This approach will provide a significant entry point to ensure that a more holistic and comprehensive legal framework is adopted.

Another benefit to a more holistic and comprehensive human rights framework supports a less State-centric approach to cultural rights. Most of the processes for the protection of cultural diversity and cultural heritage work from the top down; however, in this State-centred system, IHRL is starting to develop norms to ensure a more direct participation of the concerned communities. Here, IHRL can ensure that indigenous, local, and rural communities are included in the protection and management of their own cultural heritage. The African Commission on Human and Peoples' Rights relies on the term 'custodian communities' in defining how local populations (rather than States) are better suited to protecting and guarding their cultural heritage. This approach is part of a larger emerging connection between cultural rights and environmental protection, labelled 'biocultural rights',[165] which links the dramatic loss of biodiversity with the loss of cultural diversity.[166] By recognizing the fundamental human rights of the local communities over their cultural practices, traditional knowledge, and management of their natural resources, cultural rights over natural resources then become part of environmental law, another significantly expanding field of international law, which is examined in Chapter 6.

---

[165] See Kabir Sanjay Bavikatte and Tom Bennett. 'Community Stewardship: The Foundation of Biocultural Rights', 6(1) *Journal of Human Rights and the Environment*, 2015, 7–29.

[166] See J. Peter Brosiusand and Sarah L. Hitchner, 'Cultural Diversity and Conservation', 61(199) *International Social Science Journal*, 2010, 141–68.

6

Protecting Natural Resources

Conservation, Biodiversity, Climate Change, and Human Rights

The natural resources of the earth, including the air, water, land, flora and fauna and especially representative samples of natural ecosystems, must be safeguarded for the benefit of present and future generations through careful planning or management, as appropriate.

Principle 2, Declaration of the United Nations Conference
on the Human Environment (1972)

1. Introduction

This chapter focuses on the connection between the international legal framework governing the conservation of natural resources and international human rights law (IHRL). The conservation, protection, and sustainable use of natural resources constitute a substantial and growing area of international law. In 1972, the United Nations Conference on Human Environment played a major role launching the development of the contemporary body of international environmental law,[1] which, since then, has developed to protect natural resources. This includes several specialized treaties that address issues like the protection of certain species,[2] threatened environments,[3] the loss of biological diversity, or changes in the climate and

---

[1] Declaration of the United Nations Conference on the Human Environment, adopted in Stockholm, 16 June 1972, UN Doc. A/Conf.48/14/Rev. 1 (1973), 11 *International Legal Materials*, 1972, 1416. On the evolution of international environmental law, see Peter H. Sand (ed.), *The History and Origin of International Environmental Law* (Edward Elgar, 2015); Edith Brown Weiss, 'The Evolution of International Environmental Law', 54 *Japanese Yearbook of International Law*, 2011, 1–27.

[2] See, for example, International Convention for the Regulation of Whaling (ICRW) 1946; Convention on International Trade in Endangered Species of Wild Fauna and Flora (CITES) 1973; Convention on the Conservation of Migratory Species of Wild Animals (CMS or Bonn Convention) 1979.

[3] See, for example, Ramsar Convention on Wetlands of International Importance especially as Waterfowl Habitat 1971; UN Convention on the Law of the Sea (UNCLOS) 1982; Convention to Combat Desertification (CCD), Paris, 1994.

Natural Resources and Human Rights: An Appraisal. Jérémie Gilbert. © J. Gilbert 2018. Published 2018 by Oxford University Press.

resources depletion.[4] Although this body of international law is about the conservation of natural resources, there are some direct connections with IHRL.

The relationship between environmental law and IHRL has been the topic of
intensive debates, especially about whether IHRL should include a right to the environment, and if so, what should be its content.[5] International environmental law
and IHRL are increasingly cross-fertilizing, and UN human rights institutions have
recognized more and more the close relationship between environmental concerns
and the realization of human rights.[6] Consequently, there is a significant doctrine
and jurisprudence linking human rights and the environment, which includes the
connection between environmental concerns and human rights norms like the right
to life, food, water, health, housing, and family, as well as procedural rights like
freedom of information and participation.[7]

The aim of this chapter is not to engage in a review of the human rights norms
and procedures that are relevant to the protection of the environment. This mapping has been done in a very comprehensive manner by the (former) Independent
Expert (now Special Rapporteur) on the issue of human rights obligations relating
to the enjoyment of a safe, clean, healthy, and sustainable environment.[8] There is
also a very large body of literature and doctrine exploring the connection between
the environment and IHRL.[9] Instead, this chapter examines the potential synergies
between international environmental law and human rights when it comes to the
protection of natural resources. To do so, it focuses on three main areas of potential
convergence. It first focuses on the pollution of natural resources by analysing how
IHRL is gradually offering a potential platform to seek remedies for the victims

---

[4] In general, see Shawkat Alam, Jahid Hossain Bhuiyan, Tareq MR Chowdhury, and Erika J. Techera
(eds), *Routledge Handbook of International Environmental Law* (Routledge, 2012); Sand (n 1).

[5] See Dinah Shelton, 'Human Rights, Environmental Rights, and the Right to Environment', 28
Stanford Journal of International Law, 1991, 103; Neil A. F. Popovic, 'In Pursuit of Environmental
Human Rights: Commentary on the Draft Declaration of Principles on Human Rights and the
Environment', 27 *Columbia Human Rights Law Review*, 1995, 487; Romina Picolotti and Jorge Daniel
Taillant (eds), *Linking Human Rights and the Environment* (University of Arizona Press, 2003).

[6] See United Nations Human Resource Council (2011), Analytical Study on the Relationship between Human Rights and the Environment.

[7] See Advisory Opinion of the Inter-American Court of Human Rights, Advisory Opinion OC-23/
17: The Environment and Human Rights, November 2017.

[8] Report of the Independent Expert on the Issue of Human Rights Obligations Relating to the
Enjoyment of a Safe, Clean, Healthy and Sustainable Environment, John H. Knox, Mapping Report,
UN Doc. A/HRC/25/53 (2013). The Independent Expert Mandate has since been transformed into
one of Special Rapporteur, see UN Human Rights Council Resolution A/HRC/RES/28/11, 'Human
Rights and the Environment' (7 April 2015).

[9] See Boyle and Anderson, *Human Rights Approaches to Environmental Protection* (OUP, 1996);
Francesco Francioni, 'International Human Rights in an Environmental Horizon,' 21 *European Journal
of International Law*, 2010, 41; Donald Anton and Dinah Shelton, *Environmental Protection and
Human Rights* (CUP, 2012); and Alan Boyle, 'Human Rights and the Environment: Where Next?',
23 *European Journal of International Law*, 2012, 613; Ben Boer (ed.), *Environmental Law Dimensions
of Human Rights* (OUP, 2014); Svitlana Kravchenko and John E. Bonine, *Human Rights and the
Environment: Cases, Law and Policy* (Carolina Academic Press, 2008); Dinah Shelton, 'Human Rights
and the Environment: What Specific Environmental Rights Have Been Recognized?', 35 *Denver
Journal of International Law and Policy*, 2006, 129; Picolotti and Taillant (n 5); Federico Lenzerini, 'The
Interplay between Environmental Protection and Human and Peoples' Rights in International Law',
10(1) *African Yearbook of International Law*, 2003, 93.

of pollution. Next, it concentrates on the conservation of natural resources, particularly on the interconnection between protected areas, biodiversity, and IHRL. Finally, it examines the relationship between climate change and IHRL, focusing on the role that IHRL can play in the development of the current climate change adaptation and mitigation frameworks.

2. Human Rights and the Pollution of Natural Resources

Pollution of natural resources has direct consequences on the health and well-being of humans.[10] Nonetheless, despite such an obvious connection between environmental law and human rights, there are very few specific mentions within the main international human rights treaties of a right to a life free from pollution. While there have been theoretical debates on the need to adopt a specific right to a healthy and safe environment, in practice, the connection between pollution and human rights has been developing under the banner of other relevant rights, such as food, health, and privacy. This section examines the development of procedural rights, particularly the right to be informed of potential effects of pollution. It also explores how IHRL increasingly looks at the impact of pollution created by non-State actors, notably when the impacts of the pollution are transboundary.

2.1 Pollution and the right to a healthy environment: from theory to practice

The 'right to a healthy environment' was initially recognized in Principle 1 of the 1972 Stockholm Declaration on the Human Environment.[11] Then, in 1992 the UN Conference on Environment and Development in Rio de Janeiro affirmed that 'human beings ... are entitled to a healthy and productive life in harmony with nature'.[12] However, the right to a healthy environment remains limited within the core international human rights treaties. The UDHR, the ICCPR, and the ICESCR do not make any specific mention of the environment, and in general, international human rights treaties do not integrate specific protection against pollution.[13] Nonetheless, at the regional level, the African Charter on Human and Peoples' Rights (ACHPR) proclaims that 'all peoples shall have the right to a satisfactory

---

[10] See Article 1 of the 1979 UNECE Convention on Long-Range Transboundary Air Pollution, which defines 'pollution' as 'the introduction by man, directly or indirectly, of substance or energy into the [environment] resulting in deleterious effects of such a nature as to endanger human health'.

[11] 'Man (sic) has the fundamental right to freedom, equality and adequate conditions of life, in an environment of a quality that permits a life of dignity and well-being, and he bears a solemn responsibility to protect and improve the environment for present and future generations.' Declaration of the United Nations Conference on the Human Environment, Principle 1 (1972).

[12] Rio Declaration on Environment and Development (1992), Principle 1. For analysis, see Dinah Shelton, 'What Happened in Rio to Human Rights?', 3 *The Yearbook of International Environmental Law*, 1993, 75.

[13] See, however, the 1989 Convention on the Rights of the Child (Art. 24(2)(c)) and the 1989 ILO Convention No. 169 concerning Indigenous and Tribal Peoples (Art. 7(4)).

environment favourable to their development'.[14] The Protocol of San Salvador to the American Convention on Human Rights also states that 'everyone shall have the right to live in a healthy environment'.[15] The 2009 European Union Charter of Fundamental Rights affirms that '[a] high level of environmental protection and the improvement of the quality of the environment must be integrated into the policies of the Union and ensured in accordance with the principle of sustainable development'.[16] The Arab Charter on Human Rights and the Association of Southeast Asian Nations (ASEAN) Human Rights Declaration also proclaims a right to a healthy environment.[17] Finally, the 2007 Declaration on the Rights of Indigenous Peoples also makes explicit connection between indigenous peoples' rights and a safe and clean environment.[18] However, apart these few specific generic mentions of environmental protection, none of these instruments fully embraces a right to a clean and pollution-free environment, per se. Instead, the approach has been based on the interpretation of other relevant human rights norms, e.g. the right to life, rights to an adequate standard of living, to health, to food, or to privacy and family life. The rationale here is that States have an obligation to protect their citizens against pollution of natural resources as it could interfere with the enjoyment of some of their human rights.

At the institutional level, the Human Rights Council has noted that the protection of the environment contributes to the enjoyment of human rights, and that environmental damage can have negative implications for the effective enjoyment of human rights.[19] During the 1990s, the (former) Commission on Human Rights adopted several resolutions on the environment specifically focusing on the negative impact of the illicit dumping of toxic and dangerous wastes on the enjoyment of human rights, and decided to appoint a Special Rapporteur on the issue.[20] In 2011, the Human Rights Council decided to strengthen the mandate to cover the whole life cycle of hazardous products by nominating a Special Rapporteur on the implications for human rights of the environmentally sound management and disposal of

---

[14] African Charter on Human and Peoples' Rights, Article 24. On the connection between the environment and development, see Robin Churchill, 'Environmental Rights in Existing Human Rights Treaties'. In: Alan E. Boyle and Michael R. Anderson (eds), *Human Rights Approaches to Environmental Protection* (OUP, 1998), pp. 90–106.

[15] Organization of American States (OAS), Additional Protocol to the American Convention on Human Rights in the Area of Economic, Social and Cultural Rights ('Protocol of San Salvador'), 16 November 1999, A-52, Art. 11(1).

[16] European Union Charter of Fundamental Rights, Art. 37.

[17] League of Arab States, Arab Charter on Human Rights, Art. 38; Association of Southeast Asian Nations (ASEAN), ASEAN Human Rights Declaration, Art. 28(f).

[18] Article 29.1 states that 'indigenous peoples have the right to the conservation and protection of the environment and the productive capacity of their lands or territories and resources. States shall establish and implement assistance programmes for indigenous peoples for such conservation and protection, without discrimination', United Nations Declaration on the Rights of Indigenous Peoples (2007).

[19] Human Rights Council, Resolution on Human Rights and the Environment, A/HRC/RES/16/11.

[20] Resolution 1995/8: Adverse Effects of the Illicit Movement and Dumping of Toxic and Dangerous Products and Wastes on the Enjoyment of Human Rights, UN Doc. E/CN.4/1995/176.

hazardous substances and wastes.[21] The mandate of the Special Rapporteur includes the monitoring of the adverse effects that the generation, management, handling, distribution, and final disposal of hazardous substances and wastes may have on the full enjoyment of human rights. While the mandate is not specifically on natural resources, it details the way hazardous substances, wastes, including toxic chemicals and pesticides, might affect human rights. For example, recent reports of the Special Rapporteur have highlighted how air pollution can negatively affect human health—notably, the most vulnerable, including children, women of reproductive age, the elderly, and those of poor health.[22] Another focus of the Special Rapporteur has been the impact of the use of pesticides on the right to safe water and the right to food.[23] Other Special Rapporteurs have highlighted the connection between pollution of natural resources and human rights violations, which includes the special Rapporteur on the human right to safe drinking water and sanitation, or the Special Rapporteur on the right to food.[24]

UN human rights treaty-monitoring bodies have also increasingly focused on the negative impact of pollution. The Committee on Economic, Social and Cultural Rights (CESCR) has highlighted the strong correlation between the right to health, the right to water, and protection from pollution and hazardous materials.[25] It noted that 'the right to health embraces a wide range of socioeconomic factors that promote conditions in which people can lead a healthy life, and extends to the underlying determinants of health, such as … a healthy environment'.[26] Additionally, it declares that 'the improvement of all aspects of environmental and industrial hygiene' comprises 'the prevention and reduction of the population's exposure to harmful substances such as radiation and harmful chemicals or other detrimental environmental conditions that directly or indirectly impact upon human health'.[27] These concerns have also been raised in several of its concluding observations. For example, the CESCR noted with concern the increased use of chemical pesticides and transgenic soya seeds in regions traditionally inhabited or used by indigenous communities in Argentina. The CESCR emphasized how these have negatively

[21] Mandate of the Special Rapporteur on the Implications for Human Rights of the Environmentally Sound Management and Disposal of Hazardous Substances and Wastes, UN Doc. A/HRC/RES/18/11 (2011).

[22] See Report of the Special Rapporteur on the Implications for Human Rights of the Environmentally Sound Management and Disposal of Hazardous Substances and Wastes on his Mission to the United Kingdom of Great Britain and Northern Ireland, UN Doc. A/HRC/36/41/Add.2 (2017).

[23] See End-of-Visit Statement by the United Nations Special Rapporteur on Human Rights and Hazardous Substances and Wastes, Baskut Tuncak on his visit to Denmark and Greenland, 2–13 October 2017.

[24] For review and analysis, see 'Mapping Human Rights Obligations Relating to the Enjoyment of a Safe, Clean, Healthy and Sustainable Environment: Individual Report on the Special Procedures of the United Nations Human Rights Council', Report No. 7 (OHCHR, December 2013).

[25] UNCESCR, General Comment No. 14: The Right to the Highest Attainable Standard of Health, UN Doc. E/C.12/2000/4 (2000); General Comment No. 15: The Right to Water, UN Doc. E/C.12/2002/11 (2003).

[26] UNCESCR, General Comment No. 14: The Right to the Highest Attainable Standard of Health, UN Doc. E/C.12/2000/4 (2000), para. 4.

[27] Ibid., para. 15.

affected these communities and created obstacles to their access to safe, adequate, and affordable food.[28]

These concerns are not limited to the right to health, and the Human Rights Committee (HRC) noted the impact of pollution and hazardous waste on the right to life. In its individual opinion in *E.H.P. v Canada*, the HRC stressed that the storage of nuclear wastes near human habitation could raise 'serious issues with regard to the obligations of States parties to protect human life'.[29] The Committee on the Elimination of Discrimination against Women (CEDAW) declared that water pollution can adversely affect rights protected under the Convention on the Elimination of All Forms of Discrimination against Women.[30] The Committee on the Rights of the Child (CRC) has also focused on the negative impact that pollution can have on children. In its General Comment on the Right of the Child to the Enjoyment of the Highest Attainable Standard of Health, the CRC emphasized the dangers and risks of local environmental pollution to children's health.[31] It noted that 'States should take measures to address the dangers and risks that local environmental pollution poses to children's health in all settings'.[32] The Committee on the Elimination of Racial Discrimination (CERD) has also addressed the negative impact of the pollution of natural resources on specifically marginalized communities.[33] On many occasions, CERD has noted that pollution of natural resources can prejudice the enjoyment of the right to health of indigenous peoples.[34] Overall, most of the human rights treaty-monitoring bodies have highlighted the negative consequences that pollution can have on human health.[35]

The connection between pollution of natural resources and IHRL is also part of an increasingly expansive jurisprudence from regional human rights courts and commissions. The African Commission on Human and Peoples' Rights (ACoHPR) has examined the connection in *Social and Economic Rights Action Centre and another* concerning pollution created by oil spills in Nigeria.[36] Likewise, the Inter-American Court of Human Rights (IACtHR) and Inter-American Commission

---

[28] See, for example, Concluding Observations on Argentina, E/C.12/ARG/CO/3 (2011).

[29] *E.H.P. v Canada*, Communication No. 67/1980, U.N. Doc. CCPR/C/OP/1 at 20 (1984), para. 8.

[30] Convention on the Elimination of All Forms of Discrimination against Women (CEDAW) Report, Sect. II, n 11.

[31] General Comment No. 15 on the Right of the Child to the Enjoyment of the Highest Attainable Standard of Health, UN Doc. CRC/C/GC/15 (2013); see also Article 24(2)(c) of the Convention on the Rights of the Child.

[32] See, for example, Report of the Committee on the Convention on the Elimination of All Forms of Racial Discrimination: Slovakia, 17 October 2000, UN Doc. A/55/18, para. 265.

[33] See Report of the Committee on the Convention on the Elimination of All Forms of Racial Discrimination United States, 30 October 2001, UN Doc. A/56/18, para. 400; Decision 1(68) on the United States, 1 October 2006, UN Doc. A/61/18, paras 7–10.

[34] For references, see Study by the Expert Mechanism on the Rights of Indigenous Peoples, *Right to Health and Indigenous Peoples with a Focus on Children and Youth* UN Doc. A/HRC/33/57 (2016).

[35] For details, see the independent reports on the treaty-monitoring bodies prepared for the study on 'Mapping Human Rights Obligations Relating to the Enjoyment of a Safe, Clean, Healthy and Sustainable Environment' (n 24).

[36] *Social and Economic Rights Action Centre and another v Federal Republic of Nigeria*, Communication 155/96 (African Commission on Human and Peoples' Rights 2001).

on Human Rights (IACHR) have adopted relevant decisions linking pollution and IHRL.[37] For example, in their 1997 report on the situation of human rights in Ecuador, the IACHR stated that:

[r]espect for the inherent dignity of the person is the principle which underlies the fundamental protections of the right to life and to preservation of physical well-being. Conditions of severe environmental pollution, which may cause serious physical illness, impairment and suffering on the part of the local populace, are inconsistent with the right to be respected as a human being.[38]

The IACtHR has recognized the 'undeniable link between the protection of the environment and the enjoyment of other human rights'.[39]

Probably the most developed jurisprudence linking pollution and human rights emerges from the European Court of Human Rights (ECtHR). Despite the lack of references to the environment or pollution in the European Convention on Human Rights, the ECtHR has adopted several cases concerning the negative impact of pollution on human rights.[40] *Lopez Ostra* is often seen as a landmark case as it recognized that 'severe environmental pollution may affect individuals' well-being and prevent them from enjoying their homes in such a way as to affect their private and family life adversely'.[41] This case has been followed by several other cases putting forward the same connection between the right to privacy and family life (Art. 8) and pollution.[42] Several types of pollution have been examined by the court, including air pollution,[43] cyanide,[44] nuclear,[45] or accumulation of waste.[46] Not all

---

[37] See *Kuna of Madungandí and Emberá of Bayano Indigenous Peoples and Their Members v Panama*, Merits. Report No. 125/12, Case 12.354 (2012), para. 233; See also *Community of La Oroya v Peru*, Admissibility. Report No. 76/09 (2009); and *Case of the Kichwa Indigenous People of Sarayaku v Ecuador*, (Merits and Reparations) Case 12.465 (2012).

[38] Report on the Situation of Human Rights in Ecuador, OEA/Ser.L/V/II.96, Doc. 10 rev. 1, Chap. VIII (1997); see also *Community of San Mateo de Huanchor v Peru* and *Community of La Oroya v Peru*; and *Communities of the Maya People (Sipakepense and Mam) of the Sipacapa and San Miguel Ixtahuacán Municipalities in the Department of San Marcos v Guatemala*, IACHR PM 260/07 (2010).

[39] *Kawas-Fernández v Honduras*, Merits, Reparations, and Costs, Judgment. Series C No. 196 (2009), para. 148.

[40] See *Lopez Ostra v Spain*, 20 EHRR (1994) 277; *Guerra v Italy*, 26 EHRR (1998) 357; *Fadeyeva v Russia*, 45 EHRR (2007) 10; *Öneryildiz v Turkey*, 41 EHRR (2005) 20; *Taskin v Turkey*, 42 EHRR (2006) 50, paras 113–19; *Tatar v Romania* [2009] ECtHR, para 88; *Budayeva v Russia* [2008] ECtHR.

[41] *López Ostra*, Judgment. Application No. 16798/90 (1994), para. 51.

[42] See *Herrick v The United Kingdom*, Judgment. Application No. 11185/84 (1985), p. 275; *Buckley v The United Kingdom*, Judgment. Application No. 20348/92 (1996); *Chapman v The United Kingdom*, Judgment. Application No. 27238/95 (2001); *Beard v The United Kingdom*, Judgment. Application No. 24882/94 (2001); *Coster v The United Kingdom*, Judgment. Application No. 24876/94 (2001); *Lee v The United Kingdom*, Judgment. Application No. 25289/94 (2001); *and Jane Smith v The United Kingdom*, Judgment. Application No. 25154/94 (2001).

[43] *Surugiu v Romania*, 20 April 2004, 48995/99; *Öneryildiz v Turkey*, 30 November 2004, 48939/99; *Brânduşe v Romania*, 7 April 2009, 6586/03; *Guerra and others v Italy*, 19 February 1998, 14967/89; *Fadeyeva v Russia*, 9 June 2005, 55723/00; *Giacomelli v Italy*, 2 November 2006, 59909/00; *Bacila v Romania*, 30 March 2010, 19234/04; *Dubetska and others v Ukraine*, 10 February 2011, 30499/03.

[44] *Taskin and others v Turkey*, 10 November 2004, 46117/99; *Öçkan and others v Turkey*, 28 March 2006, 46771/99; *Lemke v Turkey*, 5 June 2007, 17381/02; *Tatar v Romania*, 27 January 2009, 67021/01.

[45] *McGinley and Egan v United Kingdom*, 9 June 1998, 21825/93 and 23414/94; *Tatar v Romania*, 27 January 2009, 67021/01.

[46] *Di Sarno v Italy*, 10 January 2012, 30765/08.

pollution can lead to a human rights violation. As noted by the ECtHR in *Fadayeva*, the adverse effects of environmental pollution must attain a certain minimum level if they are to fall within the scope of Article 8.[47] In its jurisprudence, the ECtHR has made it clear that it is not the pollution of the natural resources that is the concern of the court, per se, but the impact of such pollution on the enjoyment of protected human rights. As highlighted in *Kyrtatos*, 'the crucial element which must be present in determining whether, in the circumstances of a case, environmental pollution has adversely affected one of the rights safeguarded by paragraph 1 of Article 8 is the existence of a harmful effect on a person's private or family sphere and not simply the general deterioration of the environment.'[48]

Overall, looking at the special procedures, treaty monitoring bodies, and regional jurisprudence shows that there is a strong link between pollution of natural resources and IHRL. This jurisprudence has developed despite the lack of integration of a specific right to a healthy environment and instead has been grounded in the positive interpretation of other human rights such as the right to life, the right to health, private life, and property. This offers a solid platform to link pollution and human rights, with the limitations that the causes of pollution must have a direct impact on human rights, and that the victims can prove the direct impact of the pollution on the enjoyment of their human rights.[49]

2.2 Procedural rights, transboundary pollution, and corporations

When it comes to pollution of natural resources, probably one of the most significant contributions of IHRL comes from procedural rights. Boyle notes that 'procedural rights are the most important environmental addition to human rights law since the 1992 Rio Declaration on Environment and Development'.[50] An important procedural aspect concerns the right to receive information and be informed about potential cases of pollution. This includes the right to know whether peoples are, or may be, exposed to hazardous or toxic substances. The right to information constitutes a pivotal right, and several international human rights institutions have highlighted that public authorities have an obligation to provide access to environmental information and provide for the assessment of cases of pollution that may interfere with the enjoyment of human rights.[51]

---

[47] *Fadayeva v Russia* (No. 55723/00), 2005-IV, 16 (2005).

[48] See *Kyrtatos v Greece*, Application No. 41666/98, 22 May 2003, para. 52. The same rationale applies in *Tătar v Romania,* Application No. 657021/01, 27 January 2009.

[49] There are other legal avenues to potentially link IHRL and pollution; see Donato Vozza, 'Historical Pollution and Human Rights Violations: Is There a Role for Criminal Law?', in Francesco Centonze and Stefano Manacorda (eds), *Historical Pollution: Comparative Legal Responses to Environmental Crimes* (Springer, 2017), pp. 423–61; and see Marie-Catherine Petersmann, 'Environmental Protection and Human Rights: When Friends become Foes—Conflict Management of the CJEU'. In: Christina Voigt (ed.), *The Environment in International Courts and Tribunals: Questions of Legitimacy* (CUP, 2018).

[50] Alan Boyle, 'Human Rights and the Environment: Where Next?', 23(3) *The European Journal of International Law*, 2012, 613.

[51] For details and analysis, see Report of the Special Rapporteur on the Adverse Effects of the Illicit Movement and Dumping of Toxic and Dangerous Products and Wastes on the Enjoyment of Human Rights, Okechukwu Ibeanu, UN Doc. A/HRC/7/21 (2008).

This obligation to provide information about potential pollution constitutes an important element of the jurisprudence of the regional human rights courts and commissions. At the Inter-American level, Article 13 of the American Convention concerning Freedom of Thought and Expression has been interpreted as implying an obligation to ensure access to information. For example, in a case concerning the potential impact of a forestry exploitation project in Chile, the IACtHR highlighted that freedom of expression and though include the right to seek and receive information about potential risk to the environment.[52] In *Community of La Oroya* concerning allegations that Peru permitted a metallurgic plant to operate resulting in pollution and contamination of water resources causing the death and illness of local residents, the IACHR noted that:

the alleged lack and/or manipulation of information on the environmental pollution pervasive in La Oroya, and on its effects on the health of its residents, along with the alleged harassment toward persons who attempt to disseminate information in that regard, could represent violations of the right enshrined in Article 13 of the American Convention.[53]

The ECtHR has adopted similar reasoning in several of its cases, where it found that public authorities have an obligation to provide information about potential risk of pollution.[54] In *Öneryildiz*, which concerned the life-threatening impact of living close to a large rubbish tip, the ECtHR ruled that while the authorities knew about potentially life-threatening gas emanations from the waste disposal site, it failed to inform the concerned applicants of the risk. [55] Likewise, in *Taşkin*, the ECtHR declared that the failure to make available to the public risk-assessment documents in case of a serious and substantial threat to an environmental accident constituted a breach of the State's obligations under Article 8.[56] The ECtHR held that 'whilst Article 8 contains no explicit procedural requirements, the decision-making process leading to measures of interference must be fair and such as to afford due respect to the interests of the individual as safeguarded by Article 8'. In reaching its decision, the ECtHR referred to Rio Principle 10 and the Aarhus Convention.[57] Indeed, the obligation to provide information about potential environmental hazards is strongly embedded in international environmental law, especially the 1998 Aarhus Convention on Access to Information, Public Participation in Decision-Making

[52] *Claude-Reyes et al. v Chile*, Merits, Reparations and Costs, Judgment. Series C No. 151 (2006). In *Claude-Reyes et al.* petitioners alleged that Chile had violated their right to freedom of expression and free access to state-held information when the Chilean Committee on Foreign Investment failed to release information about a deforestation project that the petitioners wanted to evaluate in terms of its environmental impact

[53] *Community of La Oroya v Peru*, para. 75. See Spieler, 'The La Oroya Case: The Relationship between Environmental Degradation and Human Rights Violations', 18 *Human Rights Brief*, 2011, 19.

[54] See *Guerra v Italy*, 1998-I, 210, 221; *Budayeva v Russia*, Application Nos 15339/02, 21166/02, 20058/02, 11673/02, and 15343/02. (20 March 2008).

[55] *Öneryildiz v Turkey*, Application No. 48939/99; [2005] 41 EHRR 20; [2004] ECHR 657; 18 BHRC 145, (2005); [2004] Inquest LR 108.

[56] *Taşkin v Turkey*, 2004-X, 179. In this case, the applicants lived near a mine which led to the release of cyanide posing a significant risk to flora, fauna, underground water sources, and human health.

[57] Ibid., para. 201; see also *Demir and Baykara v Turkey*, 12 November 2008, 34503/97, para. 82.

and Access to Justice in Environmental Matters.[58] There is an increasingly significant integration of these international environmental norms on access to information in the human rights jurisprudence.[59]

The obligation to provide information is not only passive but requires the authorities to assess the potential risk of pollution. For example, in *Tătar*, the ECtHR
held that there had been a violation of Article 8 on account of the authorities' failure
to protect the right of the applicants, who lived in the vicinity of a gold mine, to
enjoy a healthy and protected environment. While the applicants failed to prove
the existence of a causal link between exposure to sodium cyanide and their health,
the ECtHR ruled that the existence of a serious and material risk for the applicants'
health and well-being entailed a duty to assess the risks. In doing so, it also reiterated
that public authorities have a duty to guarantee the right of members of the public
to participate in the decision-making process concerning environmental issues.[60]
Indeed, the procedural rights put forward by international human rights bodies
are wider than just getting information about potential pollution, and include fa-
cilitating public participation in decision-making processes, as well as providing
access to remedies in cases of pollution.[61] Overall, there is a significant human rights
jurisprudence on procedural rights highlighting the positive obligation of States to
ensure that proper information is provided to the concerned local population when
there are potential risks of pollution.

However, there are some limitations to this current legal approach, specifically,
regarding the involvement of non-State actors, as very often the polluters are not
public authorities, but private entities.[62] This raises the issue of the responsibilities
of private actors, especially corporations, in such cases of pollution.[63] While this
issue is part of the larger question of the responsibilities of corporations for violations of IHRL, specific cases connecting pollution of natural resources by corporations and human rights violations have started to surface. The main approach of
the tribunals is still to put the responsibility on the public authorities for not acting
to prevent the pollution by the corporations. For example, in *SERAP*, the Court of
Justice of the Economic Community of West African States (ECOWAS) focused

---

[58] For a compelling analysis on the human rights aspects of the 1998 Aarhus Convention on Access to
Information, see Alan Boyle, 'Human Rights and the Environment: Where Next?', 23(3) *The European
Journal of International Law*, 2012, 621–3. See also the Rotterdam Convention on the Prior Informed
Consent Procedure for Certain Hazardous Chemicals and Pesticides in International Trade (Art.
15), the Stockholm Convention on Persistent Organic Pollutants (Art. 10), and the United Nations
Framework Convention on Climate Change (Art. 6(a)).

[59] The IACtHR has also made references to the Aarhus Convention in its decisions; see *Claude-Reyes
et al. v Chile*, Merits, Reparations and Costs, Judgment. Series C No. 151 (2006).

[60] However, this is limited to direct victims and not the public at large, see *L'Erablière A.S.B.L. v
Belgium*, Application No. 49230/07 (2009); and *Athanassoglou and Others v Switzerland* (Grand
Chamber, 2009).

[61] See Donald M. Zillman, Alastair Lucas, and George (Rock) Pring (eds), *Human Rights in Natural
Resource Development* (OUP, 2002).

[62] See Leonard H. Jeffrey, *Pollution and the Struggle for the World Product: Multinational Corporations,
Environment, and International Comparative Advantage* (CUP, 2006); Juliette Jowit, 'World's Top Firms
Cause $2.2tn of Environmental Damage, Report Estimates', *The Guardian*, 18 February 2010.

[63] See Elisa Morgera, *Corporate Accountability in International Environmental Law* (OUP, 2009).

on the governmental obligation to hold accountable actors who infringe human rights through oil pollution, and to ensure adequate reparation for victims.[64] Several other cases have adopted a similar line of reasoning by focusing on the obligations of public authorities to ensure that the pollution committed by private actors is addressed, since States have a human rights obligation to control and punish these violations.[65] Shelton notes that 'as these cases make clear, human rights tribunals hold the State responsible whether pollution or other environmental harm is directly caused by the State, or whether the State's responsibility arises from its failure to properly regulate private-sector activities'.[66]

Yet, putting the onus on governments to control acts of corporations and guarantee obligations to inform, prevent, and ensure participation in decisions that might lead to pollution perpetuates a very State-centric approach. Very often pollution breaches are transboundary, both in their effects (pollution taking place across borders) and in terms of the actors (with multinational corporations involved).[67] Transboundary pollution is generally not well addressed under a State-centric approach, as governments will only take responsibilities for actions taking place in their own territory.[68] Moreover, the fact that large-scale pollution usually involves multinational corporations makes the traditional legal approach focusing on States' jurisdictions also inadequate. The inadequacy of the IHRL approach to transboundary pollution committed by private actors was illustrated in *Trafigura*, a case concerning toxic waste disposal in the Ivory Coast.[69] Ultimately, the victims had to take legal actions in at least three different countries and under very different legal approaches, none of which included human rights violations.[70]

The complex saga of cases regarding pollution of the Amazon in Ecuador provides another illustration of the inadequacy of this approach.[71] Again, in this case,

---

[64] *SERAP v Nigeria*, Court of Justice of the Economic Community of West African States, Judgment No. ECW/CCJ/JUD/18/12 (14 December 2012).

[65] See for example, *Gbemre v Shell Petroleum Development Company of Nigeria Ltd et al.* (Federal Court of Nigeria, 2005). For review and analysis of other relevant cases, see Dinah Shelton, 'Whiplash and Backlash: Reflections on a Human Rights Approach to Environmental Protection', 13 *Santa Clara Journal of International Law*, 2015, 11.

[66] Ibid., 26.

[67] See also the discussion in *Arial Herbicide Spraying (Ecuador v Columbia)* [2008] ICJ 4–28 General List No. 138 (31 March 2008).

[68] See ILC Draft Articles on Prevention of Transboundary Harm from Hazardous Activities, Report of the ILC 53rd Session, GAOR, UN Doc. A/56/10 (2001); 1982 UN Convention on the Law of the Sea, Arts 192–222; Advisory Opinion on the Legality of the Threat or Use of Nuclear Weapons [1996] ICJ Rep 226, para. 29; *Pulp Mills*, paras 101, 187–97; Advisory Opinion on Responsibilities and Obligations of States with Respect to Activities in the Area [2011] ITLOS, paras 111–31.

[69] See Olanrewaju A. Fagbohun, 'The Regulation of Transboundary Shipments of Hazardous Waste: A Case Study of the Dumping of Toxic Waste in Abidjan, Cote d'Ivoire', 37 *Hong Kong Law Journal*, 2007, 831; Amnesty International and Greenpeace, *The Toxic Truth* (2012).

[70] These included cases in the United Kingdom, the Netherlands, and France. See Jan Wouters and Cedric Ryngaert, 'Litigation for Overseas Corporate Human Rights Abuse in the European Union: The Challenge of Jurisdiction', 40 *George Washington International Law Review*, 2008, 939.

[71] See Chiara Giorgetti, 'Mass Tort Claims in International Investment Proceedings: What Are the Lessons from the Ecuador-Chevron Dispute', 34 *University of Pennsylvania International Law Journal*, 2012, 787; James Rochlin, 'Development, the Environment and Ecuador's Oil Patch: The Context and Nuances of the Case Against Texaco', 28(2) *Journal of Third World Studies*, 2011, 11.

the victims had to take legal action in several different countries, over several years, and with no proper access to remedies for human rights violations. The complexity of bringing legal actions in these cases exemplifies the lack of proper forum to put forward human rights claims for pollution by corporations.[72] The fact that multinational corporations will have *locus standi* in several countries creates a gap in the current human rights legal approach, which focuses mainly on States' responsibilities to control acts of pollution within their territories. Cases of pollution of natural resources find themselves at the heart of a much wider debate within IHRL regarding the responsibilities of corporations as well as the exterritorial applications of human rights.[73] The agenda to push for a more developed legal framework governing the relationship between IHRL and corporations is currently being developed; it will undoubtedly have a profound effect on the relationship between pollution of natural resources and IHRL.[74]

3. Nature Conservation, Biodiversity, and Human Rights: From Wildlife to Biocultural Rights

This section focuses on the conservation of natural resources and the role of human rights in supporting such effort. The first line of enquiry concerns the relationship between natural protected areas and IHRL. The creation of protected areas across the globe to safeguard various natural resources and promote biodiversity has increasingly led to tensions regarding the rights of local communities. The following analysis examines how IHRL can play an important role in supporting more positive interaction between the goal of protection of nature and the rights of local populations. The second line of enquiry is on the relationship between the international legal framework on biodiversity and IHRL.

---

[72] See Jorge Viñuales, 'Extraterritorial Dimension of Environmental Protection'. In: Nehal Bhuta (ed.), *The Frontiers of Human Rights* (OUP, 2016); Jennifer A. Zerk, 'Extraterritorial Jurisdiction: Lessons for the Business and Human Rights Sphere from Six Regulatory Areas' (Corporate Social Responsibility Initiative Working Paper No. 59, 2009).

[73] See *Al-Skeini v United Kingdom* [2011] ECtHR, paras 130–42; *Öcalan v Turkey*, 41 EHRR (2005) 985, para. 91; *Ilascu v Moldova and Russia*, 40 EHRR (2005) 46, paras 310–19, 376–94; *Issa et al. v Turkey*, 41 EHRR (2004) 567, para. 71; *Cyprus v Turkey*, 35 EHRR (2002) 30, para. 78; *Bankovic v Belgium and Ors* [2001] ECtHR 333, *Alejandre, Costa, de la Pena y Morales v Republica de Cuba* [1999] IACHR Report No. 86/99, para. 23.

[74] For updates, see the Open-Ended Intergovernmental Working Group on Transnational Corporations and other Business Enterprises with Respect to Human Rights. Available at: http://www.ohchr.org/EN/HRBodies/HRC/WGTransCorp/Pages/IGWGOnTNC.aspx; see also Pierre-Marie Dupuy and Jorge E. Viñuales (eds), *Harnessing Foreign Investment to Promote Environmental Protection: Incentives and Safeguards* (CUP, 2013); Jorge E. Viñuales, *Foreign Investment and the Environment in International Law* (CUP, 2012); Lorenzo Cotula, *Human Rights, Natural Resource, and Investment Law in a Globalised World: Shades of Grey in the Shadow of the Law* (Routledge, 2012); Francesco Francioni (ed.), *Environment, Human Rights and International Trade* (Hart, 2001).

3.1 From 'fortress conservation' to 'stewardship rights'

A large part of the earth is covered by protected areas.[75] Protected areas include national parks, wilderness areas, nature reserves, and any other areas for which access and exploitation is restricted due to its intrinsic natural and ecological value.[76] Protected areas are designated with the objective of conserving natural resources.[77] The emergence of contemporary nature reserves took place during the nineteenth century, an era that witnessed the establishment of significant protected areas in North America.[78] At the time, the dominant doctrine advocated a return to a 'pure' and 'pristine' wilderness free from human interaction.[79] Under this approach, a dichotomy between humans and nature was created, where human interaction with nature was seen as detrimental to 'wildlife'.[80] This dominant vision led to the establishment of many protected areas across the globe, often resulting in the forced expulsion of local and indigenous populations living on the concerned territories.[81] Local and indigenous communities were forcedly, and often violently, removed from their territories, despite having forged a centuries-old relationship with their natural environment. This approach became labelled as 'fortress conservation', referring to a model based on the belief that biodiversity protection is best achieved by creating protected areas where ecosystems can function in isolation from human

[75] Estimation indicates that there are more than 161,000 protected areas in the world representing about 15 per cent of the world's land surface area. See Protected Planet Report 2016 (UNEP-WCMC and IUCN 2016). There are plans to expand protected area coverage to 17 per cent of terrestrial and inland water areas and 10 per cent of coastal and marine areas by 2020: see the Strategic Plan for Biodiversity 2011–2020, Aichi Biodiversity Target 11. See UNEP/CBD/COP/10/INF/12/Rev.1.

[76] The International Union for Conservation of Nature (IUCN) defines 'protected area' as 'geographical space, recognised, dedicated and managed, through legal or other effective means, to achieve the long-term conservation of nature with associated ecosystem services and cultural values'. UNEP-WCMC, 'About Protected Areas'. In: Nigel Dudley (ed.), *Guidelines for Appling Protected Areas Management Categories* (IUCN, 2008), pp. 8–9. On the definition of 'intrinsic natural value', see Michael Bowman, 'Biodiversity, Intrinsic Value, and the Definition and Valuation of Environmental Harm'. In: Michael Bowman and Alan Boyle (eds), *Environmental Damage in International and Comparative Law: Problems of Definition and Valuation* (OUP, 2002).

[77] The Convention on Biological Diversity defines a protected area as 'a geographically defined area which is designated or regulated and managed to achieve specific conservation objectives', CBD, Art. 2.

[78] The modern notion of protected areas probably started with the establishment of the Yosemite Valley as public trust land in 1864, followed by the establishment of Yellowstone National Park in 1872. For analysis, see Bernhard Gissibl, Sabine Höhler, and Patrick Kupper (eds), *Civilizing Nature: National Parks in Global Historical Perspective* (Berghahn Books, 2012).

[79] See William M. Denevan, 'The Pristine Myth: Landscape of the Americas in 1492', 82 *Annals of the Association of American Geographers*, 1992, 369–438; Richard H. Grove, *Green Imperialism: Colonial Expansion, Tropical Island Edens and the Origins of Environmentalism, 1600–1800* (CUP, 1996); John McCormick, *Reclaiming Paradise: The Global Environmental Movement* (Indiana University Press, 1991).

[80] For references, see George Perkins Marsh, *Man and Nature or, Physical Geography as Modified by Human Action* (C. Scribner, 1864); see also Marie-Catherine Petersmann, 'Narcissus' Reflection in the Lake: Untold Narratives in Environmental Law beyond the Anthropocentric Frame', 30 *Journal of Environmental Law*, 2018, 1–25.

[81] See Stan Stevens (ed.), *Conservation Through Cultural Survival: Indigenous Peoples and Protected Areas* (Island Press, 1997); Mark David Spence, *Dispossessing the Wilderness: Indian Removal and the Making of the National Parks* (OUP, 2009); Mark Dowie, *Conservation Refugees: The Hundred-Year Conflict between Global Conservation and Native Peoples* (MIT Press, 2009).

disturbance.[82] Most of the protected areas that were established between the 1930s and the end of the 1990s were embedded in this approach,[83] which led to the establishment of many protected areas across Africa and Asia, and subsequently, in the forced removal of local peoples in the name of restoring 'pristine' nature.[84]

More recently, many local and indigenous communities have challenged this exclusive wilderness model. This has resulted in an important shift, most notably within the World Park Congress, which is the landmark global forum on protected areas. At the 1992 World Park Congress it was established that all existing and future protected areas shall be managed and established in full compliance with the rights of indigenous peoples, mobile peoples, and local communities.[85] In 2003, the World Parks Congress recognized the role that local communities can play in conservation.[86] Although at the international policy level a paradigm change took place, this change in international policy documents has not yet been translated to the local level, with many communities still facing forced eviction, displacement, and loss of access to natural resources due to wildlife conservation measures. The legacy of 'fortress conservation' is still felt by many communities across the globe who are expelled from their ancestral lands in the name of conservation.[87] This particularly affects indigenous peoples who live in areas that are often designed as protected areas, resulting in forced displacement and serious restrictions on access to natural resources, which then leads to violations of fundamental human rights.[88]

An important element of the human rights approach has been to highlight that protection of natural resources through the establishment of protected areas and the rights of indigenous peoples over these natural resources are not necessarily antinomical.[89] Conversely, the human rights approach underlines that conservation of natural resources and indigenous peoples' rights could be complementary.[90]

---

[82] See Amity A. Doolittle, 'Fortress Conservation'. In: Paul Robbins (ed.), *Encyclopedia of Environment and Society* (Sage, 2007).

[83] See Convention Relative to the Preservation of Fauna and Flora in their Natural State (1933); Convention on Nature Protection and Wild Life Preservation in the Western Hemisphere (1940); African Convention on the Conservation of Nature and Natural Resources (1968).

[84] See Lotte Hughes, *Moving the Maasai: A Colonial Misadventure* (Palgrave Macmillan, 2006); Christopher Kidd, *Development Discourse and the Batwa of South West Uganda: Representing the 'Other': Presenting the 'Self'* (Unpublished PhD thesis, University of Glasgow, 2008); Navjot S. Sodhi, Gerg Acciaioli, Maribeth Erb, and Alan Khee-Jin Tan (eds), *Biodiversity and Human Livelihoods in Protected Areas: Case Studies from the Malay Archipelago* (CUP, 2008).

[85] See Recommendation 5.13 on Cultural and Spiritual Values of Protected Areas of the IV International Union for Conservation of Nature World Parks Congress, February 1992, Caracas, Venezuela.

[86] The Durban Accord and Action Plan were adopted, see IUCN–The World Conservation Union, *Benefits Beyond Boundaries: Proceedings of the Vth IUCN World Parks Congress: Durban, South Africa 8–17 September 2003* (IUCN, 2005).

[87] See Stan Stevens (ed.), *Indigenous Peoples, National Parks and Protected Areas: A New Paradigm Linking Conservation, Culture and Rights* (University of Arizona Press, 2014).

[88] See UN Special Rapporteur on the Rights of Indigenous Peoples, Victoria Tauli-Corpuz, Report on Conservation and Indigenous Peoples' Rights, UN Doc. A/71/150 (2016); and Report of the Special Rapporteur on the Issue of Human Rights Obligations Relating to the Enjoyment of a Safe, Clean, Healthy and Sustainable Environment, UN Doc. A/HRC/34/49 (2017).

[89] See Ellen Desmet, *Indigenous Rights Entwined with Nature Conservation* (Intersentia, 2011).

[90] See UNDRIP Art. 29 and ILO 169, Art. 7.4.

This approach has been developed quite strongly in the jurisprudence of both the Inter-American and African systems of human rights,[91] and followed cases in both jurisdictions concerning forced evictions and serious human rights violations faced by indigenous peoples due to the establishment of protected areas on their territories.[92] The IACtHR has developed a substantive jurisprudence recognizing the link between environmental protection and indigenous peoples' rights.[93] *Kaliña and Lokono Peoples* constitutes an important milestone as it was one of the first times the IACtHR had to specifically examine the relationship between protected areas and indigenous peoples.[94] The concerned communities had seen their access to natural resources curtailed after the creation of protected areas on their ancestral territories. In its argument, the government had justified these restrictions on the need to protect the natural resources. Consequently, the IACtHR had to look specifically at the issue of 'the compatibility of the right of the indigenous peoples with the protection of the environment'.[95] On this issue, the IACtHR stated that it found

that a protected area consists not only of its biological dimension, but also of its socio-cultural dimension and that, therefore, it requires an interdisciplinary, participatory approach. Thus, in general, the indigenous peoples may play an important role in nature conservation since certain traditional uses entail sustainable practices and are considered essential for the effectiveness of conservation strategies. Consequently, respect for the rights of the indigenous peoples may have a positive impact on environmental conservation. Hence, the rights of the indigenous peoples and international environmental laws should be understood as complementary, rather than exclusionary, rights.[96]

The IACtHR added that participation and benefit from nature conservation are essential elements to ensure the fair and adequate participation of indigenous peoples to the management of protected areas.

An important legacy of *Kaliña and Lokono Peoples* is to recognize that respect for the rights of indigenous peoples is an essential element of good practice to establish protected areas, as well as the importance of ensuring their right to effective participation in conservation management. The decision also highlights that traditional practices can contribute to the sustainable care and protection of the environment

---

[91] See Marie-Catherine Petersmann, 'The Integration of Environmental Protection Considerations within the Human Rights Law Regime: Which Solutions Have Been Provided by Regional Human Rights Courts?', 24 *Italian Yearbook of International Law*, 2014, 191–218.

[92] See *Xákmok Kásek Indigenous Community v Paraguay*, Merits, Reparations, and Costs, Judgment. Series C No. 214 (2010); African Commission on Human and Peoples' Rights: *Centre for Minority Rights Development (Kenya) and Minority Rights Group International on behalf of Endorois Welfare Council v Kenya* (February 2010).

[93] See *Kalina and Lokono Peoples v Suriname*, Merits, Reparations and Costs (2015); *Comunidad Garífuna Triunfo de la Cruz y Sus Miembros v Honduras*, Merits, Reparations and Costs (2015); *Kichwa Indigenous People of Sarayaku v Ecuador*, Judgment. Series C No. 245 (2012); *Xàkmok Kàsek Indigenous Community v Paraguay*, Judgment (2010); *Kawas-Fernandez v Honduras*, Judgment. Series C No. 196 (2009); *Maria Salvador Chiriboga v Ecuador*, Preliminary Objection and Merits, Judgment. (2008); *Sawhoyamaxa Indigenous Community v Paraguay*, Judgment. Series C No. 146 (2006); *Yakye Axa Indigenous Community v Paraguay*, Merits, Reparations and Costs, Judgment. Series C No. 125 (2005); *Mayagna (Sumo) Awas Tingni Community v Nicaragua*, Judgment. Series C No. 79 (2001).

[94] *Kaliña and Lokono Peoples v Suriname* (n 93).   [95] Ibid., para. 171-ss.

[96] Ibid., para 173 (references omitted).

and should be maintained, protected, and promoted.[97] A similar approach is found in the jurisprudence of the African system. In two cases concerning Kenya, both the ACoHPR and the Court have highlighted that the goal of nature preservation should not be seen as antinomic with the rights of indigenous peoples over these territories.[98] International human rights monitoring bodies and special procedures have also adopted a similar line of reasoning.[99] CERD has been paying particular attention to the violations of indigenous peoples' rights resulting from the establishment of protected areas, highlighting that the non-recognition of indigenous peoples' rights over their land and natural resources in protected areas constitutes a form of racial discrimination.[100] In general, international human rights bodies have highlighted that protected areas should be established and managed with the full and effective participation of the indigenous peoples affected and in respect of their own forms of use and management of natural resources.[101]

Looking at the different cases, decisions, and recommendations of international human rights bodies, it appears that IHRL supports a 'stewardship rights' approach to indigenous peoples' rights over protected areas.[102] It is grounded in the recognition of indigenous peoples' fundamental rights to land and natural resources contained in the protected areas, as well their right to participate in the management of these protected areas in their role of 'stewards' or 'custodians' of their natural resources. Here, ancestral practices connected to the use of natural resources could have a positive and supportive role to protect natural resources. The establishment of protected areas often results in narrow restrictions on traditional practices and activities, such as hunting, gathering, farming, or animal husbandry, in violation of the cultural and subsistence rights of indigenous peoples.[103] The human rights approach to conservation challenges this approach in highlighting that indigenous peoples' traditional practices and management of natural resources should be integrated in

---

[97] For further analysis, see Fergus Mackay, 'The *Case of the Kaliña and Lokono Peoples v Suriname*: Convergence, Divergence and Mutual Reinforcement', *Erasmus Law Review*, forthcoming 2019.

[98] See African Commission on Human and Peoples' Rights, *Endorois Welfare Council v Kenya*, No. 276/2003 (2010); African Court on Human and Peoples' Rights, *ACHPR v Kenya*, Application No. 006/2012, Judgment of African Court of Human and Peoples' Rights, issued 26 May 2017 ('*Ogiek* Judgment').

[99] See Report of the Special Rapporteur of the Human Rights Council on the Rights of Indigenous Peoples (Conservation and Indigenous Peoples' Rights), UN Doc. A/71/229 (2016); Report of the Special Rapporteur on the Rights of Indigenous Peoples on her visit to Honduras, UN Doc. A/HRC/33/42/Add.2, 21 (July 2016).

[100] See, for example, Concluding Observations: Rwanda, UN CERD/C/RWA/CO/18-20 (2016); Suriname, UN CERD/C/SUR/CO/13-15 (2015); see also Early Warning/Urgent Action: Thailand, UA/EW, 3 October 2016.

[101] See Jérémie Gilbert, *Indigenous Peoples' Land Rights under International Law: From Victims to Actors*, 2nd edition (Brill, 2016).

[102] On notion of stewardship rights, see Rebecca Tsosie, 'Tribal Environmental Policy in an Era of Self-Determination: The Role of Ethics, Economics and Traditional Ecological Knowledge', 21 *Vermont Law Review*, 1996, 225; Mark Poffenberger, 'People in the Forest: Community Forestry Experiences from Southeast Asia', 5(1) *International Journal of Environment and Sustainable Development*, 2006, 57–69; Kelbessa Workineh, 'The Rehabilitation of Indigenous Environmental Ethics in Africa', 52 *Diogenes*, 2005, 17–34.

[103] On the cultural aspects of such restrictions, see Chapter 5.

the conservation effort. This does not mean 'romanticizing' indigenous peoples' traditions by assuming that these are inherently protecting nature, but rather focusing on the need to include indigenous peoples' values on an equal footing with other more formal conservationist approaches.[104] Stewardship rights are also integrated in some of the more recent international environmental norms and national practices that recognize the role of 'custodianship and guardianship' local and indigenous peoples can play in the effort to protect natural resources.[105] These developments on stewardship rights are part of the larger increasing complementarity between IHRL and the international legal framework governing biodiversity.

3.2 Biodiversity, human rights, and the emergence of biocultural rights

This section discusses the area of potential complementary between biodiversity law and IHRL. The dramatic loss of biological diversity has triggered the emergence of a very developed international legal framework on biodiversity, with the 1992 Convention on Biological Diversity as its foundation. Since then, a comprehensive legal framework of norms and mechanisms has been developed on biodiversity law,[106] where biodiversity refers to 'the variability among living organisms from all sources including, inter alia, terrestrial, marine and other aquatic ecosystems and the ecological complexes of which they are part; this includes diversity within species, between species and of ecosystems'.[107] It does not only concern species and ecosystem diversity, but also the different ways natural resources are used, including the interaction between ecosystems, natural resources, and humans.[108]

In terms of IHRL, while biodiversity in itself is not specifically included in any treaties, there is an increasingly important synergy between the two fields.[109] This interaction is notably triggered by the references made to the role of traditional knowledge of indigenous and local communities made in international biodiversity law.[110] The Nagoya Protocol on Access to Genetic Resources and the Fair and Equitable Sharing of Benefits arising from their Utilization recognizes the

[104] See Leena Heinamaki, 'Protecting the Rights of Indigenous Peoples – Promoting the Sustainability of the Global Environment?', 11 *International Community Law Review*, 2009, 3.
[105] See, for example, the increasing number of Indigenous and Community Conserved Areas (ICCAs) across the globe. See Ashish Kothari, Colleen Corrigan, Harry Jonas, Aurélie Neumann, and Holly Shrumm (eds), *Recognising and Supporting Territories and Areas Conserved by Indigenous Peoples and Local Communities: Global Overview and National Case Studies* (Natural Justice, 2012); Dudley (n 76); Stan Stevens, 'Implementing the UN Declaration on the Rights of Indigenous Peoples and International Human Rights Law Through the Recognition of ICCAs', 17 *Policy Matters*, 2010, 181–94.
[106] See Alexander Gillespie, *Conservation, Biodiversity and International Law* (Edward Elgar, 2013); Elisa Morgera and Jona Razzaque, *Biodiversity and Nature Protection Law* (Elgar Encyclopedia of Environmental Law, 2017).
[107] CBD, Art. 2.
[108] See Sarah A. Laird (ed.), *Biodiversity and Traditional Knowledge: Equitable Partnerships in Practice* (Earthscan, 2002).
[109] See Elisa Morgera, 'No Need to Reinvent the Wheel for a Human Rights-Based Approach to Tackling Climate Change: The Contribution of International Biodiversity Law'. In: Erikki Hollo, Kati Kulovesi, and Michael Mehlin (eds), *Climate Change and the Law* (Springer, 2013).
[110] See Articles 8(j) and 10(c) of the CBD. Chapter 5 examines the cultural rights connection between biodiversity and traditional knowledge.

importance of the traditional knowledge of local and indigenous communities for the conservation of biological diversity and the sustainable use of its components.[111] Likewise, the Akwé:Kon Voluntary Guidelines aim at providing general advice on the incorporation of cultural, environmental (including biodiversity-related), and social considerations of indigenous and local communities within impact assessment procedures.[112]

While the connection between biodiversity and IHRL is recent and still evolving, it has received increasing attention from human rights bodies. In 2017, the Special Rapporteur on the environment presented a specific report on the human rights obligations relating to the conservation and sustainable use of biological diversity.[113] The report demonstrates that several direct links between biodiversity and the realization of IHRL exist, including access to diversity of plants and seeds to ensure the realization of the right to food and the right to health, or the importance of diversity of minerals and water sources to ensure access to clean and safe water. The report shows an abundant variety of examples of direct connections between biodiversity and IHRL, notably the importance of ecosystem services for the realization of several key human rights such as the right to life and the right to non-discrimination. The report concludes that a human rights-based approach to biodiversity has three main advantages: (1) it clarifies that the loss of biodiversity also undermines the full enjoyment of human rights; (2) it heightens the urgent need to protect biodiversity; and (3) it promotes policy coherence and legitimacy in the conservation and sustainable use of biodiversity.[114]

One of the most developed areas linking biodiversity and IHRL relates to the rights of indigenous peoples,[115] especially in situations concerning the violations of indigenous peoples' rights over their land and natural resources. In *Kaliña and Lokono Peoples*, the IACtHR referred to provisions of the CBD in its interpretation of the ACHR.[116] International human rights treaty bodies have also highlighted the link between indigenous peoples' rights to land and natural resources and the protection of biodiversity. In its concluding observations, the CESCR declared that the loss of biodiversity leads to the violations of indigenous peoples' rights. [117]

---

[111] For an analysis of the Nagoya Protocol, see Elisa Morgera, Elsa Tsioumani, and Matthias Buck, *Unraveling the Nagoya Protocol: A Commentary on the Nagoya Protocol on Access and Benefit-Sharing to the Convention on Biological Diversity* (Brill, 2014); Kabir Bavikatte and Daniel F. Robinson, 'Towards a People's History of the Law: Biocultural Jurisprudence and the Nagoya Protocol on Access and Benefit Sharing', 7(1) *Law, Environment and Development Journal*, 2011, 35.

[112] CBD COP VII (2004), Decision VII/16, Annex, para. 2.

[113] Report of the Special Rapporteur on the Issue of Human Rights Obligations Relating to the Enjoyment of a Safe, Clean, Healthy and Sustainable Environment, UN Doc. A/HRC/34/4 (January 2017).

[114] Ibid., para. 65.

[115] As noted by the IACHR: 'Many indigenous and tribal peoples live in areas rich in living and non-living resources, including forests that contain abundant biodiversity, water, and minerals.' IACHR, *Indigenous and Tribal Peoples' Rights Over Their Ancestral Lands and Natural Resources*. OEA/Ser.L/V/II, (2009), p. 197.

[116] *Kaliña and Lokono Peoples*, 177 (quoting and incorporating Arts 8(j) and 10(c) of the CBD).

[117] See Concluding Observations of the Committee on Economic, Social and Cultural Rights: Democratic Republic of the Congo, UN Doc. E/C.12/COD/CO/4 (2009), para. 14; Concluding Observations of the Committee on Economic, Social and Cultural Rights: Cambodia, UN Doc E/C.12/KHM/CO/1 (2009), para. 15.

References to biodiversity are not limited to indigenous peoples as international human rights bodies have increasingly started to recognize the impact of biodiversity on treaty rights of other vulnerable groups, including children, rural women, or small-scale farmers. For example, CEDAW has highlighted the importance of biodiversity for rural women in Argentina.[118] The CRC has noted the particularly negative impact that the loss of biodiversity can have on the realization of children rights in the Seychelles.[119] International human rights institutions not only focus on the negative impact that the loss of biodiversity can have on human rights, but also on the positive contribution that specific rights-holders can have on the protection of biodiversity. On this front, a significant area of engagement concerns the right to access to diversity of seeds and plants for small-scale farmers.[120] The former Special Rapporteur on the right to food devoted a whole report to the issue of seed policies and the right to food highlighting the threats to seeds and biological diversity that peasants and other people working in rural areas face, and concluded that these need stronger protection under IHRL.[121] During the official visit to Mexico in 2012, the Special Rapporteur noted the negative impact that the cultivation of transgenic maize posed to the diversity of native maize, leading to loss of agro-biodiversity.[122] Likewise, as an outcome of an official visit to the Philippines, the Special Rapporteur invited the authorities to actively 'promote the conservation and management of agricultural biodiversity to ensure genetic diversity in order to sustain the natural resource base for farmer resilience, innovation and adaptation to climate change'.[123]

The issue of the protection of biodiversity and access to a variety of seeds for peasants and farmers is also at the heart of the negotiations for the eventual adoption of a Declaration on the Rights of Peasants and Other People Working in Rural Areas.[124] The draft of the declaration affirms that peasants have the right to maintain, control, protect, and develop their seeds and traditional knowledge, and more generally proclaims that:

[p]easants and other people working in rural areas have the right, individually or collectively, to conserve, maintain and sustainably use and develop biological diversity and associated knowledge, including in agriculture, fishing and livestock. They also have the right to maintain their traditional agrarian, pastoral and agroecological systems upon which their subsistence and the renewal of agricultural biodiversity depend.[125]

---

[118] Concluding Observations: Argentina, UN Doc. CEDAW/C/ARG/CO/7 (2016), para. 38.

[119] Concluding Observations: Seychelles, UN Doc. CRC/C/SYC/CO/2-4 (2012), para. 7.

[120] See Christophe Golay, 'Negotiation of a United Nations Declaration on the Rights of Peasants and Other People Working in Rural Areas', Geneva Academy, Geneva (2015).

[121] See Report of the Special Rapporteur on the Right to Food, Olivier De Schutter (on Seed Policies and the Right to Food), UN Doc. A/64/170, 23 July 2009.

[122] Report of the Special Rapporteur on the Right to Food, Mission to Mexico, UN Doc. A/HRC/19/59/Add.2 (2012), para. 52.

[123] Report of the Special Rapporteur on the Right to Food on her mission to Philippines, UN Doc. A/HRC/31/51/Add.1 (2015), para. 65.

[124] See Draft Declaration on the Rights of Peasants and Other People Working in Rural Areas, presented by the Chair-Rapporteur of the Working Group, UN Doc. A/HRC/WG.15/4/2 (2017). See also the discussion on food sovereignty in Chapter 1, and right to seeds in Chapter 5.

[125] Ibid., Arts 19 and 20.

This focus on biodiversity and agroecological knowledge is part of the larger push from other fields of international law to emphasize the importance of recognizing agro-diversity and farmer's rights.[126] The International Treaty on Plant Genetic Resources for Food and Agriculture acknowledges 'the enormous contribution that the local and indigenous communities and farmers of all regions of the world [...] have made and will continue to make for the conservation and development of plant genetic resources which constitute the basis of food and agriculture production throughout the world'.[127] The FAO guidelines also acknowledge the direct connection between biodiversity and well-being and rights of farmers and small-scale fisheries.[128]

Put together, this body of norms, recommendations, and jurisprudence highlights how IHRL participates in the emergence of what has been labelled 'biocultural rights', which include the stewardship rights that have been examined earlier, as well as the rights to the participation, management, and benefit from natural resources and the cultural rights and traditional knowledge examined in Chapter 5. 'Biocultural rights' refers to the emergence of a body of international norms recognizing the rights of indigenous and local rural communities to protect, promote, and enjoy their cultural and traditional use of natural resources as part of the overall agenda for the protection of biodiversity. This emergence arises from the junction between the fields of environmental, cultural, and human rights and, more specifically, based on the notion of biocultural diversity.[129] Bavikatte suggests that biocultural rights are emerging from several of the international biodiversity norms which acknowledge the stewardship role of indigenous and local communities over natural resources.[130] These rights are based on a community's long-established right, in accordance with its customary practices to steward its lands, waters, and resources. Bavikatte and Bennet note that 'these rights differ from the general category of indigenous rights because they presuppose an explicit link to the conservation and the sustainable use of biological diversity, and because the group need not necessarily be indigenous'.[131] They add that 'biocultural rights also differ significantly from other group rights in that the nature of the rights they seek to assert is not necessarily based on ethnicity, religion or minority status but instead on a history of stewardship'.[132] From this perspective, the overarching concept of biocultural rights offers a very

---

[126] See Juliana Santili, *Agrobiodiversity and the Law: Regulating Genetic Resources, Food Security and Cultural Diversity* (Routledge, 2012).

[127] International Treaty on Plant Genetic Resources for Food and Agriculture, Art. 9.

[128] FAO, *Voluntary Guidelines for Securing Sustainable Small-Scale Fisheries in the Context of Food Security and Poverty Eradication* (Small-Scale Fisheries Guidelines), 2014; see also *Voluntary Guidelines to Support the Progressive Realization of the Right to Food in the Context of National Food Security*, Guideline 8.12.

[129] See Luisa Maffi and Ellen Woodley, *Biocultural Diversity Conservation: A Global Sourcebook* (Earthscan, 2010); Giulia Sajeva, 'Rights with Limits: Biocultural Rights–Between Self-Determination and Conservation of the Environment', 6(1) *Journal of Human Rights and the Environment*, 2015, 30–54.

[130] See Kabir Sanjay Bavikatte, *Stewarding the Earth: Rethinking Property and the Emergence of Biocultural Rights* (OUP, 2014).

[131] Kabir Sanjay Bavikatte and Tom Bennett, 'Community Stewardship: The Foundation of Biocultural Rights', 6(1) *Journal of Human Rights and the Environment*, 2015, 10.

[132] Ibid., 27

attractive platform to adopt a much more cohesive, holistic, and comprehensive approach to the rights over natural resources essential to local communities.[133] This more cohesive approach addresses many of the issues that have been raised about the fragmentation of international law when it comes to cultural heritage, biodiversity, and human rights norms.[134] The umbrella concept of biocultural rights offers a great avenue to challenge this fragmentation and avoid the segregation between cultural and environmental rights that currently exists in international law. Overall, while it is hard to predict to what extent IHRL will specifically integrate biocultural rights in its future jurisprudence, it is certain that IHRL will play an increasingly significant role when it comes to the protection and conservation of biodiversity.

4. Climate Change, Natural Resources, and Human Rights

International law has started to fully embrace the fact that climate change represents an urgent and potentially irreversible threat to human societies and the environment. This change is taking place at different levels, either as part of specific environmental treaties and agreements or within already existing treaties or mandates.[135] The impact of climate change on human rights has also been acknowledged, as global warming could leave many without access to adequate food, water, or housing, affecting their socio-economic and cultural rights.[136] Climate change has undeniable long-term consequences on natural resources, which, in turn, bears serious consequences on human rights of the most affected populations.

In the context of this book, the aim is not to review the human rights contribution to the fight against climate change, as a very large literature is available on the issue.[137] Instead, it is to examine how a human rights-based approach to climate change could contribute to a more comprehensive understanding of peoples' rights over their natural resources. It explores the contribution of IHRL to the emergence of 'climate justice', and focuses on the human rights aspects of the discriminatory impact that the degradation of natural resources has on some of the most exposed

---

[133] See Chapter 5.

[134] See Study by the Expert Mechanism on the Rights of Indigenous Peoples, Promotion and Protection of the Rights of Indigenous Peoples with Respect to their Cultural Heritage, UN Doc. A/HRC/30/53 (2015).

[135] See Daniel Bodansky, Jutta Brunnée, and Lavanya Rajamani, *International Climate Change Law* (OUP, 2017); Kevin R. Gray, Cinnamon Piñon Carlarne, and Richard Tarasofsky, *The Oxford Handbook of International Climate Change Law* (OUP, 2016); Erkki Hollo, Kati Kulovesi, and Michael Mehling (eds), *Climate Change and the Law: A Global Perspective* (Springer, 2012).

[136] See Michael Burger and Jessica Wentz, *Climate Change and Human Rights* (UNEP Report, 2015).

[137] For references, see Ron Dudai, 'Climate Change and Human Rights Practice', 1(2) *Journal of Human Rights Practice*, 2009, 294–307; John H. Knox, 'Linking Human Rights and Climate Change at the United Nations', 33 *Harvard Environmental Law Review*, 2009, 477–98; Sumudu Atapattu, *Human Rights Approaches to Climate Change: Challenges and Opportunities* (Routledge, 2015); Ottavio Quirico and Mouloud Boumghar (eds), *Climate Change and Human Rights: An International and Comparative Law Perspective* (Routledge, 2016).

communities. [138] It also explores the role that human rights can play in the adjudication of claims against the degradation of natural resources due to climate change. Furthermore, it examines the impact of the mechanisms that have been developed to mitigate the impact of climate change on peoples' rights over their natural resources.

4.1 Climate justice, discrimination, and adjudication

The specialized legal framework governing climate, which is established by the United Nations Framework Convention on Climate Change (UNFCCC), does not specifically integrate a human rights-based approach to climate change. One of the first specific references to IHRL came only in 2010 with the adoption of the Cancun Agreement urging States to 'fully respect human rights' in all climate change-related actions.[139] Following pressure from civil society actors and international organizations, the 2015 Paris Agreement included specific statements linking the fight against climate change with the protection of IHRL.[140] The preamble declares that:

States Parties should, when taking action to address climate change, respect, promote and consider their respective obligations on human rights, the right to health, the rights of indigenous peoples, local communities, migrants, children, persons with disabilities and people in vulnerable situations and the right to development, as well as gender equality, empowerment of women and intergenerational equity.[141]

However, apart from this very generic statement in the Preamble, the specialized field of climate change law has not fully integrated a human rights-based approach to climate change.[142] On the other hand, human rights institutions have increasingly focused their attention on the human rights consequences of climate change. The UN Human Rights Council has adopted several resolutions and statements connecting the fight against climate change with the protection of human rights.[143] The main approach has been to highlight the negative consequences that climate change has on human rights. For example, it notes that:

---

[138] See Tracey Skillington, *Climate Justice and Human Rights* (Springer, 2016); Dominic Roser and Christian Seidel, *Climate Justice: An Introduction* (Taylor & Francis, 2016); Henry Shue, *Climate Justice: Vulnerability and Protection* (OUP, 2014).

[139] Cancún Agreement, adopted at the 2010 United Nations Climate Change Conference, COP16/CMP6 (10 December 2010), para. 8.

[140] See Daniel Bodansky, Jutta Brunnée, and Lavanya Rajamani, *International Climate Change Law* (OUP, 2017), pp. 310–12.

[141] 'Paris Agreement,' FCCC/CP/2015/L.9/Rev.1, Preamble, United Nations, 12 December 2015.

[142] See Lavanya Rajamani, *Rights-Based Perspectives in the International Negotiations on Climate Change* (Center for Policy Research, 2010); Sébastien Jodoin, *Lost in Translation: Human Rights in Climate Negotiations* (Center for International Sustainable Development Law, 2010); Gregor Beck, Cora Ditzel, Sofia Ganter, and Olga Perov, 'Mind the Gap: The Discrepancy between the Normative Debate and Actual Use of Human Rights Language in International Climate Negotiations', 2 *Consilience: The Journal for Sustainable Development*, 2015, 25–45.

[143] See Human Rights Council Resolution 7/23, 'Human Rights and Climate Change,' UN Doc A/HRC/7/78 (2008), Human Rights Council Resolution 10/4, 'Human Rights and Climate Change', UN Doc A/HRC/RES/10/4, 'Human Rights Council Resolution 18/22, Human Rights and Climate Change,' UN Doc A/HRC/RES/18/22 (2009), 'Human Rights Council Resolution 26/27, Human Rights and Climate Change,' UN Doc A/HRC/RES/26/27 (2010).

climate change-related impacts have a range of implications, both direct and indirect, for the effective enjoyment of human rights including, *inter alia*, the right to life, the right to adequate food, the right to the highest attainable standard of health, the right to adequate housing, the right to self-determination and human rights obligations related to access to safe drinking water and sanitation, and recalling that in no case may a people be deprived of its own means of subsistence.[144]

The Office of the UN High Commissioner for Human Rights (OHCHR) has also adopted several documents articulating the importance of adopting a human rights-based approach to tackle climate change. [145] In connection to natural resources, this approach highlights how climate fluctuations directly and negatively impact access to essential resources for the livelihood and well-being of millions of people around the globe. The approach has been dual by highlighting the consequences of climate change on the concerned resources (substantive rights approach) as well as underlining the negative impact of resources degradation on specifically vulnerable populations (rights-holders approach).

In terms of the substantive rights that are affected by climate change, human rights institutions have generally put the emphasis on the direct connection between the degradation and rarefication of essential natural resources and the impact on the right to food, right to health, right to water, and the right to an adequate standard of living.[146] For example, the Special Rapporteur on the Right to Food noted that 'climate change, which translates in more frequent and extreme weather events, such as droughts and floods and less predictable rainfall, is already having a severe impact on the ability of certain regions and communities to feed themselves'.[147] The Special Rapporteur on the human right to safe drinking water and sanitation has underlined the negative impact of climate change on the quality and quantity of water resources.[148] The negative consequences of climate change on the right to health have also been highlighted, ranging from increased vector-borne diseases to increased likelihood of undernutrition.[149]

[144] UNHRC Resolution 10/4 (2009) on Human Rights and Climate Change.

[145] See 'Understanding Human Rights and Climate Change: Key Messages,' Office of the UN High Commissioner on Human Rights, 2015.

[146] See Alessandra Franca, 'Climate Change and Interdependent Human Rights to Food, Water and Health'. In: Quirico and Boumghar (n 137).

[147] Report submitted by the Special Rapporteur on the Right to Food, Olivier De Schutter, 20 December 2010, UN Doc. A/HRC/16/49, para. 9.

[148] See Special Rapporteur on the Human Right to Safe Drinking Water and Sanitation, Mission to El Salvador, UN Doc. A/HRC/33/49/Add.1 (2016), para. 96. See also *Climate Change and the Human Rights to Water and Sanitation, Position Paper* (undated). Available at: http://www.ohchr.org/ Documents/Issues/Water/Climate_Change_Right_Water_Sanitation.pdf; see also Laura Westra, 'Climate Change and the Human Right to Water', 1(2) *Journal of Human Rights and the Environment*, 2010, 161, 174.

[149] See Office of the United Nations High Commissioner for Human Rights, Analytical Study on the Relationship between Climate Change and the Human Right of Everyone to the Enjoyment of the Highest Attainable Standard of Physical and Mental Health, UN Doc. A/HRC/32/23 (2016); see also Paul Hunt and Rajat Khosla, 'Climate Change and the Right to the Highest Attainable Standard of Health'. In: Stephen Humphreys (ed.), *Human Rights and Climate Change* (CUP, 2010), pp. 238–ss.

One of the key contributions of IHRL has been to highlight the discriminatory impact of climate change.[150] While international climate change law has put some focus on the specific vulnerability of certain populations (especially low islands nations), IHRL adds another element in underlining the discrimination faced by certain groups when it comes to the impact of climate change, notably due to inequality in access to natural resources. Climate change has a disproportionate effect on marginalized, vulnerable, and excluded individuals and groups, especially those whose ways of life are inextricably linked to access to essential natural resources threatened by climate change. For example, the negative impacts of climate change are not gender neutral, and women suffer more from it due to their predominant role across the globe in providing household nutrition that is often dependent on natural resources.[151] Hence, the degradation and reduction of the access to essential natural resources due to climate change tends to affect rural women more dramatically than their more urban counterparts.[152] The CEDAW Committee has systematically highlighted the need for public authorities to ensure that a specific gender perspective is adopted in their efforts to address climate change.[153] The OHCHR has also undertaken a specific analytical study on the relationship between climate change and the full enjoyment of the rights of the child, which highlights that shortages of safe drinking water and food (will) have disproportionate impacts on children.[154] Human rights bodies have also highlighted the negative impact of climate change and resources degradation on the rights of indigenous peoples. [155]

More generally, the increased rarefication of access to essential natural resources due to climate change will have significant effects on the poorest segments of society. The Special Rapporteur on extreme poverty stated that '[e]xtreme weather events caused by climate change can create vicious circles by increasingly forcing persons living in extreme poverty to over-exploit natural resources as a coping mechanism to ensure survival'.[156] In general, it has been noted that 'the erosion of livelihoods, in part provoked by climate change, is considered a key push factor for the increase in rural-to-urban migration, most of which will be to urban slums and informal

---

[150] See the Advisory Opinion of the Inter-American Court of Human Rights, Advisory Opinion OC-23/17 Concerning the Environment and Human Rights, November 2017.

[151] See Irene Dankelman, *Gender and Climate Change: An Introduction* (Routledge, 2012); Fatma Denton, 'Climate Change Vulnerability, Impacts, and Adaptation: Why Does Gender Matter?', 20(2) *Gender and Development*, 2010, 12.

[152] See Lena Bendlin, 'Women's Human Rights in a Changing Climate: Highlighting the Distributive Effects of Climate Policies', 27(4) *Cambridge Review of International Affairs*, 2014, 680–98.

[153] See, for example, Thailand: UN Doc. CEDAW/C/THA/CO/6-7 (2017), para. 47; Nigeria: UN Doc. CEDAW/C/NGA/CO/7-8 (2017), para. 40; Niger: UN Doc. CEDAW/C/NER/CO/3-4 (2017), para. 37; Barbados: UN Doc. CEDAW/C/BRB/CO/5-8 (2017), para. 48.

[154] Office of the United Nations High Commissioner for Human Rights, Analytical Study on the Relationship between Climate Change and the Full and Effective Enjoyment of the Rights of the Child, UN Doc. A/HRC/35/13 (2017).

[155] See Permanent Forum on Indigenous Issues: Report on the Seventh Session (21 April–2 May 2008), UN Doc. E/C.19/2008/13. See also Special Rapporteur on the Situation of Human Rights and Fundamental Freedoms of Indigenous Peoples, UN Doc. A/HRC/4/32, para. 49.

[156] Report of the Special Rapporteur on Extreme Poverty and Human Rights (Magdalena Sepúlveda Carmona), 9 August 2010, UN Doc. A/65/259, para. 38.

settlements offering precarious living conditions'.[157] The Special Rapporteur on the human rights of migrants identified various impacts from climate change on migrant workers, noting 'that the effects of climate change will likely play a significant and increasingly determinative role in international migration'.[158] These increased migration flows will severely impact the level of poverty and vulnerability faced by populations forced to migrate due to climate change. According to the Special Rapporteur on adequate housing, climate change-induced extreme weather events pose risks to the right to adequate housing in urban settlements, smaller settlements, and small islands.[159] The Special Rapporteur also cautioned that the implications of climate change will be severe, particularly for low-income groups and those living in countries that lack the resources, infrastructures, and overall capacity necessary to protect their populations.[160]

Besides the reports and recommendations of international human rights bodies, another important entry point in relation to climate change comes via litigation and adjudication. 'Climate litigation' has become an important element in seeking remedies against the negative effects of climate change, and IHRL plays an increasingly important role in these cases of litigation.[161] However, despite the mounting importance of IHRL in climate litigation, there is not (yet) a great record of successful argumentation on the discriminatory impact of climate change on access to natural resources. To date, one of the most relevant cases of adjudication concerns the 2005 petition to the Inter-American Commission on Human Rights (IACHR) from Inuit communities from northern Canada and Alaska.[162] These communities challenged the impact that global warming had on their rights to life, health, culture, and subsistence due to changes of snowfall, thinning of sea ice, melting of permafrost, and changes in animals' movements. However, the IACHR declared the petition inadmissible due to insufficient information to determine a violation of the rights protected by the American Declaration.[163]

One of the challenges relates to the legal complexity in proving a direct and immediate link between climate change and human rights violations.[164] The OHCHR

---

[157] Protection of and Assistance to Internally Displaced Persons, 9 August 2011, UN Doc. A/66/285, para. 66.

[158] Report of the Special Rapporteur on the Human Rights of Migrants to the General Assembly, 13 August 2012, UN Doc. A/67/299, para. 17.

[159] Report of the Special Rapporteur on Adequate Housing as a Component of the Right to an Adequate Standard of Living, and on the Right to Non-Discrimination in this Context, UN Doc. A/64/25 (2009).

[160] Ibid., para. 65.

[161] See Marilyn Averill, 'Linking Climate Litigation and Human Rights', 18 *Review of European Community and International Environmental Law*, 2009, 139; Eric A. Posner, 'Climate Change and International Human Rights Litigation: A Critical Appraisal', 155 *University of Pennsylvania Law Review*, 2007, 1925; William Burns and Hari Osofsky (eds), *Adjudicating Climate Change* (CUP, 2009).

[162] Sheila Watt-Cloutier, Petition to the Inter-American Commission on Human Rights Seeking Relief from Violations Resulting from Global Warming Caused by Acts and Omissions of the United States (7 December 2005).

[163] For analysis, see Hari Osofsky, 'The Inuit Petition as a Bridge: Beyond Dialectics of Climate Change and Indigenous Peoples' Rights', 31 *American Indian Law Review*, 2007, 675.

[164] See Jorge Viñuales, 'Extraterritorial Dimension of Environmental Protection'. In: Nehal Bhuta (ed.), *The Frontiers of Human Rights* (OUP, 2016), pp. 214–ss.

report on climate change notes that '[w]hile climate change has obvious implications for the enjoyment of human rights, it is less obvious whether, and to what extent, such effects can be qualified as human rights violations in a strict legal sense'.[165]
The long-term effect of climate change is an issue difficult to qualify under IHRL,
which usually focuses on immediate and measurable violations. The OHCHR report notes that:

> human rights litigation is not well-suited to promote precautionary measures based on
> risk assessments, unless such risks pose an imminent threat to the human rights of specific
> individuals.[166]

More precisely, in the context of this book, one of the difficulties is to 'prove' the
direct causality between climate change, loss of access to natural resources, and
human rights violations. This does not mean that IHRL is not relevant to legally
challenge the negative impact of climate change in courts, as across the globe more
and more cases are using human rights arguments in litigation against climate
change.[167] Crucially, these cases not only focus on the lack of governmental efforts
to fight climate change, but also increasingly involve investors and corporations for
lack of measures to reduce the negative impact of climate change.[168] This is a significantly important potential legal avenue for adjudication in that international
law usually does not provide legal remedies for individuals against large corporate
carbon producers for their contribution to climate change.[169] However, at the time
of writing, this is very much an area in development. Yet, as cases of adjudication
emerge on a daily basis, there is no doubt that they will greatly contribute to the increased connection between IHRL and the degradation of natural resources due to
climate change.

All these recent developments linking climate change, IHRL, and natural resources are part of what has been labelled as 'climate justice', which includes an effort
to develop a human rights-based approach to climate change.[170] The development
of such a body of law will have important consequences regarding the management
of natural resources, as it will provide a human rights-based approach to the extremely discriminatory and unequal impact that climate change creates in terms of
access to natural resources.

---

[165] UN HRC, Report of the OHCHR on the Relationship between Climate Change and Human
Rights, UN Doc. A/HRC/10/61, 15 January 2009, at para. 70.
[166] Ibid., para. 91.
[167] See Tessa Khan, 'Accounting for the Human Rights Harms of Climate Change', 25 *SUR-
International Journal on Human Rights*, 2017, 89.
[168] Damilola S. Olawuyi, 'Climate Justice and Corporate Responsibility: Taking Human Rights
Seriously in Climate Actions and Projects', 34 *Journal of Energy & Natural Resources Law*, 2016, 27–44.
[169] For illustrations of recent cases against corporations, see Keely Boom, Julie-Anne Richards,
and Stephen Leonard, *Climate Justice: The International Momentum Towards Climate Litigation* (The
Green Political Foundation, 2016); see also Anna Riddell, 'Human Rights Responsibility of Private
Corporations for Climate Change?'. In: Quirico and Boumghar (n 137).
[170] 'The Mary Robinson Foundation—Climate Justice' describes climate justice as an effort to link
'human rights and development to achieve a human-centred approach, safeguarding the rights of the
most vulnerable and sharing the burdens and benefits of climate change and its resolution equitably and
fairly'. See Mary Robinson Foundation—Climate Justice, 'Principles of Climate Justice', at 1.

4.2 Carbon trading and the commodification of natural resources

An important element of the international response to climate change has been to develop a specific mechanism to mitigate the impact of climate change. Many of these measures aim at reducing greenhouse gas emissions, either by setting targets to reduce emissions or by developing new technologies to produce fewer carbon emissions. Several market incentives have been put in place to support these mechanisms, leading to the emergence of a significant carbon trading market, where certified emission reduction credits can be exchanged. However, these approaches can seriously undermine and restrict access to natural resources for many local communities.

Due to the enormous impact of deforestation on climate change, the programme on Reducing Emissions from Deforestation and Forest Degradation (REDD/REDD+) has become a central element of the international mitigation strategies on climate change.[171] In short, it is a mitigation mechanism whose purpose is to address greenhouse gas emissions due to different forms of deforestation and forest degradation in developing countries and to act as an incentive to maintain forest cover. One of the mechanisms established under this scheme invites industrialized countries to make financial transfer to developing countries to compensate them for the cost of avoiding emissions from deforestation—an approach that has led to the development of a carbon trading market.[172] On top of the controversial issue of reliance on a market-based approach to climate change, the REDD process also leads to human rights violations for local forest communities.[173] The list of human rights issues raised by REDD+ is extensive, including that the commodification of forest carbon sequestration has resulted in forced eviction and loss of land rights for many local and indigenous forest communities.[174] It has also resulted in the loss of forest peoples' territories to large-scale commercial forest operations and restriction of access and use of natural resources. Other issues concern the process itself, as often there are no consultations with local communities before forests are put on a REDD platform. The lack of benefit-sharing for the local communities is also an issue of contention. In general, there has been a lack of direct participation in the design and implementation of REDD+ activities, as well as a lack of equitable benefit-sharing of forest communities.[175]

---

[171] The programme was formally endorsed by the Warsaw Framework for REDD+ in 2013, officially becoming 'Reducing Emissions from Deforestation and forest Degradation, plus the sustainable management of forests, and the conservation and enhancement of forest carbon stocks (REDD+), UNFCCC document FCCC/CP/2013/10/Add.

[172] For an insightful analysis, see Frances Seymour, 'Forest, Climate Change and Human Rights'. In: Humphreys (n 149) 207–37.

[173] See Kate Wilkinson, 'Payment for "Ecosystem Services" and the "Green Economy": Green-Washing or Something New?', 5(2) *Journal of Human Rights and the Environment*, 2014, 168–91, 179; Naomi Klein, *This Changes Everything: Capitalism vs. the Climate* (Penguin, 2014).

[174] See Malayna Raftopoulos, 'REDD+ and Human Rights: Addressing the Urgent Need for a Full Community-Based Human Rights Impact Assessment', 20(4) *The International Journal of Human Rights*, 2016, 509–30.

[175] See Annalisa Savaresi, 'REDD+ and Human Rights: Addressing Synergies between International Regimes', 18(3) *Ecology and Society*, 2013, 5.

However, there have been some improvements regarding the policy documents defining REDD processes, for example, the REDD+ Safeguards calling upon States to respect the knowledge of indigenous and local communities.[176] According to the Guidelines on Stakeholder Engagement in REDD+ Readiness, the design of benefit-sharing systems for equitable and effective distribution of REDD+ revenues shall be part of the issues for consultation with stakeholders, including forest-dependent communities.[177] There is also an increasingly positive impact of policies and mechanisms developed under biodiversity law to support the rights of the local and indigenous communities to participation, consent, and benefit-sharing in the use of their ecosystems.[178] However, despite these policy statements, at the local level there is still a very dominant top-down approach to REDD+ activities, which often results in reduction of access to natural resources located in the concerned forests for local communities, as well as loss of land rights and violations of their cultural rights.

Another area of potential clashes between IHRL and climate change mitigation processes relates to the increased marketization of clean development mechanisms (CDMs). Under the CDM, industrialized countries can support green investments in other countries to gain certified emissions credits.[179] This has led to the development of many CDM projects across the globe, ranging from geothermal, wind, hydro, and biogas power projects, and any other form of green energies that would allow for reduced release of carbon into the atmosphere. While undoubtedly these technological progresses positively tackle greenhouse gases emissions, there are some potentially negative effects on the human rights of local populations living near these large-scale developments. Many indigenous and local communities have been negatively impacted by the increased production of bioenergies or agrofuels.[180] These include the establishment of palm oil, hydroelectric dams, or wind farms on marginalized indigenous or local communities territories, leading to forced displacement, loss of livelihood, and food insecurity.[181] Indigenous peoples have been particularly affected by the large-scale development of palm oil plantations on their traditional forestlands, leading to the loss of their land and access to natural

---

[176] REDD+ Social and Environmental Standards (2010).

[177] Forest Carbon Partnership Facility (FCPF), UN-REDD, Guidelines on Stakeholder Engagement in REDD+ Readiness (2012) with a Focus on the Participation of Indigenous Peoples and Other Forest-Dependent Communities.

[178] On this interaction between biodiversity law and climate change frameworks, see Morgera (n 109) 350–90; Federico Lenzerini and Erika Piergentili, 'A Double-Edged Sword: Climate Change, Biodiversity and Human Rights', In: Quirico and Boumghar (n 137).

[179] Article 12 of the Kyoto Protocol to the United Nations Framework Convention on Climate Change, 11 December 1997, 37 *International Legal Materials* 22.

[180] See Jeanette Schade and Wolfgang Obergassel, 'Human Rights and the Clean Development Mechanism', 27(4) *Cambridge Review of International Affairs*, 2014, 717; Wolfgang Obergassel, Lauri Peterson, Florian Mersmann, Jeanette Schade, Jane Alice Hofbauer, and Monika Mayrhofer, 'Human Rights and the Clean Development Mechanism: Lessons Learned from Three Case Studies', 8(1) *Journal of Human Rights and the Environment*, 2017, 51–71.

[181] See Naomi Roht-Arriaza, 'Human Rights in the Climate Change Regime', 1 *Journal of Human Rights and the Environment*, 2010, 211; Sonja Vermeulen and Lorenzo Cotula 'Over the Heads of Local People: Consultation, Consent, and Recompense in Large-Scale Land Deals for Biofuels Projects in Africa', 37 *Journal of Peasant Studies*, 2010, 899; Kanyinke Sena, *Renewable Energy Projects and the Rights of Marginalised/Indigenous Communities in Kenya* (IWGIA, Report 21, 2015).

resources.[182] Indigenous peoples, especially across southeast Asia, have seen their forest land transformed into palm oil farms, leading to forced displacement and loss of access to essential sources of livelihood.[183]

The potential negative impact is not limited to displacement; additionally, the production of biofuels can negatively impact food production as crops previously used to feed livestock or people instead are going into fuel production. As noted by the (former) Special Rapporteur on the right to food, the increased production of biofuels has led to the reduction of lands and water resources available to produce food, and also contributed to increasing the price of food commodities, both of which have negatively impacted on the realization of the right to food.[184] The increasing investment in bioenergy or in climate geoengineering can also have consequences on the amount of land and water that are necessary for such technologies.[185] It is worth noting that many of these investments in the development of bioenergy production are part of large-scale investments that are very often covered and protected under investment treaties, adding another complex layer of legal obligations to the already complex mix of climate change law, human rights, and biodiversity law. [186] Moreover, due to the very specific nature of international investment law, IHRL is very often ignored and disregarded in arbitration disputes that might concern local peoples' rights over their natural resources.[187]

There is no doubt that carbon credit schemes and investments in green technologies play an increasingly important role in both climate change adaptation and mitigation.[188] In this context, the integration of the human rights-based approach to climate change becomes an even more important and pressing issue. In the interaction between these different fields of international law, IHRL has an important role to play in supporting a sustainable use of natural resources based on the fundamental rights of peoples over their natural resources. In many ways, IHRL is a latecomer to the law on climate change, but the dominant focus on market and financial approaches to climate change mitigation processes is adding another urgent call to recognize the importance of human rights in future mechanisms that will be developed to alleviate the effects of climate change.

---

[182] See Victoria Tauli-Corpuz and Aqqaluk Lynge, 'Impact of Climate Change Mitigation Measures on the Territories and Lands of Indigenous Peoples', UN Doc. E/2007/43 E/C.19/2007/12 (2007), para. 52.

[183] See, for example, CERD, Report on the Situation in Indonesia, UN. CERD/C/IDN/CO/3, para. 17; Marcus Colchester (ed.), *Oil Palm Expansion in South East Asia: Trends and Implications for Local Communities and Indigenous Peoples* (Forest Peoples Programme, 2011).

[184] Report of the Special Rapporteur on the Right to Food, UN Doc. A/62/289 (2007), paras 21–41.

[185] See the analysis by William C. G. Burns, 'Human Rights Dimensions of Bioenergy with Carbon Capture and Storage: A Framework for Climate Justice in the Realm of Climate Geoengineering'. In: Randall Abate (ed.), *Climate Justice: Case Studies in Global and Regional Governance Challenges* (Environmental Law Institute, 2016), pp. 149–76.

[186] See Valentina Vadi, 'Balancing Human Rights, Climate Change and Foreign Investment Protection'. In: Quirico and Boumghar (n 137).

[187] See discussion on this point in Chapter 2, and Cotula (n 74).

[188] See the proposal to establish new mechanisms to contribute to the mitigation of greenhouse gas emissions, United Nations, Paris Agreement, Art. 6.4 (2015).

5. Conclusion

This chapter has taken a wide approach to the protection of natural resources in connecting environmental concerns and IHRL. It is not possible to do justice to the very complex, rich, and ever-changing legal jurisprudence and doctrine emerging on environmental human rights. The aim here is to offer an analysis on the emerging connections, synergies, and potential clashes regarding the protection of natural resources within other fields of international law. The chapter has focused on three areas of increased interaction between environmental law, human rights, and management of natural resources: pollution, biodiversity, and climate change. As to whether IHRL should specifically cater for a specific right to the environment, there is no doubt that the engagement of IHRL with environmental concerns and, more specifically, with the protection of natural resources has increased over the last few years. There might not be a straightforward affirmation of a human right to a clean and healthy environment, but the expanding jurisprudence recognizing that States have a duty to prevent severe environmental pollution that could put human life and health in danger is certainly a path in the right direction. The rationale is that public authorities have an obligation to ensure that their actions do not lead to the pollution of natural resources which could be detrimental to the health and livelihood of local populations. In terms of the content of a human rights-based approach to natural resources management, this adds a specific emphasis on a right to be free from pollution of natural resources that are essential to the realization of the right to health, food, and water. One of the challenges ahead concerns the increased potential liability of corporations, notably in cases of transboundary pollution.

The other significant area of progress examined the evolution of 'biocultural rights' and the increasing synergies between the legal frameworks governing protected areas, biodiversity, and human rights. This evolution has come as a reaction to the historically one-sided dominant approach to wilderness, which resulted in serious violations of the rights of local and indigenous communities. While this is still a very fragile evolution lacking proper implementation at the local level, the recognition of the rights of indigenous and local populations in protected areas offers some new perspectives on future potential co-management and stewardship approaches to the protection of endangered natural areas. One of the most promising legal developments is probably the recognition of the role that indigenous peoples and local communities can play in the protection of biodiversity. From this perspective, the emergence of biocultural rights which join concerns on biodiversity, cultural heritage, and human rights certainly offers one of the most dynamic and promising changes in terms of the protection of natural resources. To support the maturing of biocultural rights, IHRL needs to engage more wholeheartedly with the protection of biodiversity, recognizing the legal value of traditional ecosystem knowledge and the legal value of community biocultural protocols.

Lastly, one of the front lines of engagement between IHRL and environmental concerns centres on climate change and the emergence of climate justice. Here, IHRL plays an important role by ensuring that the increasingly dominant market and financial approach to climate change mitigation keeps a human face. Most of the recent initiatives to lessen the negative impact of the emission of greenhouse gases have relied on the commodification of natural resources. While, undoubtedly, in the current dominant capitalistic economic market this approach is essential to ensure practical and fast solutions to climate change, human rights are equally necessary to ensure that the carbon market respects the fundamental access to natural resources from the most marginalized and discriminated populations. In such a context, IHRL can also provide a platform to ensure that the resilience and adaptation of populations that are the most at risk are integrated and valued in the effort to combat climate change. For the time being, the dominance of financial and investment norms over IHRL is a worrying sign that the commodification of natural resources will lead to even further degradation of very fragile ecosystems.

Overall, taking stock of the different approaches examined in this chapter, IHRL plays an increasingly important role in environmental policies and litigation. The contribution of a human rights-based approach to the protection of natural resources is manifold. It brings a more human focus to the protection of natural resources as environmental law is largely driven by State-to-State relationships, with little space for the rights of the individuals or the local communities directly affected by these regulations. From this perspective, one attraction of a human rights-based approach to the protection of natural resources relates to the fact that it can create possibilities for individuals and civil society to engage in litigation to seek remedies and changes to protect natural resources. This possibility is lacking under more general environmental treaties that are usually based on State-to-State processes.[189]

Another important contribution of IHRL is to build bridges between distant areas of international environmental law. Conservation, biodiversity, and climate change law often work in silos, and despite touching on similar issues, these legal frameworks remain extremely specialized and have little interconnection. The language of IHRL is not only important in conceptualizing the rights-based approach to natural resources' protection, but it also encompasses a more holistic and comprehensive approach to the relationship between humans and natural resources. Indeed, one of the complexities of environmental law is the division between different approaches to natural resources, including the laws governing protected areas, resources depletion, fragile environments, water and marine resources, biodiversity, natural heritage, and climate change. In offering an approach grounded on biocultural rights, IHRL can potentially offer a more holistic approach to our relationship with natural resources by recognizing the fundamental cultural and spiritual connections to our environment. There is undoubtedly an inherent danger to this human-centred approach to natural resources, which could lead to an even more anthropocentric

---

[189] This is the case under most Non-Compliance Procedures (NCPs) under international environmental law, with the notable exception of the Aarhus Convention Compliance Mechanism, see Svitlana Kravchenko, 'The Aarhus Convention and Innovations in Compliance with Multilateral Environmental Agreements', 18 *Colorado Journal of International Environmental Law & Policy*, 2007, 1; Veit Koester, 'The Compliance Committee of the Aarhus Convention', 37 *Environmental Policy and Law*, 2007, 84.

dominance of the legal framework governing the protection of nature.[190] But as the threats to natural resources and the new technologies to extract and exploit natural resources are relentless,[191] the emergence of norms on biocultural rights are putting forward notions of stewardship and custodianship of natural resources rather than notions of ownership, sovereignty, and management which have thus far dominated the international legal framework.

[190] See Marie-Catherine Petersmann, 'Narcissus' Reflection in the Lake: Untold Narratives in Environmental Law beyond the Anthropocentric Frame', 30 *Journal of Environmental Law*, 2018, 1–25.

[191] For more recent challenges, see issues concerning Tar Sands and Fracking, Damien Short, Jessica Elliot, Kadin Norder, Edward Lloyd-Davies, and Joanna Morley, 'Extreme Energy, "Fracking" and Human Rights: A New Field for Human Rights Impact Assessments?', 19(6) *The International Journal of Human Rights*, 2015, 697–736; Jennifer Huseman and Damien Short. ' "A Slow Industrial Genocide": Tar Sands and the Indigenous Peoples of Northern Alberta', 16(1) *The International Journal of Human Rights*, 2012, 216–37.

Conclusion

1. Human Rights and the Legalization of Natural Resources Management

The 'quest' for natural resources and their subsequent exploitation is continuing to expand, leading to 'unprecedented crisis of resource depletion'.[1] An important effect of this expansion is the accompanying levels of legalization of natural resources management. Conventionally, the international legal framework governing natural resources has been restricted to a few very specialized areas of international law. This traditional specialization has increasingly been challenged with more and more legal fields touching on issues of natural resources management. This growth has resulted in a complex and fragmented international legal framework encompassing public international law, international investment law, international trade law, international environmental law, international biodiversity law, international cultural heritage law, international criminal law, international humanitarian law, international law of the sea and watercourses, international space law, international development law, and international human rights law. It has also led to a dramatic rise in the number of cases of adjudication about natural resources management in investment arbitration, State territorial disputes, trade-related disputes, environmental litigation, and human rights cases. In this context, a human rights-based approach to natural resources management can play a very important role in ensuring a better and fairer inclusion of local communities. This chapter examines what the content of a human rights-based approach to natural resources might be, who the right-holders of a human rights-based approach to natural resources might be, and who the potential duty-bearers are of such an approach. Lastly, it asks what might the value be of a human rights-based approach to natural resources and looks at its prospects, potential challenges, and limitations.

2. What is the Content of a Human Rights-Based Approach to Natural Resources?

A human rights-based approach to natural resources management is not based on any specific human rights treaty, or any specific provision, but rather emerges as part of an

---

[1] Michael T. Klare, *The Race for What's Left: The Global Scramble for the World's Last Resources* (Picador, 2012).

Natural Resources and Human Rights: An Appraisal. Jérémie Gilbert. © J. Gilbert 2018. Published 2018 by Oxford University Press.

enlarged approach to different elements of human rights law scattered across several different treaties and instruments. The right to self-determination contains one of the clearest references to natural resources by proclaiming that 'all peoples may, for their own ends, freely dispose of their natural wealth and resources'. Although this was proclaimed within the overall caveat of States' permanent sovereignty over natural resources, it offers a strong legal statement highlighting that sovereignty over natural resources should be exercised to benefit peoples. Although often lacking practical implementation, the right to self-determination over natural resources represents an important vindication of human rights law's relevance to natural resources management and of a human rights-based approach to natural resources. Indigenous peoples have successfully revived the promise of self-determination by pushing for the development of norms and jurisprudence recognizing their right to self-determination over the natural resources located in their ancestral territories. The revival of self-determination over natural resources continues under the principle of food sovereignty, advocated by transnational farmers' movements. In this context, self-determination serves as an overarching principle to reclaim control over natural resources that are essential to food production based on Article 1 of the two International Covenants that proclaim peoples should freely dispose of their natural resources.

The right to property, which guarantees and protects the rights to use, access, and dispose of natural resources, has increasingly been connected to indigenous peoples' land ownership and includes property rights over natural resources.[2] Outside the rights of indigenous peoples, there is a developing jurisprudence on usage, access, and collective tenure rights to forests and fisheries for local communities. The right to development and its progressive integration in the governance of natural resources has been integrated as an important legal principle to ensure the participation of local populations in the management of natural resources. The breakthrough of the emergence of a right to participation and consultation for indigenous peoples, which led the way for the proclamation of the right to FPIC, is now a significant legal tool in the governance of natural resources. The right to participation and consultation are also integrated in the governance of natural resources for non-indigenous communities. These legal developments linking governance of natural resources with principles of consultation, consent, and participation produced ripple effects on the overall governance of natural resources, stressing that ensuring a participatory approach to development also means benefiting from these developments. This approach is embedded in the right to development, but also grounded in the right to self-determination, the right to public participation, and the principle of non-discrimination.

The right to life also constitutes an important legal basis to the human rights-based approach to natural resources. A substantial jurisprudence and doctrine have emerged connecting the right to life and access to essential natural resources, including water and other natural resources that are essential to ensure access to adequate and sufficient food and health. The connection applies to the increased targeting and killing of persons that are involved in protests against project involving the exploitation and degradation of natural resources. In these contexts, the human

---

[2] See Jérémie Gilbert, *Indigenous Peoples' Land Rights under International Law* (Brill, 2016).

rights to freedom of assembly, freedom of association, freedom of expression, and the right to the physical integrity of the person are important elements of a human rights-based approach to the management of natural resources.

Additionally, cultural rights constitute a significant component of the human rights-based approach to natural resources management. These rights include the protection and promotion of cultural practices and traditions connected to the use of natural resources. Human rights law recognizes that the protection of both cultural practices and traditional methods of using natural resources is essential to ensure the cultural survival of indigenous peoples. It also recognizes the importance of traditional knowledge connected to the use of natural resources. Human rights law acknowledges that sacred and spiritual connections to natural resources constitute important elements of religious and spiritual practices of many communities. As such, the right to freedom of thought, conscience, and religion is an important ingredient of the human rights-based approach to natural resources management.

This approach is also shaped by environmental law. Despite debate over what constitutes an international human right to a healthy environment, there is substantial jurisprudence on the impact of the pollution of natural resources on the enjoyment of human rights. This jurisprudence includes procedural rights, such as the right to information and the right to access remedies, as well as biocultural rights, including cultural rights, participatory rights, environmental rights, and self-determination. The impact of climate change on the right to food, right to water, and, more generally, on the right to an adequate standard of living creates another area of interaction between human rights law and the management of natural resources.

Overall, there is a solid legal foundation to support a human-rights based approach to the management, use, and protection of natural resources. The catalogue of rights relevant to natural resources includes both civil and political rights, such as the right to life, personal integrity of the person or freedom of assembly, expression and speech, as well as economic-social and cultural rights such as the right to food, water, or health; this variety of rights is testimony to the inherent independence and indivisibility of human rights law. Based on the findings of the book, Box 1 proposes

---

Box 1 Proposition for a human rights-based approach to natural resources management

I. Overarching principles

    a. The right to self-determination over natural resources
    b. Non-discrimination and equality

II. Fundamental rights
    a. Right to life
    b. Right to adequate standards of living
      i. Right to food
      ii. Right to water
      iii. Right to health
    c. Right to personal integrity of the person

III. Essential freedoms
   a. Freedom of expression and speech
   b. Freedom of assembly and protest
   c. Freedom of information

IV. Participatory rights
   a. Right to development
   b. Public participation and consultation
   c. Fair and Equitable benefit-sharing
   d. Right to free, prior, and informed consent
   e. Access to remedies

V. Cultural rights
   a. Rights for minorities to enjoy their own culture, to profess and practise their own religion, or to use their own language
   b. Right to freedom of thought, conscience, and religion
   c. Biocultural rights

VI. Environmental rights
   a. Freedom from pollution
   b. Right to family and private life
   c. Participation and access to information

a comprehensive, coherent, and workable framework on the content of a human rights-based approach to natural resources management.

This overview and classification is not meant to be comprehensive and definitive, but rather aims at supporting the development of future research and advocacy regarding the role of human rights law as it applies to natural resources. Hopefully, it will support further development and enhancement of what the content of a human rights-based approach to natural resources might look like.

3. Specific Rights-Holders: Indigenous Peoples, Rural Women, Farmers, and Local Communities

The most advanced developments made by human rights law in addressing natural resources have occurred around groups of specific rights-holders; peoples, individuals, and communities for whom access, control, and management of natural resources are essential to the enjoyment of their fundamental human rights.

Over the last few decades, indigenous peoples have successfully pushed human rights law to recognize their fundamental human right to natural resources. This recognition has taken place at several levels, including normative, jurisprudential, and policy levels. In terms of the normative development, the United Nations Declaration on the Rights of Indigenous Peoples makes several specific references to indigenous peoples' right to natural resources, including ownership, cultural, and spiritual elements.[3] Likewise,

---

[3] See UN Declaration on the Rights of Indigenous Peoples (UNDRIP), Preamble, Arts 8, 25, 26, 27, 28, 29, 31, and 32.

the ILO Convention 169 also integrates relevant provisions concerning indigenous peoples' rights over natural resources. International human rights-monitoring bodies have provided a large body of decisions, recommendations, and comments on the rights of indigenous peoples to natural resources. In terms of the jurisprudence, a very substantive body of rulings and decisions concerns indigenous peoples' rights to natural resources in the African and Inter-American human rights courts and commissions. Most international organizations have adopted specific policies recognizing the importance of the human rights to natural resources for indigenous peoples.

Additionally, many international human rights bodies recognize rural women's rights over natural resources as a specific area, which includes participatory rights, management rights, and property rights. The Committee on the Elimination of Discrimination against Women (CEDAW) has focused on the importance of guaranteeing access, property rights, and rights to land, water, and other natural resources for rural women.[4] CEDAW has noted how rural women face systemic discrimination in accessing natural resources,[5] and it has also emphasized the extremely important and positive contribution that rural women make to the protection of biodiversity, as well as the important role they play in the fight against climate change.[6]

Furthermore, peasants, small-scale farmers, subsistence farmers, and agricultural workers also appear in human rights documents. For example, in 2017 the Human Rights Council highlighted the importance of traditional sustainable agricultural practices, e.g. traditional seed supply systems, for many small-scale and subsistence farmers.[7] There is a lack of consistency in the terminology used with references to small-scale farmers, landless peasants, or subsistence farmers; however, there does exist an overarching agreement that small-scale and exploited farmers are lacking protection in terms of the rights to natural resources. This push to recognize the rights of peasants and small-scale farmers to natural resources is influencing the negotiations to adopt a UN Declaration on the Rights of Peasants and Other People Working in Rural Areas.[8] The draft text defines peasants as

any person who engages or who seeks to engage alone, or in association with others or as a community, in small-scale agricultural production for subsistence and/or for the market, and who relies significantly, though not necessarily exclusively, on family or household labour and other non-monetized ways of organizing labour, and who has a special dependency on and attachment to the lands.[9]

---

[4] For references, see CEDAW, General Recommendation No. 34 on the Rights of Rural Women, UN Doc. CEDAW/C/GC/34 (2016).

[5] See, for example, CEDAW, General Recommendation No. 21 on Equality in Marriage and Family Relations, para. 27 (contained in A/49/38, Chapter I, A).

[6] See, for example, Concluding Observations: Argentina, UN Doc. CEDAW/C/ARG/CO/7 (2016), para. 38.

[7] Human Rights Council, UN Doc. A/HRC/34/L.21 (21 March 2017).

[8] See Open-Ended Intergovernmental Working Group on a United Nations Declaration on the Rights of Peasants and Other People Working in Rural Areas, Human Rights Council, Promotion and Protection of the Human Rights of Peasants and Other People Working in Rural Areas, UN Doc. A/HRC/RES/21/19 (2012).

[9] Draft Declaration on the Rights of Peasants and Other People Working in Rural Areas presented by the Chair-Rapporteur of the working group, UN Doc. A/HRC/WG.15/4/2 (6 March 2017), Art. 1.

Article 5, dedicated exclusively to natural resources, declares that '[p]easants and other people working in rural areas have the right to have access to and to use the natural resources present in their communities that are required to enjoy adequate living conditions. They have the right to participate in the management of these resources and to enjoy the benefits of their development and conservation in their communities.'[10]

The Declaration's final content and its adoption are still uncertain, but irrespective of the outcome, its draft state alone highlights a need to recognize the rights of small-scale farmers and peasants over natural resources.

Human rights institutions also refer to very specific categories of rights-holders, such as pastoralists, hunter-gatherers, or fisher-folk, based on the special relationship that these groups have with natural resources. Likewise, human rights institutions have referred to 'forest communities' and 'fishing communities'. In its Resolution on the Protection of Sacred Natural Sites and Territories, the African Commission referred to 'custodian communities'.[11] These references to specific rights-holders are part of the larger references made to the rights of 'local communities'. International legal instruments and human rights institutions are increasingly referring to the generic category of 'local communities'.

Originally, the term appeared in international legal instruments concerning biodiversity law. For example, the text of the Convention on Biological Diversity (CBD) and the decisions of the Conference of the Parties and its subsidiary bodies use the term 'indigenous and local communities'.[12] There is no absolute or binding definition on the use of such terminology, but the CBD has put forward several characteristics used to define local communities,[13] including lifestyles linked to traditions associated with natural cycles, or the community's occupation of a definable territory that has traditionally been occupied and/or used, either permanently or periodically.[14] The term 'local communities' is also used in the 2003 UNESCO Convention on the Safeguarding of the Intangible Cultural Heritage,[15] which also refers to these rights.[16] The 1994 United Nations Convention to Combat

---

[10] Ibid.

[11] African Commission on Human and Peoples' Rights, Resolution on the Protection of Sacred Natural Sites and Territories, ACHPR/Res. 372 (LX) 2017. The term 'custodian communities' refers to communities 'who maintain customary governance systems to protect sacred natural sites and territories'.

[12] Convention on Biological Diversity, 1992. See the Preamble, which recognizes 'the close and traditional dependence of many indigenous and local communities embodying traditional lifestyles on biological resources, and the desirability of sharing equitably benefits arising from the use of traditional knowledge, innovations and practices relevant to the conservation of biological diversity and the sustainable use of its components'.

[13] On the debates that lead to the adoption of the terminology 'indigenous peoples and local communities', see CBD Decision XI/14 G (2012), para. 2.

[14] Report of the Expert Group Meeting of Local Community Representatives within the context of Article 8(j) and related provisions of the Convention of Biological Diversity (4 Sept 2011), UNEP/CBD/WG8J/7/8/Add.1, Annex I.

[15] For analysis, see Janet Blake, *Commentary of the UNESCO 2003 Convention on the Safeguarding of the Intangible Cultural Heritage* (Institute of Art & Law, 2006).

[16] For analysis, see Sabrina Urbinati, 'The Role for Communities, Groups and Individuals under the Convention for the Safeguarding of the Intangible Cultural Heritage'. In: Silvia Borelli and Federico

Desertification (UNCCD) calls for the participation of 'traditional local communities' in the design and implementation of programmes to combat desertification.[17] The 2006 International Tropical Timber Agreement (ITTA) encourages States to support and develop land reforestation and management 'with due regard for the interests of local communities dependent on forest resources'.[18] Overall, under international environmental and cultural heritage law, the terms 'local' and 'traditional' communities are used to refer to local stakeholders in the management of natural resources.[19]

International human rights institutions use a similar approach regarding the local communities who claim a right to those natural resources located in their vicinity. In doing so, human rights law refers to peoples whose life is directly connected to the use of natural resources, and that their fundamental human rights often depend on the protection of these resources. Clarke notes that:

these local communities should have human rights protection in respect to the resources they utilise collectively simply by virtue of their local identity, and not by virtue of any special consideration that should be given to them because of the indigenous or minority status of the community, or because their resource use is integral to the cultural identity of the community.[20]

This broad approach does not mean that the complexity of identity markers between individuals and groups or their social constructs are ignored.[21] Rather, it acknowledges that the management of natural resources constitutes an important element of the human rights of the local communities, not only as individual rights, but also as collective rights.

4. Duty-Bearers: States, International Organizations, Financial Institutions, and Corporations

Human rights law traditionally addresses the relationship between public authorities and peoples; as such, the main duty-bearer of human rights law is the State. However, this is gradually changing as potential non-State duty-bearers are identified, including public international institutions, financial institutions, private

---

Lenzerini (eds), *Cultural Heritage, Cultural Rights, Cultural Diversity. New Developments in International Law* (Leiden, 2012), pp. 201–ss.

[17] United Nations Convention to Combat Desertification in those Countries Experiencing Serious Drought and/or Desertification, Particularly in Africa (1994), Art. 3(a).

[18] International Tropical Timber Agreement (2006), Art. 1(j).

[19] For analysis, see Adriana Bessa, 'Traditional Local Communities: What Lessons Can Be Learnt at the International Level from the Experiences of Brazil and Scotland?', 24(3) *Review of European Community & International Environmental Law*, 2015, 330–40.

[20] Alison Clarke, 'Property, Human Rights and Communities'. In: Ting Xu and Jean Alain (eds), *Property and Human Rights in a Global Context* (Hart Publishing, 2015), p. 20.

[21] For a critical analysis on the notion of 'communities', see Eric Hobsbawm and Terence O. Ranger, *The Invention of Tradition* (CUP/Canto, 1992); Peter Geschiere, *The Perils of Belonging: Autochthony, Citizenship and Exclusion in Africa and Europe* (University of Chicago Press, 2009); Dorothy L. Hodgson, 'Becoming Indigenous in Africa', 52(9) *African Studies Review*, 2009, 1–32; Emma Waterton

corporations, and armed groups.[22] Permanent State sovereignty over natural resources comes with the duty to ensure the well-being of their peoples. This stewardship approach entails that States have a duty to ensure the 'best' use of these resources, despite the lack of international monitoring on the delivery of this obligation. In this context, human rights law offers an important platform to support this overall 'stewardship' duty of public authorities by monitoring how the States' management of natural resources affects the human rights of their citizens. From this viewpoint, it guides what the duties of the States might be regarding the relationship between their sovereignty over natural resources and their people.

There are both positive and negative obligations that form part of this 'stewardship' role of the State. Public authorities have a duty to refrain from inducing conditions that impede peoples from attaining the necessities of life, including accessing natural resources that are essential to ensure life. It also calls on States to ensure that citizens have access to information about any potential pollution of natural resources. In terms of positive obligations, human rights law supports a participatory approach to the management of natural resources, putting forward the right to participation and benefit from the use of natural resources. It also calls for public authorities to respect the cultural rights of their citizens regarding the use of natural resources. States also have an obligation to guarantee the enjoyment of human rights without discrimination and to ensure the equal right to the enjoyment of these rights, which has some important repercussion on the ways the access and use of natural resources are guaranteed.

The State has an obligation to achieve the progressive realization of economic, social, and cultural rights while utilizing the maximum of its available resources. This has repercussions for fiscal and taxation regimes emerging from the exploitation of natural resources. Public authorities also must intervene to protect their citizens' human rights against actions of other actors who might endanger these rights. With this in mind, a human rights-based approach to the management of natural resources means that States have an obligation to respect the cultural, livelihood, and property rights of local populations over natural resources, and that they have an obligation to protect their citizens against any loss of access to natural resources because of actions from other enterprises or individuals. Finally, public authorities have an obligation to fulfil their citizens' access to and utilization of resources and means to ensure livelihoods, including food security, as well as support a participatory approach to the management of national natural resources.

and Laurajane Smith, 'The Recognition and Misrecognition of Community Heritage', 16(1–2) *International Journal of Heritage Studies*, 2010, 4–15.

[22] See Kurt Mills and David J. Karp (eds), *Human Rights Protection in Global Politics: Responsibilities of States and Non-State Actors* (Springer, 2015); John Gerrard Ruggie, *Just Business: Multinational Corporations and Human Rights* (W.W. Norton, 2013); David J. Karp, *Responsibility for Human Rights: Transnational Corporations in Imperfect States* (CUP, 2014); Surya Deva and David Bilchitz (eds), *Human Rights Obligations of Business: Beyond the Corporate Responsibility to Respect?* (CUP, 2013); Juan Pablo Bohoslavsky and Jernej Letnar Černič (eds), *Making Sovereign Financing and Human Rights Work* (Hart, 2014); Andrew Clapham, 'Focusing on Armed Non-State Actors'. In: Andrew Clapham and

International organizations play a very significant role in the management and protection of natural resources and their obligation to respect human rights law is essential.[23] International human rights treaty-monitoring bodies increasingly refer UN specialized agencies, including UNESCO, the ILO, and other relevant bodies within the United Nations system, to their obligations to respect human rights.[24] This also includes the World Bank, regional development banks, the International Monetary Fund, and the World Trade Organization.[25] In general, international organizations are now subject to scrutiny about their fulfilling these obligations to respect and protect human rights law,[26] especially in more recent treaties.[27] As such, international organizations are gradually integrating human rights language into their own the policy instruments. For example, the Food and Agriculture Organization (FAO) voluntary guidelines include direct references to the human rights of peasants, fisher-folk, pastoralists, and rural workers.[28]

Financial institutions, including private investment funds, banks, and others involved in the exploitation, protection, and management of natural resources, have a direct impact on the human rights of local individuals and communities over their natural resources. There is still a gap regarding their obligations due to the conflicts between international investment law and human rights law. There is currently intensive arbitration activity in this field of law; hopefully, these cases will lead to a better articulation of the obligations of private financial institutions. Private corporations play a dominant role in the exploitation of natural resources, and the human rights obligations of corporations, especially extractive industries, are set out in several international human rights institutions. For example, in 2017 the CESCR General Comment on the Impact of Business on Human Rights noted that:

[a]mong the groups that are often disproportionately affected by the adverse impact of business activities are women, children, indigenous peoples, particularly in relation to the development, utilization or exploitation of lands and natural resources, peasants, fisherfolk

---

Paola Gaeta (eds), *The Oxford Handbook of International Law in Armed Conflict* (OUP, 2014), pp. 766–810, at 802–5.

[23] See Nico Schrijver, *Development without Destruction: The UN and Global Resource Management* (Indiana University Press, 2010).

[24] For analysis and references, see Andrew Clapham, 'Human Rights Obligations for Non-State-Actors: Where are We Now?'. In: Fannie Lafontaine (ed.), *Doing Peace the Rights Way: Essays in International Law and Relations in Honour of Louise Arbour* (Intersentia, 2018).

[25] See Report of the Independent Expert on the Promotion of a Democratic and Equitable International Order, UN Doc. A/HRC/36/40 (2017); Report of the Special Rapporteur on the Right to Food, UN Doc. A/HRC/10/5/Add.2 (2009).

[26] See Jan Wouters, Eva Brems, Stefan Smis, and Pierre Schmitt (eds), *Accountability for Human Rights Violations by International Organisations* (Intersentia, 2010).

[27] See, for example, Convention on the Rights of Persons with Disabilities, Arts 42–4. For analysis, see Martin Faix, 'Binding International Organisations to Human Rights Obligations—Some Underlying Questions'. In: Pavel Šturma and Narciso Leandro Xavier Baez (eds), *International and Internal Mechanisms of Fundamental Rights Effectiveness*, (RW&W, 2015), pp. 37–52 at 51–2; Martin Faix, 'Are International Organisations Bound by International Human Rights Obligations?', 5 *Czech Yearbook of Public and Private International Law*, 2014, 267–90.

[28] FAO, *Voluntary Guidelines for Securing Sustainable Small-Scale Fisheries in the Context of Food Security and Poverty Eradication* (Small-Scale Fisheries Guidelines), 2014.

and other people working in rural areas, and ethnic or religious minorities where these minorities are politically disempowered.[29]

The former UN Special Rapporteur on the rights of indigenous peoples noted that corporations bear a responsibility to respect indigenous peoples' right to participate in decisions concerning activities potentially affecting their lands and resources. This obligation is independent of the States' duty to consult with indigenous peoples prior to the implementation of measures affecting them.[30]

Endorsed by the UN Human Rights Council in 2011, the UN Framework on Business and Human Rights and its Guiding Principles has launched several complementary initiatives to support the development of the law on business and human rights. The ongoing negotiations of the UN Human Rights Council Open-Ended Intergovernmental Working Group on Transnational Corporations and Other Business Enterprises with Respect to Human Rights regarding the 'content, scope, nature and form' of a future international instrument indicate the importance given to this topic by the international community.[31] Irrespective of the future of this potential instrument, there is an increased volume of litigation and adjudication regarding the violations of the human rights of local communities over their natural resources by corporations. This increase will undoubtedly lead to a more systematic and comprehensive doctrine regarding the relationship between human rights law and corporations.

5. The Value of a Human Rights-Based Approach to Natural Resources: Prospects, Challenges, and Limitations

In terms of its prospects, human rights law supports a people-centred approach to the use and management of natural resources. Most of the international legal processes for the management and governance of natural resources are State-centric and usually dominated by top-down processes controlled by governments and specialized international governmental organizations, where there is little space for the concerned local communities. The only real legal challenge to this States-dominant approach comes from international environmental law as it concerns the protection of natural resources. Human rights law puts fundamental human rights over natural resources in the equation, championing the idea that indigenous peoples, local communities, and rural women should be included in the protection, use, and management of their own natural resources. In offering an overarching legal framework to support indigenous peoples and local communities' rights to participate directly in and benefit

---

[29] General Comment No. 24 (2017) on State Obligations under the International Covenant on Economic, Social and Cultural Rights in the Context of Business Activities, UN Doc. E/C.12/GC/24, para. 8.

[30] Report to the Human Rights Council A/HRC/15/37. Summary of Activities, Corporate Responsibility with Respect to Indigenous Peoples (19 July 2010), para. 67.

[31] For updates on this process, see their website. Available at: http://www.ohchr.org/EN/HRBodies/HRC/WGTransCorp/Pages/IGWGOnTNC.aspx.

directly from the governance of natural resources, human rights law supports a more 'bottom-up' approach to the management of natural resources. It gives space for individuals and communities to take part in the law governing natural resources.

The focus on more participatory and beneficial management of natural resources can greatly contribute to fighting the so-called 'curse of natural resources'. A human rights-based approach to the management of natural resources ensures direct benefits for the local population. The High-Level Panel of Experts on Food Security and Nutrition of the Committee on World Food Security noted in its 2011 report that:

[n]ational governments often simply assert underlying ownership of all resources, managed by and held in trust for the benefit of the citizenry. This leaves millions of smallholders vulnerable to dispossession.[32]

The principles of participation and benefit-sharing, as well as a non-discriminatory approach to property rights, offer tools to challenge the high poverty levels faced by many marginalized rural communities by ensuring much more inclusive and beneficial participation of local communities. In supporting not only participation to developmental projects but also benefit-sharing, human rights law has an important role to dispel the curse of natural resources.

A human rights-based approach also recognizes a culturally embedded understanding of laws and customs governing the use of natural resources. In most situations, natural resources are considered according to their economic potential; human rights law supports a more culturally based approach to natural resources by recognizing and protecting the value of natural resources from this point of view. While international cultural heritage law and international environmental law also support biocultural rights, sustainable development, and more local management of natural resources, these processes are still very much State-centred and remain fragmented. Under the broad heading of cultural rights, human rights law offers a more holistic approach to ensure protection of cultural heritage, traditional knowledge, and spiritual ties to natural resources.

Additionally, human rights law can address some of the past damage done through the top-down approaches to environmental protection. It supports the reconciliation between conservation goals that emerged under the paradigm of pristine nature and local communities' traditional rights and management of natural resources. It challenges the presumption that participants in open-access systems lack sufficient incentive to conserve resources or protect the environment, disputing the legacy of the 'tragedy of the commons', which wrongly pointed toward communities' collective forms of property over natural resources as a source of resource degradation.[33]

---

[32] Committee on World Food Security (CWFS), 'Land Tenure and International Investments in Agriculture: A Report by the High-Level Panel of Experts on Food Security and Nutrition', July 2011, 40. Available at: http://www.fao.org/fileadmin/user_upload/hlpe/hlpe_docu ments/HLPE-Land-tenure-and-international-investments-in-agriculture-2011.pdf.

[33] See Elinor Ostrom, *Governing the Commons: The Evolution of Institutions for Collective Action* (CUP, 1990).

More space should be provided for human rights law in the natural resources management framework, not only for its potential beneficial impact, but also as a way to address the fragmentation of the international legal framework. Human rights law finds itself at the junction between several other specialized fields of international law, where there are often inextricable contradictions and a lack of harmonization and collaboration between these specialized fields. Human rights law is one of the few areas of international law that addresses all the issues at the heart of international law governing natural resources. A better integration of human rights obligations in other fields of international law could serve as a benchmark for the other areas governing the international law on natural resources.

In the overall architecture dominating international resources law, there are very few avenues for individuals and communities to claim their rights to control the way natural resources are used. The human rights language offers a platform to push for policy changes by empowering indigenous peoples, local communities, small-scale farmers, and rural women to challenge the lack of respect, protection, and fulfilment of their fundamental rights over natural resources. A human rights-based approach to natural resources might not lead to direct implementation and compliance at local levels, but it offers a supportive platform to argue for change.[34] It will not be a simple or expedient process; yet, identifying common elements that connect human rights law and natural resources law can support local communities in reclaiming their fundamental rights. Ultimately, the value of human rights law is to provide a platform to claim a rights-based approach to the management of natural resources, highlighting that the most directly concerned individuals, peoples, and communities should be directly involved in managing their own natural resources.

---

[34] See Thomas Risse, Stephen C. Ropp, and Kathryn Sikkink (eds), *The Persistent Power of Human Rights: From Commitment to Compliance* (CUP, 2013); Courtney Hillebrecht, *Domestic Politics and International Human Rights Tribunals: The Problem of Compliance* (CUP, 2014).

Selected Bibliography

Aaron, E., 'The Application of International Criminal Law to Resource Exploitation: Ituri, Democratic Republic of the Congo', 47 *Natural Resources Journal*, 2007, 225–45.

Aguire, D., *Human Right to Development in a Globalized Context* (Ashgate Publishing, 2008).

Alam, S., Bhuiyan, J. H., and Razzaque, J., (eds), *International Natural Resources Law, Investment and Sustainability* (Routledge, 2017).

Alden Wily, L., ' "The Law is to Blame": The Vulnerable Status of Common Property Rights in Sub-Saharan Africa', 42(3) *Development and Change*, 2011, 733–57.

Allison, E., Åsgård B., and Willmann, R., 'Human Rights Approaches to Governing Fisheries', 10 *Maritime Studies*, 2011, 5–13.

Allison, E., Ratner, B. D., Åsgård, B., Willmann, R., Pomeroy, R., and Kurien, J., 'Rights-Based Fisheries Governance: From Fishing Rights to Human Rights', 13(1) *Fish and Fisheries*, 2012, 14–29.

Anton, D., and Shelton, D., *Environmental Protection and Human Rights* (CUP, 2011).

Aponte, M-L., 'The U'WA and Occidental Petroleum: Searching for Corporate Accountability in Violations of Indigenous Land Rights', 31(2) *American Indian Law Review*, 2006, 651–73.

Atapattu, S., *Human Rights Approaches to Climate Change: Challenges and Opportunities* (Routledge, 2015).

Barnes, R., *Property Rights and Natural Resources* (Hart Publishing, 2009).

Barrera-Hernandez, L., 'Sovereignty over Natural Resources under Examination: The Inter-American System for Human Rights and Natural Resource Allocation', 12 *Annual Survey of International and Comparative Law*, 2006, 43.

Barrera-Hernández, L., Barton, B., Godden, L., Lucas, A., and Rønne, A., (eds), *Sharing the Costs and Benefits of Energy and Resource Activity: Legal Change and Impact on Communities* (OUP, 2016).

Bavikatte, K. S., *Stewarding the Earth: Rethinking Property and the Emergence of Biocultural Rights* (OUP, 2014).

Bavikatte, K. S., and Bennett, T., 'Community Stewardship: The Foundation Of Biocultural Rights.' 6 *Journal of Human Rights and the Environment*, 2015, 7–29.

Bessa, A., 'Traditional Local Communities: What Lessons Can Be Learnt at the International Level from the Experiences of Brazil and Scotland?', 24(3) *Review of European Community & International Environmental Law*, 2015, 330–40.

Blanco, E., and Razzaque, J., (eds), *Globalisation and Natural Resources Law: Challenges, Key Issues and Perspectives* (Edward Elgar, 2011).

Boer, B., (ed.), *Environmental Law Dimensions of Human Rights* (OUP, 2014).

Borelli, S., and Lenzerini, F. (eds), *Cultural Heritage, Cultural Rights, Cultural Diversity: New Developments in International Law* (Brill, 2012).

Boyd, D. R., *The Rights of Nature: A Legal Revolution That Could Save the World* (ECW Press, 2017).

Boyle, A., 'Human Rights and the Environment: Where Next?', 23 *European Journal of International Law*, 2012, 613.

Bungenberg, M., and Hobe, S., (eds), *Permanent Sovereignty over Natural Resources* (Springer, 2015).

Claeys, P., 'Food Sovereignty and the Recognition of New Rights for Peasants at the UN: A Critical Overview of La Via Campesina's Rights Claims over the Last 20 Years', 12(2) *Globalizations*, 2015, 452–65.

Claeys, P., *Human Rights and the Food Sovereignty Movement: Reclaiming Control* (Routledge, 2015).

Cotula, L., *Human Rights, Natural Resource and Investment Law in a Globalised World: Shades of Grey in the Shadow of the Law* (Routledge, 2012).

Cotula, L., 'Land, Property and Sovereignty in International Law,' 25 *Cardozo Journal of International and Comparative Law*, 2017, 219, 286.

Dam-de Jong, D., *International Law and Governance of Natural Resources in Conflict and Post-Conflict Situations* (CUP, 2015).

Darcy, S., ' "The Elephant in the Room"; Corporate Tax Avoidance and Business and Human Rights', 2(1) *Business and Human Rights Journal*, 2017, 1–30.

De Schutter, O., and Vanloqueren, G., 'The New Green Revolution: How Twenty-First-Century Science Can Feed the World', 2(4) *Solutions*, 2011, 33–44.

Desmarais, A., Claeys, P., and Trauger, A., (eds), *Public Policies for Food Sovereignty Social Movements and the State* (Routledge, 2017).

Desmet, E., *Indigenous Rights Entwined with Nature Conservation* (Intersentia, 2011).

Disko, S., and Tugendhat, H., (eds), *World Heritage Sites and Indigenous Peoples Rights* (International Work Group for Indigenous Affairs, 2014).

Djoyou, Kamga S., *The Right to Development in the African Human Rights System* (Routledge, 2018).

Doyle, C., *Indigenous Peoples, Title to Territory, Rights and Resources: The Transformative Role of Free Prior and Informed Consent* (Routledge, 2014).

Duruigbo, E., 'Permanent Sovereignty and Peoples' Ownership of Natural Resources in International Law', 38 *George Washington International Law Review*, 2006, 33.

Errico, S., 'The Controversial Issue of Natural Resources: Balancing States' Sovereignty with Indigenous Peoples' Rights'. In: Stephen Allen and Alexandra Xanthaki (eds), *Reflections on the UN Declaration on the Rights of Indigenous Peoples* (Hart Publishing, 2011), pp. 329–66.

Farmer, A., 'Towards a Meaningful Rebirth of Economic Self-Determination: Human Rights Realization in Resource-Rich Countries', 39 *NYU Journal of International Law and Politics*, 2007, 417, 424.

Francioni, F., 'International Human Rights in an Environmental Horizon', 21 *European Journal of International Law*, 2010, 41.

Gess, K., 'Permanent Sovereignty Over Natural Resources: An Analytical Review of the United Nations Declaration and its Genesis', 13 *International & Comparative Law Quarterly*, 1964, 398, 449.

Gibson, J., *Community Resources: Intellectual Property, International Trade and Protection of Traditional Knowledge* (Routledge, 2016).

Gilbert, J., 'The Right to Freely Dispose of Natural Resources: Utopia or Forgotten Right', 31 *Netherlands Quarterly of Human Rights*, 2013, 314.

Gilbert, J., *Indigenous Peoples' Land Rights under International Law*, 2nd edition (Brill, 2016).

Gillespie, A., *Conservation, Biodiversity and International Law* (Edward Elgar, 2013).

Godden, L., and Tehan, M., (eds), *Comparative Perspectives on Communal Lands and Individual Ownership: Sustainable Futures* (Routledge, 2010).

Golay, C., 'The Right to Food and the Right to Life'. In: David Fraser and Graça Almeida Rodrigues (eds), *Disrespect Today, Conflict Tomorrow* (Critical, Cultural and Communications Press, 2009), pp. 151–8.

Haugen, H-M., 'The Right to Self-Determination and Natural Resources: The Case of Western Sahara', 3(1) *Lead Law, Environment and Development Journal*, 2007, 70–81.

Haugen, H-M., 'Food Sovereignty—An Appropriate Approach to Ensure the Right to Food?', 78(3) *Nordic Journal of International Law*, 2009, 263–92.

Heinämäki, L., and Herrmann, T. M. (eds), *Experiencing and Protecting Sacred Natural Sites of Sámi and Other Indigenous Peoples* (Springer Polar Sciences, 2017).

Keenan, P., 'Conflict Minerals and the Law of Pillage', 14(2) *Chicago Journal of International Law*, 2014, 524–58.

Khan, T., 'Accounting for the Human Rights Harms of Climate Change', 25 *SUR International Journal on Human Rights*, 2017, 89.

Klare, M., *The Race for What's Left: The Global Scramble for the World's Last Resources* (Picador, 2012).

Knox, J. H., 'Linking Human Rights and Climate Change at the United Nations', 33 *Harvard Environmental Law Review*, 2009, 477–98.

Kröger, M., *Contentious Agency and Natural Resource Politics* (Routledge, 2013).

Laird, S., (ed.), *Biodiversity and Traditional Knowledge: Equitable Partnerships in Practice* (Routledge, 2010).

Le Billon, P., *Fuelling War: Natural Resources and Armed Conflicts* (Routledge, 2005).

Lenzerini, F., and Vrdoljak, A. F., (eds), *International Law for Common Goods: Normative Perspectives on Human Rights, Culture and Nature* (Hart Publishing, 2014).

Martínez-Torres, M-E., and Rosset, P., 'La Vía Campesina: the Birth and Evolution of a Transnational Social Movement', 37(1) *The Journal of Peasant Studies*, 2010, 149–75.

McGee, B., 'The Community Referendum: Participatory Democracy and the Right to Free, Prior and Informed Consent to Development', 27 *Berkeley Journal of International Law*, 2009, 570.

McHarg, A., Barton, B., Bradbrook, A., and Godden, L. (eds), *Property and the Law in Energy and Natural Resources* (OUP, 2010).

Miranda, L., 'The Role of International Law in Intrastate Natural Resource Allocation: Sovereignty, Human Rights, and Peoples-Based Development', 45(3) *Vanderbilt Journal of Transnational Law*, 2012, 12–17.

Morgera, E., 'Against All Odds: The Contribution of the Convention on Biological Diversity to International Human Rights Law'. In: Alland, D., Chetail, V., de Frouville, O., and Viñuales, J. E., (eds), *Unity and Diversity of International Law. Essays in Honour of Professor Pierre-Marie Dupuy* (Brill, 2014), p. 983.

Morgera, E., 'The Need for an International Legal Concept of Fair and Equitable Benefit-sharing', 27 *European Journal of International Law*, 2016, 353.

Morgera, E., and Kulovesi, K., (eds), *Research Handbook on International Law and Natural Resources* (Edward Elgar, 2016).

Morgera, E., and Razzaque, J., 'Biodiversity and Nature Protection Law', *Elgar Encyclopaedia of Environmental Law* (Edward Elgar, 2017).

Newell, P., and Wheeler, J., (eds), *Rights, Resources and the Politics of Accountability* (Zed Books, 2006).

O'Faircheallaigh, C., 'Community Development Agreements in the Mining Industry: An Emerging Global Phenomenon', 44 *Community Development*, 2013, 222–38.

Pasqualucci, J., 'The Right to a Dignified Life (*Vida Digna*): The Integration of Economic and Social Rights with Civil and Political Rights in the Inter-American Human Rights System', 31 *Hastings International & Comparative Law Review*, 2008, 1.

Petersmann, M-C., ' "Narcissus" Reflection in the Lake: Untold Narratives in Environmental Law beyond the Anthropocentric Frame', 30 *Journal of Environmental Law*, 2018, 1–25.

Pichler, M., Staritz, C., Küblböck, K., Plank, C., Raza, W., and Ruiz Peyré, F., (eds), *Fairness and Justice in Natural Resource Politics* (Routledge, 2016).

Quirico, O. and Boumghar, M., (eds), *Climate Change and Human Rights: An International and Comparative Law Perspective* (Routledge, 2016).

Raftopoulos, M., 'Contemporary Debates on Social-Environmental Conflicts, Extractivism and Human Rights in Latin America', 21(4) *International Journal of Human Rights*, 2017, 387–404.

Razzaque, J., and Blanco, E., (eds), *Natural Resources and the Green Economy: Redefining the Challenges for People, States and Corporations* (Brill, 2012).

Resurreccion, B., and Elmhirst, E., (eds), *Gender and Natural Resource Management: Livelihoods, Mobility and Interventions* (Earthscan, 2008).

Sajeva, G., 'Rights with Limits: Biocultural Rights–Between Self-Determination and Conservation of the Environment', 6(1) *Journal of Human Rights and the Environment*, 2015, 30–54.

Sato, J., *Governance of Natural Resources: Uncovering the Social Purpose of Materials in Nature* (United Nations University Press, 2013).

Schrijver, N., *Sovereignty over Natural Resources: Balancing Rights and Duties* (CUP, 2008).

Schrijver, N., *Development without Destruction: The UN and Global Resource Management* (Indiana University Press, 2010).

Shelton, D., 'Human Rights and the Environment: What Specific Environmental Rights Have Been Recognized?', 35 *Denver Journal of International Law and Policy*, 2006, 129.

Shelton, D., 'Whiplash and Backlash—Reflections on a Human Rights Approach to Environmental Protection', 13 *Santa Clara Journal of International Law*, 2015, 11.

Sikor, T., and Stahl, J., (eds), *Forests and People: Property, Governance, and Human Rights* (Routledge, 2012).

Stevens, S., (ed.), *Indigenous Peoples, National Parks and Protected Areas: A New Paradigm Linking Conservation, Culture and Rights* (University of Arizona Press, 2014).

Tan, C., and Julio Faundez, J., *Natural Resources and Sustainable Development: International Economic Law Perspectives* (Edward Elgar Publishing, 2017).

Tramontana, E., 'The Contribution of the Inter-American Human Rights Bodies to Evolving International Law on Indigenous Rights over Lands and Natural Resources', 17(2) *International Journal on Minority and Group Rights*, 2010, 241–63.

van den Herik, L., and Dam-De Jong, D., 'Revitalizing the Antique War Crime of Pillage: The Potential and Pitfalls of Using International Criminal Law to Address Illegal Resource Exploitation during Armed Conflict', 22(3) *Criminal Law Forum*, 2011, 237–73.

Vasquez, P. I., *Oil Sparks in the Amazon: Local Conflicts, Indigenous Populations, and Natural Resources* (University of Georgia Press, 2014).

Verschuuren, B., (ed.), *Sacred Natural Sites: Conserving Nature and Culture* (Routledge, 2010).

Warris, A., *Tax & Development: Solving Kenya's Fiscal Crisis through Human Rights: A Case Study of Kenya's Constituency Development Fund* (Law Africa, 2013).

Westra, L., (ed.), *Environmental Justice and the Rights of Indigenous Peoples: International and Domestic Legal Perspectives* (Earthscan, 2012).

Williams, A., and Le Billon, P., (eds), *Corruption, Natural Resources and Development: From Resource Curse to Political Ecology* (Edward Elgar, 2017).

Winkler, I., *The Human Right to Water: Significance, Legal Status and Implications for Water Allocation* (Hart Publishing, 2012).

Wittman, H., Desmarais, A., and Wiebe, N., (eds), *Food Sovereignty: Reconnecting Food, Nature and Community* (Fernwood Publishing/Food First Books, 2010).

Xanthaki, A., Valkonen, S., Heinämäki, L., and Nuorgam, P., (eds), *Indigenous Peoples' Cultural Heritage: Rights, Debates, Challenges* (Brill, 2017).

Xu, T., and Alain, J., (eds), *Property and Human Rights in a Global Context* (Hart Publishing, 2015).

Xu, T., and Clarke, A., (eds), *Legal Strategies for the Development and Protection of Communal Property* (OUP, 2017).

Young, H., and Goldman, L., (eds), *Livelihoods, Natural Resources, and Post-Conflict Peacebuilding* (Routledge, 2015).

Ziegler, J., Golay, C., Mahon, C., and Way, S., *The Fight for the Right to Food: Lessons Learned* (Springer, 2011).

Zillman, D. M., Lucas, A., and Pring, G., (eds), *Human Rights in Natural Resource Development* (OUP, 2002).

Index